The Fate of the Man of God from Judah

The Fate of the Man of God from Judah

A Literary and Theological Reading of 1 Kings 13

MAN HEE YOON

Foreword by Christopher Seitz

◆PICKWICK *Publications* · Eugene, Oregon

THE FATE OF THE MAN OF GOD FROM JUDAH
A Literary and Theological Reading of 1 Kings 13

Copyright © 2020 Man Hee Yoon. All rights reserved. Except for brief quotations in critical publications or reviews, no part of this book may be reproduced in any manner without prior written permission from the publisher. Write: Permissions, Wipf and Stock Publishers, 199 W. 8th Ave., Suite 3, Eugene, OR 97401.

Pickwick Publications
An Imprint of Wipf and Stock Publishers
199 W. 8th Ave., Suite 3
Eugene, OR 97401

www.wipfandstock.com

PAPERBACK ISBN: 978-1-7252-5083-3
HARDCOVER ISBN: 978-1-7252-5084-0
EBOOK ISBN: 978-1-7252-5085-7

Cataloguing-in-Publication data:

Names: Yoon, Man Hee, author. | Seitz, Christopher R., foreword.

Title: The fate of the man of God from Judah : a literary and theological reading of 1 Kings 13 / Man Hee Yoon ; with a foreword by Christopher Seitz.

Description: Eugene, OR: Pickwick Publications, 2020. | Includes bibliographical references.

Identifiers: ISBN 978-1-7252-5083-3 (paperback). | ISBN 978-1-7252-5084-0 (hardcover). | ISBN 978-1-7252-5085-7 (ebook).

Subjects: LCSH: Bible.—Kings, 1st, XIII—Criticism, interpretation, etc.

Classification: BS1335.52 Y66 2020 (print) | BS1335.52 (ebook)

Manufactured in the U.S.A.   01/17/20

Unless otherwise indicated, Scripture quotations are the author's own translations. Scripture quotations marked (NRSV) come from the New Revised Standard Version Bible, copyright © 1989 National Council of the Churches of Christ in the United States of America. Used by permission. All rights reserved worldwide.

Contents

List of Tables | vii
Foreword by Christopher Seitz | ix
Preface | xi
Acknowledgments | xiii
Abbreviations | xiv

Introduction | 1

1 A Survey of Modern Scholarship on 1 Kings 13 and Hermeneutical Suggestions | 9

2 Exegesis of 1 Kings 13 | 40

3 A Literary Analysis of the Jeroboam Narrative | 93

4 A Theological Approach to the Jeroboam Narrative | 126

Conclusion & Future Study | 157

Bibliography | 161

Tables

Parallels between 1 Kings 13:3–6 and 1 Kings 13:20–26 | 47
Parallels between 1 Kings 13:7–10 and 1 Kings 13:15–19 | 48

Foreword

NO ONE WILL DISPUTE that the story of the man of God and the lying prophet, as related in 1 Kings 13, is a strange text, even by Old Testament standards (compare the story of Judah and Tamar in Genesis 38). It is a provocative and challenging text on a number of different levels. What is it doing here, in the context of a longer set of episodes concerning King Jeroboam, after the cleavage of the Kingdom of Israel? Does God tell prophets to lie—how does that work, measured against prophecy as we more generally understand it? The poor man of God—is he just set up? The start of his career as we see it is exemplary. And ironically, given his punishment by God, so is his ending: the old prophet who spoke against him in the name of God asks to be buried with him when his own days draw to a close. Perhaps the story is really about something else (true and false prophecy; the monarchy more widely understood). Or are these just ways to divert our attention from details and facts that otherwise unfold straightforwardly, if provocatively?

In this accessible, thoroughly researched, and carefully written study, Man Hee Yoon takes us straight into the heart of the problems noted above, and others as well. He does not avoid the details of the story in the name of relocating the problems into a different sphere of reflection, even as he countenances the strong likelihood that the details serve more than one purpose in the wider narrative of the Deuteronomistic History. The story of the man of God and the lying prophet is about what it says and also about the House of Jeroboam in just how it goes about saying that. The story is about an obedience to God that is asked to risk everything, even when confronted by a prophet of God who has been sent, as we learn, to test his resolve in strictest terms.

Yoon examines the story from various angles, testing the many explanations that have been given in previous scholarship to guide our

Foreword

interpretation. What he is able to show is that the priorities of the story must be carefully determined so as not to allow subsidiary themes to overtake our reading. Indeed, several of these subsidiary themes are sufficiently engaging—precisely because provocative—that they tempt us to do just that; that is their artful purpose. We too, the readers, are tested just as is the man of God. And so too, in the wider scheme of things, is King Jeroboam. The narrative has been carefully constructed so as to create a moral and theological dilemma for characters and readers both, from whom a costly obedience is also required in the journey with God.

By turns Yoon examines the function of the lying motif; the ethical and theological dimensions of the story—why the sevenfold repetition of "by the word of the LORD"—and the fate of the man of God as a warning, unheeded by the King of Israel and ending in his own judgment; the false trail of true/false prophecy as an intended subject taken up in distinctive fashion by the author; the reason for the story's present placement; and the way the story functions hermeneutically as a drama, with some similarities to the brief notice at 1 Kings 20:35–36.

Yoon's multi-faceted "close reading" of this carefully constructed biblical account, given shape in the final form of the thirteenth chapter of 1 Kings, is the means by which its distinctive literary unfolding and its serious theological purpose are both unlocked and shown to be inextricably related. Be prepared for a journey into the heart of a demanding and rewarding biblical text.

Christopher Seitz
Senior Research Professor of Biblical Interpretation,
Wycliffe College in the University of Toronto

Preface

THIS MONOGRAPH IS A revised version of my doctoral dissertation, which was submitted in 2016 to the faculty of Wycliffe College (at the University of Toronto) and the biblical department of the Toronto School of Theology. This book focuses on a story in 1 Kings 13 of the encounters that the man of God from Judah had with King Jeroboam and with the old prophet of Bethel. This rather puzzling and bizarre story has confounded biblical scholars as well as the general reader of the Bible throughout many generations. Scholarship has not reached a consensus as to what its main theme is; this may be due to the lack of any agreed hermeneutical principles to employ for the interpretation of the story. In this book, I analyze the narrator's (or the implied author's) intention, as expressed in the final form of the text, and argue, based on the hermeneutical principles framed by the aim, that a) the main theme of 1 Kings 13 is the certainty of God's judgment on Jeroboam, which is visualized in the prophecy and fulfillment structure of the story, and b) the story is best categorized as consisting of prophetic symbolic acts (or prophetic drama) in which the narrator configured the actions of prophets in a way to illustrate and prefigure the fate of Jeroboam's dynasty. This study is an attempt to read the story literarily and theologically—an approach that has not been undertaken enough for this chapter—and to present a coherent interpretation of the story in light of this approach.

Acknowledgments

I WOULD LIKE TO express my deepest gratitude to Dr. Christopher Seitz, who has constantly provided full support for me throughout the writing and editing process. It has been a true blessing from God to benefit from his vast scholarly knowledge and kind advice. I also want to thank Dr. Marion Taylor for her encouragement and timely challenges for me, which has helped me to continue my academic journey. I am expressing my thanks to Dr. Glen Taylor for having provided good friendship and mentorship at the times when I needed them. Dr. Keith Bodner at Crandall University has also made himself available to my calls for help and made valuable contributions to the completion of this book. Without these teachers, the completion of this book may have not been possible. Thanks also go to my wife, Hyun Jung Lee, and my two children, Esther and Micah, who always support me with their constant prayers and unconditional love. Most of all, I give glory to the living God and Jesus Christ who saved me and gave me a new life.

Abbreviations

AB	Anchor Bible
ABD	*The Anchor Bible Dictionary*. 6 vols. Edited by David Noel Freedman. New York: Doubleday, 1992
ACCS	Ancient Christian Commentary on Scripture
ATD	Das Alte Testament Deutsch
AOTC	Abingdon Old Testament Commentaries
ASV	American Standard Version
AYB	The Anchor Yale Bible
BAR	*Biblical Archaeology Review*
BDB	Francis Brown, S. R. Driver, and Charles A. Briggs. *Hebrew and English Lexicon of the Old Testament*. Oxford: Clarendon, 1907
BE	Biblical Encyclopedia
BHS	*Biblia Hebraica Stuttgartensia*
BI	*Biblical Interpretation*
BLS	Bible and Literature Series
BTCB	Brazos Theological Commentary on the Bible
BZ	*Biblische Zeitschrift*
BZAW	Beihefte zur Zeitschrift für die alttestamentliche Wissenschaft
CBQ	*Catholic Biblical Quarterly*
CBQMS	Catholic Biblical Quarterly Monograph Series
CBR	*Currents in Biblical Research*

Abbreviations

ESV	English Standard Version
FOTL	Forms of Old Testament Literature Series
HALOT	The Hebrew and Aramaic Lexicon of the Old Testament
HSM	Harvard Semitic Monographs
HUCA	*Hebrew Union College Annual*
ICC	International Critical Commentary
ISBL	Indiana Studies in Biblical Literature
ITC	International Theological Commentary
JANES	*Journal of the Ancient Near Eastern Society*
JSJ	*Journal for the Study of Judaism in the Persian, Hellenistic and Roman Period*
JBL	*Journal of Biblical Literature*
JBQ	*Jewish Bible Quarterly*
JSOT	*Journal for the Study of the Old Testament*
JSOTSup	Journal for the Study of the Old Testament Supplement Series
KJV	King James Version
LHBOTS	Library of Hebrew Bible/ Old Testament Studies
LXX	Septuagint
MT	Masoretic Text
NAC	The New American Commentary
NASB	New American Standard Bible
NEB	New English Bible
NICOT	New International Commentary on the Old Testament
NIDOTTE	*New International Dictionary of Old Testament Theology & Exegesis.* 5 vols. Edited by Willem A. VanGemeren. Grand Rapids: Zondervan, 1997
NIV	New International Version
NRSV	New Revised Standard Version
OBO	Orbis Biblicus et Orientalis
OTL	Old Testament Library

Abbreviations

RSV	Revised Standard Version
SBL	Society of Biblical Literature
SBLSP	*Society of Biblical Literature Seminar Papers*
SBT	Studies in Biblical Theology
SBTS	Sources for Biblical and Theological Study
SCJ	*Stone-Campbell Journal*
SJOT	*Scandinavian Journal of the Old Testament*
SP	*Studies on Prophecy*
STI	Studies in Theological Interpretation
TOTC	The Tyndale Old Testament Commentaries
UBCS	Understanding the Bible Commentary Series
VT	*Vetus Testamentum*
VTSup	Vetus Testamentum Supplements
WBC	Word Biblical Commentary
ZAW	*Zeitschrift für die alttestamentliche Wissenschaft*

Introduction

BACKGROUND

MOST READERS OF THE Book of Kings find 1 Kings 13 mysterious and difficult to understand because of, among other things, its eccentricity. The man of God arrives at the altar in Bethel and proclaims a message of judgment against the altar. He was commanded not to eat or drink in Bethel, and not to return the way he came to Bethel. Deceived by the old prophet of Bethel, however, the man of God disobeys the command that he received and, as a punishment, gets killed by a lion. The old prophet brings back his body, buries it in his own grave, and laments over him. A few questions immediately arise in the mind of the reader. Why was the man of God from Judah given such a command in the first place? What was the motive of the old prophet of Bethel when he deceived the man of God from Judah? Why was the man of God punished when he was deceived into disobeying the word of God innocently, whereas the old prophet of Bethel who led the man of God from Judah to disobedience went unpunished and, more surprisingly, became a messenger of the true word of God? Where is God and what is his role in this story? What is the theology of the story?

A number of historical critics have investigated the story and suggested a variety of hypotheses regarding the composition of the story. J. Morgenstern, for example, argued that the second half of the story (vv. 11–32) is a secondary expansion of the first half (vv. 1–10, 33–34),[1] whereas Würthwein held the view that the first part (vv. 1–10) was added secondarily to an earlier tradition (vv. 11–32).[2] These views are supported in part

---

1. Morgenstern, *Amos Studies I*, 161.
2. Würthwein, *Die Bücher der Könige*, 168.

Introduction

by the fact that, while King Jeroboam takes an important part in the first part of the story, he does not appear in the second (vv. 11–32). As Keith Bodner points out, moreover, it is not clear "why this narrative [the second part of the story] is placed in the midst of the account of Jeroboam's reign, or precisely how it contributes to the larger storyline."³ These observations indicate the difficulties of interpretation and raise questions about the unity of the story; hence many scholars have exerted themselves to show that the text represents "a combination of different redactional layers."⁴

More recently, new literary critics have shown that the story in 1 Kings 13 is a well-designed literary unit that displays literary artistry.⁵ Robert Cohn, for example, sees in the Jeroboam narrative "a fine example of . . . composite artistry" (1 Kgs 11:16—14:20).⁶ He argues that the narrative "bears the marks of a talented author who, by ordering and editing, created a unified story."⁷ The literary function of 1 Kings 13 in the larger context of the Jeroboam narrative has also been explored. Cohn argues that the Jeroboam narrative might have been designed by the Judahite historian to explain "why God allowed Jeroboam to inherit the greatest part of the kingdom promised to the descendants of David, but also why Jeroboam's dynasty and his kingdom, having been so favored, came to ruin."⁸ First Kings 13 is arguably situated at the center of the Jeroboam narrative and provides a turning point in terms of Jeroboam's destiny. Moreover, the location of 1 Kings 13 in the Book of Kings deserves attention, as the story provides a framework for the rest of the Deuteronomistic History running from the division of the kingdom to the fall of Judah. Set right after the division of the nation into two kingdoms, the eccentric story of 1 Kings 13 and the sin of Jeroboam provides a framework by which all the subsequent Northern Kingdom kings are measured.

Despite the generally agreed on literary function of 1 Kings 13 in the Jeroboam narrative, the main theme and theology of 1 Kings 13 and how the chapter, especially the second part (vv. 11–32), contributes to the storyline of the whole Jeroboam narrative need more clarification. In exploring

3. Bodner, *Royal Drama*, 97.
4. Kruger, "880 ",מוֹפֵת.
5. See Simon, "Prophetic Sign," 81–117; Bosworth, *The Story within a Story*, 118–65; Bodner, *Royal Drama*, 97–119.
6. Cohn, "Literary Technique," 23–35.
7. Cohn, "Literary Technique," 24.
8. Cohn, "Literary Technique," 25.

the theme and theology of the story, scholars have adopted many different approaches. Most historical critics focused their studies on reconstructing the pre-Deuteronomistic form of the text (Dietrich,[9] Jepsen,[10] Noth,[11] and Würthwein[12]) and, based on their reconstructions, proposed various themes for the story (Dozeman,[13] and Gross.[14]). Redaction critics have traced the redactional developments of the text, focusing on the differences in perspective. Narrative critics read the text more synchronically using the methods, such as characterization and gap filling.[15] They have noticed literary connections between the narrative of 1 Kings 13 and its larger context and tried to show the narrator's literary techniques.

Numerous themes have been proposed for the story: the problematic nature of prophecy; the importance of obedience; the triumph of the word of God over anything or anyone that opposes it; the relationship of Judah and Israel; the relationship of true and false prophecy; a polemic against the belief in angels; election and rejection, etc. The plethora of proposed themes indicates the difficulty of interpretation and the presence of many different ideas in the story.

This study will argue that the story has been shaped in the framework of prophecy and fulfillment, one of the theological frameworks employed in the Deuteronomistic History, as has been clearly delineated by von Rad.[16] The structural analysis of the story reveals that 1 Kings 13 contains two sets of prophecy and fulfillment within itself (vv. 3–6, 20–26), which serve to emphasize that the prophecy against the altar (1 Kgs 13:2) will certainly be fulfilled in the future. This structural analysis leads to a conclusion that the theme of the narrative is the certainty of God's judgment on the house (or dynasty) of Jeroboam, and the function of the narrative is to justify God's judgment on Jeroboam, who turned away from the way of Yahweh and continued in his evil way.

---

9. Dietrich, *Prophetie und Geschichte*, 115.
10. Jepsen, "Gottesmann und Prophet," 171–82.
11. Noth, *Könige*, 291.
12. Würthwein, *Die Bücher der Könige*, 150.
13. Dozeman, "Way of the Man," 379–93.
14. Gross, "Lying Prophet," 97–135.
15. For a discussion on gap-filling, see Sternberg, *The Poetics of Biblical Narrative*, 186–229.
16. Von Rad, *Deuteronomy*, 82.

Introduction

OUTLINE

The main goal of this study is to grasp the narrator's (or the implied author's) intention expressed in the text. This study will argue that, in delineating the certainty of the fulfillment of prophecy, the narrator depicts the story in a particular way so that what happens to the man of God from Judah could prefigure Jeroboam's beginning and end. This study will pay special attention to the symbolism employed in the story and propose that the story be read as centered on prophetic symbolic actions.

In chapter 1 I will review and critique some of the modern scholars' views on the composition and theme of 1 Kings 13 and suggest several hermeneutical principles for the interpretation of our text. I will examine various historical approaches applied to the text which may be grouped into three categories. The first approach argues for a pre-Deuteronomistic state of the text. The second can be called form-critical and historical study, which focuses on the genres of the narratives. Lastly, the third examines redactional developments of the text. In addition, I will also review a more recent approach, called narrative criticism. By and large, the historical-critical approaches have severed our story from its surrounding context, highlighting the "*disconnectedness* within the history,"[17] and hence failed to see its place and function as it stands in its setting in the completed history. Our story, however, is interwoven with the Deuteronomist's other material and, most likely, was shaped by the Deuteronomist's hand, so when severed from its literary context, the benefits of reading the text in light of the Deuteronomist's concerns and theology are lost.

In the second part of chapter 1, I will suggest my own hermeneutical principles for interpreting the text. In interpreting this story, many previous interpreters have taken wrong paths by speculating on what the text does not tell. Some have read into the text ethical issues that are foreign to our story. Others have focused too much on the psychology and motives of the characters in the story.[18] I will assume that the narrator's (the Deuteronomist's) intentions are displayed in the present form of the text. Therefore, I will analyze the details of the text as closely as possible.

---

17. Beal, *The Deuteronomist's Prophet*, 41.

18. See Gross, "Lying Prophet," 97–135. Some of his hermeneutical principles hold value for this study, though the thesis of his article is not agreed with by the current writer. His induction of the role analysis theory is foreign to the text, and reading the story based on this role theory, in my judgment, does not do justice to the text.

Introduction

For the interpretation of the text, I will suggest a few guidelines. First, a well-executed analysis of the structural form avoids the mistake of raising up individual features to the status of the primary message of the story.[19] Though we do not rule out the possibility of the presence of more than one idea in the story, I would argue that most parts (if not all) of the story were arranged by the narrator so as to contribute to the primary message of the story that the structure of the present form of the story reveals to the reader. Second, identifying the genre/form of a story is a key to the correct interpretation of biblical narratives, especially in the case of 1 Kings 13. Understanding the primary characteristics of a certain form of narrative—the symbolic narrative in our case—will clear away some interpretive directions, such as judging the statements of the text according to moral and theological value categories that are imposed on the text, or speculating on the motives of Yahweh's prohibition (v. 9) and of the characters' actions (e.g., the old prophet's lie). Third, the comparison of this text with other Deuteronomistic texts and intertextual readings will help the reader recognize the literary skills and expressions that the Deuteronomist frequently employed, which will help us with filling the gaps in the text, when necessary for the interpretation of our text.[20] The common Deuteronomistic phrases and expressions shared by different bodies of the texts in the Deuteronomistic History might also draw attention to the narrative emphasis that the narrator tried to convey to the intended reader.

Chapter 2 presents an exegesis of the narrative. The analysis of the structure of the text will give special attention to key motifs repeated in the story and clarify the literary scheme that the narrator uses to emphasize the main theme of the chapter. Through this structural analysis, it will become clear that our text has been shaped around the structure of prophecy and fulfillment and was designed in such a way to show that the prophecy against the altar in v. 2 would certainly come true; its fulfillment is described

---

19. Barth and Klopfenstein saw a role reversal between the man of God and the old prophet of Bethel as a key to interpreting the story. See Barth, *Church Dogmatics* 2/2, 393–409, and Klopfenstein, "1 Könige 13," 668. John Gray sees in our story the contrast between the disobedient man of God and the obedient beast. For this see Gray, *I & II Kings*, 302. The analysis of the structure of 1 Kings 13, however, will show that a role reversal between the man of God and the old prophet of Bethel or the contract between the man of God and the lion do not receive as much emphasis in the text and also that the scholars have read the oppositions into the text that do not exist in the text.

20. Sternberg, *Biblical Narrative*, 189.

Introduction

in 2 Kings 23:15–20.[21] I will also gather insights from methods such as narrative criticism and rhetorical criticism to read the text more synchronically for the purpose of getting at the narrator's literary techniques. Through the exegesis, the main theme of the story will become apparent.

Through my exegesis the narrator's (Deuteronomist's) understanding of prophets' roles in delivering God's message will be revealed. Bosworth and some New Criticism scholars understood the second part of the story (13:11–32) as "a play within a play"[22] or "a story within a story."[23] Bodner argues, "The man of God is configured as a picture of Jeroboam"[24] and reads 13:11–32 as "a type of political allegory that functions as a subtle reflection on the fate of Jeroboam's kingship."[25] Basically agreeing with this view, this study will focus more on the narrator's understanding of the roles of prophets in delivering God's messages. It is not likely that the prophets (the man of God from Judah and the old prophet from Bethel) expected their actions to be symbolic, but it is argued that at least the narrator intended them to be read as prophetic symbolic actions that prefigure the final destiny of Jeroboam's dynasty as a consequence of his disobedience to the word of Yahweh. In effect, this symbolic role unknown to the prophet might function to redeem—through the sovereignty/Providence of God implied by the symbolic link, or even by the inscripturation of this event vis-à-vis the narrator—the confused/ambiguous state of prophecy when left to the prophets themselves at the time (cf. 1 Kgs 22).

First Kings 13 will be compared to 1 Kings 20:35–37, which is similar to our text in milieu and genre, and, arguably, is another instance of prophetic symbolic actions. The connection between 1 Kings 13 and 1 Kings 20:35–36 is highlighted by the shared motifs which are noted by most readers. Our story will also be compared to 1 Kings 22 which also shares similar motifs with 1 Kings 13 (for example, two different voices from two groups of prophets, lying, reversal of prediction, prophecy being fulfilled through God's sovereignty regardless of human's response). Lastly, I will expand on

---

21. Jepsen argues that 1 Kings 13 is made complete when 2 Kings 23:16–18 is attached to it (see Jepsen, "Gottesmann und Prophet," 171–82). I acknowledge that the narrator might have had the later event (2 Kgs 23:16–18) in mind, as he was narrating the story in 1 Kings 13, but I would argue that the story in 1 Kings 13 should be read on its own terms first, before it is read in association with other texts.

22. Bosworth, *Story within a Story*, 118–65.

23. Bodner, *Royal Drama*, 110.

24. Bodner, *Royal Drama*, 112.

25. Bodner, *Royal Drama*, 98.

Introduction

the genre of the prophetic symbolic actions and show how our story fits the category.

Chapter 3 will turn the focus to broader contexts, that is, the Jeroboam narrative. Most scholars focused on the theme of the story in itself and then felt uneasy about making connections between the story and the Jeroboam narrative. In other words, they failed to read the story in the literary context of the Jeroboam narrative. I will examine how this story contributes to the larger Jeroboam narrative, especially in light of the theme of prophecy and fulfillment (e.g., 11:29—12:24 and 14:1–18). I will identify literary connections existing between our text and the surrounding texts in the Jeroboam narrative. It will become clearly visible that the different parts of the Jeroboam narrative communicate with one another and thereby build up the theme of the Jeroboam narrative together. Lastly, the location of 1 Kings 13 in the Jeroboam narrative will be discussed.

Chapter 4 will focus on the Deuteronomist's theology reflected in the Jeroboam narrative as well as in 1 Kings 13. I will argue that John Gray's judgment that 1 Kings 13 betrays "the mechanical and a-moral conception of the operation of the word of God" does not do justice to the story.[26] Instead, I will attempt to understand the Deuteronomist's theology in terms of how the Israelite history was advanced by the prophets' messages. I will also look into the Deuteronomistic understanding of the roles of the prophets. This perspective understood prophets' actions and behaviors to illustrate things relevant to Israelite kings and the history of Israel. Second, I will expand on the schema of prophecy and fulfillment of the Deuteronomist(s), which raises an interesting question: what here is the Deuteronomistic understanding of the relationship between God's will (prophecy) and human's decisions (Jeroboam's sin)?

Lastly, I will focus on the story's literary effects on the intended reader. The events in the story served initially as a warning to Jeroboam, but the narrator shaped the story in a particular way to demand a certain response from the reader. I will see how the theme of the chapter could have been received by the intended reader. The purpose of this story alongside other parts of the Jeroboam narrative is to show that God's words surely find their fulfillments in the history. The narrator urges the reader in the exile to respond to this warning properly and to repent and *come back* (שוב) to God, one of the frequently repeated motifs in the story.[27]

---

26. Gray, *I & II Kings*, 294.
27. Wolff, "Kerygma," 62–78.

1

A Survey of Modern Scholarship on 1 Kings 13 and Hermeneutical Suggestions

INTRODUCTION

MORE THAN THREE DECADES ago, Lemke said in his article titled "The Way of Obedience" that

> This story [1 Kings 13] has been subject to widely divergent scholarly estimates. As yet no consensus has emerged in regard to such basic questions as its date of composition, authorship, form-critical classification, tradition history and significance within the larger structural and ideological framework of the Deuteronomistic History.[1]

Though there has been some advancement since Lemke regarding the interpretation of 1 Kings 13, most of the issues that Lemke mentioned above have not yet been resolved.

In the first part of this chapter, I will review major approaches to 1 Kings 13 taken by modern scholarship on the issues mentioned previously, especially the issues of the composition and theme. The history of interpretation of 1 Kings 13 has been summarized by some scholars,[2] so it is not

---

1. Lemke, "The Way of Obedience," 303.

2. For concise reviews of modern scholarship on 1 Kings 13, see Gross, "Lying Prophet," 97–135; Lemke, "The Way of Obedience," 301–26; Knoppers, *Two Nations*

necessary to reiterate them here. Rather, it will suffice to summarize some of the main paths that scholars have taken and the major shifts made in interpretation in the last several decades. The secondary literature treated in our discussion is by no means comprehensive, but they might be enough to show the trends in the interpretation of 1 Kings 13. The second half of this chapter summarizes the current status of the study of 1 Kings 13 and makes some suggestions for the analysis and interpretation of the story.

A SURVEY OF MODERN SCHOLARSHIP ON 1 KINGS 13

In the following survey of past scholarship on 1 Kings 13, I will review interpreters and commentators coming from three major approaches: (1) historical-critical approaches, (2) theological/literary interpretations, and (3) narrative criticism.

Historical-Critical Approaches

As in the case with most biblical texts, modern scholars have taken various historical-critical approaches to interpreting 1 Kings 13 such as reconstructing the pre-deuteronomistic state of the text, form-critical and historical studies that focus on the genre of the narrative, and tracing redactional developments of the text.

Historical-Critical Issues Regarding the Date and Composition of 1 Kings 13

The presence of 1 Kings 13 in the larger Jeroboam narrative (1 Kgs 11:26—14:20) has prompted debates among scholars as to whether or not it originally belonged to the Jeroboam narrative. At first glance, 1 Kings 13 seems irrelevant to King Jeroboam. Scholars have noted that the name Jeroboam appears only twice (vv. 1, 4) in the story, and Jeroboam is referred to more often as king (vv. 6, 7, 8, and 11), suggesting perhaps that "Jeroboam" could have been inserted to make this story about Jeroboam. Thus, some historical critics have seen it to be disrupting the Jeroboam narrative, which otherwise would have been a typical narrative that describes a royal reign in Israel. Further, historical critics surmise that there may have existed two

---

under God, 2:45–71; Bosworth, *Story within a Story*, 118–30.

different traditions or stories behind the present form of the story (vv. 1–10 and 11–32).

While the first part (vv. 1–10) does seem to relate to the Jeroboam's reign, it is not as clear how the second half of the story (vv. 11–32)—describing the interactions between the man of God from Judah and an old prophet of Bethel—could be related to the surrounding narratives.[3] This suspicion is supported by the facts that Jeroboam disappears from the scene after v. 10 until he reappears in vv. 33–34 and that the issue being addressed in vv. 11–32 seems to have nothing to do with the "sin" of Jeroboam (1 Kgs 12:30; 13:34). These views reflect the seeming differences that may exist in different parts of the story. As a result, some scholars have concluded that the two stories might have been joined together, because of the coincident connection of the character "the man of God" that the two stories share, but they did not investigate further as to why the stories would have been inserted in the present location. Other scholars (e.g., Julian Morgenstern), however, consider vv. 11–32 as a secondary *expansion* of a primary narrative (vv. 1–10, 33–34).[4]

Multiple suggestions have been made as to who is responsible for the insertion of the story. The almost verbatim repetition of Jeroboam's inventions in 1 Kings 12:30–32 and 13:33–34 suggests for some scholars that 1 Kings 13 is an insertion by a Deuteronomist, while for others, it is an indication that 1 Kings 13 is an insertion by a later editor.[5] Some scholars consider the story in 1 Kings 13 a secondary, post-Deuteronomistic insertion,[6] whereas other scholars would assign the story's present position in the Jeroboam narrative to a Deuteronomistic redaction.[7] By and large, most scholars admit the antiquity of the story, but they assign the final form of the chapter to the time of Josiah.[8] For those who would assign

---

3. Bosworth, "Revisiting Karl Barth's Exegesis," 360–83.

4. Morgenstern, *Amos Studies* I; Noth, *Könige*, 291–5; Gray, *I & II Kings*, 320–23; Sweeney, *I & II Kings*, 179–80.

5. See Knoppers, *Two Nations under God*, 2:50–51.

6. See Wellhausen, *Die Composition des Hexateuchs*, 280; Benzinger, *Die Bücher der Könige*, 90–93; Jepsen, *Die Quellen des Königsbuches*, 104; Eissfeldt, *The Old Testament*, 290.

7. For example, Noth, *Könige*, 294–5; Gray, *I & II Kings*, 293–4; Simon, "Prophetic Sign," 100–101; Crenshaw, *Prophetic Conflict*, 43; Knoppers, *Two Nations under God*, 2:55.

8. Sweeney, *I & II Kings*, 178–82. See also Šanda, *Die Bücher der Könige*, 359, and Klopfenstein, "1 Könige 13," 639–72. Klopfenstein assigns its redaction or the final form

THE FATE OF THE MAN OF GOD FROM JUDAH

the present position of the story to the time of Josiah, the mention of the name "Josiah"—a king of some three hundred years later—specifically as the individual who will fulfill the prophecy against the Bethel altar (v. 2) provides strong evidence for such a view.[9]

Key Historical Critics of 1 Kings 13

With the above-mentioned critical issues in mind, I will now consider some of the key interpreters of 1 Kings 13 of the past few decades, mostly in a chronological order. This list of interpreters is far from comprehensive but may lead us to see the trends and progress that have been made in recent years.

John Gray, *1 & 2 Kings: A Commentary* (1964), considers 1 Kings 13 an instance of the prophetic midrash, "which, in spite of the nucleus of fact, is not based on historical events."[10] For him, 1 Kings 13:1–10 and 13:11–32 are two different prophetic traditions, which have been put together by a later hand (or the Deuteronomist), and especially 13:11–32 was "elaborated in the light of the reformation of Josiah, the later hand being apparent in the anachronistic reference to 'the high places which are in the cities of Samaria' (v. 32)."[11] Gray provides a detailed analysis of the Deuteronomic influence reflected in the present form of the text.

Crenshaw, *Prophetic Conflict* (1971, 2007), includes 1 Kings 13 in his study on the topic of false prophecy.[12] He, like John Gray, views 1 Kings 13 as a "prophetic legend" that contains "a kernel of historical fact."[13] He conjectures that the story originally circulated at Bethel and reflects a northern perspective.[14] Crenshaw attributes the addition of this story to the Deuteronomist. He argues

---

of the story to the time of Josiah.

9. Bosworth notes that "all other prophecy-fulfillment notices in the former prophets name the person only in the fulfillment notice, if at all" ("Revisiting Karl Barth's Exegesis," 366). Thus, it is not odd to treat the present form of the text as the result of the redactional work from the Josianic time. See also Sweeney, *I & II Kings*, 178–82.

10. Gray, *I & II Kings*, 293.

11. Gray, *I & II Kings*, 298.

12. Crenshaw, *Prophetic Conflict*, 47.

13. Crenshaw, *Prophetic Conflict*, 41.

14. Crenshaw, *Prophetic Conflict*, 42.

an oral tradition about a man of God who confronted Jeroboam with a pronouncement concerning the desecration of the altar of Bethel and who rejected the king's hospitality has been added by the Deuteronomic compiler (or perhaps a subsequent editor) after Josiah's reform, the occasion of the accidental discovery and intentional preservation of the grave alluded to in the tradition.[15]

The reason for the inclusion of the story in the Deuteronomic history was to emphasize "Jeroboam had ample warning from a genuine man of God, thus magnifying his guilt."[16] Crenshaw discusses the function of the story in the larger context of the Deuteronomistic History, but it still lacks a more complete explanation, especially on how the second half of the story fits in his understanding of the function of the story.

Lemke, in his article "The Way of Obedience: 1 Kings 13 and the Structure of the Deuteronomistic History" (1976), argues against the view, mainly through linguistic analysis, that 1 Kings 13 is "a secondary, post-Deuteronomistic interpolation" (e.g., Wellhausen, Jepsen, Eissfeldt) and contends that 1 Kings 13 is Deuteronomistic.[17] He argues that a Deuteronomistic editor inserted and even partially shaped the story, which most likely originated from northern prophetic circles. Hence 1 Kings 13 in its present position and formulation "forms an integral part of the structure and theology of the Deuteronomistic History."[18] His emphasis is on proving that there exists "an integral relationship between our pericope and the larger structure and theology of the Deuteronomistic History"[19] in an effort to demonstrate that 1 Kings 13 has "significance for an assessment of the structure and theology of the Deuteronomistic History."[20]

Walter Gross, in his article "Lying Prophet and Disobedient Man of God in 1 Kings 13: Role Analysis as An Instrument of Theological Interpretation of an OT Narrative Text" (1979), provides a good summary of past scholarship on 1 Kings 13 and raises problems related to the interpretative approaches taken by scholars.[21] He takes a literary (source) critical approach to the text and reconstructs the pre-Deuteronomistic state of the

---

15. Crenshaw, *Prophetic Conflict*, 43.
16. Crenshaw, *Prophetic Conflict*, 43.
17. Lemke, "The Way of Obedience," 303.
18. Lemke, "The Way of Obedience," 304. See also Sweeney, *I & II Kings*, 178–8.
19. Lemke, "The Way of Obedience," 312.
20. Lemke, "The Way of Obedience," 303.
21. Gross, "Lying Prophet," 97–135.

text.²² Gross suggests "obedience/disobedience" as the main theme of the present form of the story. He writes, "Whatever may have been the significance of the oracle against the altar and the burial in earlier stages of the tradition, both have been subordinated to the main theme obedience/disobedience in a way that can be demonstrated literally."²³

Gross's article is very informative and deserves more attention. His method of role analysis clears away some of the vexing problems raised by previous commentators, such as ethical and/or theological problems.²⁴ His analysis, however, may be problematic, because it assumes that the story has been structured according to that perspective. In my judgment, it is a perspective foreign to the text and thus is brought into the reading of the text, rather than being a perspective that the text itself suggests. Second, Gross bases his analysis of the pre-Deuteronomistic text on the structure of the content, not on the structure of the expression side of the text, thus often resulting in rearranging the material according to the "logical/temporal sequence," as he understands the story.²⁵ This may cause the intention of the narrator to be lost, which may be betrayed in the layout of the present form of the text. Third, his analysis of the text is limited to 13:7–28,²⁶ where he argues the theme of obedience/disobedience is mainly dealt with. Consequently, his analysis leaves out the rest of the text, and more importantly, it does not consider the function of 1 Kings 13 in its surrounding literary context.

As is the case with Walter Gross, the endeavors to reconstruct the pre-Deuteronomistic stage of the text has continued. Some scholars produced a theme out of the reconstructed pre-Deuteronomistic form of the story.²⁷ One example of this is Thomas Dozeman's article titled "The Way of the Man of God from Judah: True and False Prophecy in the Pre-Deuteronomic Legend of 1 Kings 13" (1982).²⁸ Dozeman focuses on reconstructing the pre-Deuteronomic stage of the "legend" and argues that "the unifying

22. Gross, "Lying Prophet," 4–30, comes up with 12:33b, c, 13:1, b, 2ab, 3bcd.

23. Gross, "Lying Prophet," 108.

24. Gross's role analysis focuses on establishing precisely the individuals' relationship to one another in 1 Kings 13 ("Lying Prophet," 110).

25. Gross, "Lying Prophet," 112.

26. Gross, "Lying Prophet," 113.

27. See Dozeman, "Way of the Man," 379–93; Eynikel, "Prophecy and Fulfillment," 227–37; Gray, *I & II Kings*; Gross, "Lying Prophet," 97–135; Knoppers, *Two Nations under God 2*.

28. Dozeman, "Way of the Man," 379–93.

theme of the pre-deuteronomic legend is true and false prophecy."²⁹ His view is evaluated in more detail later in this chapter (in a section titled "The Theme of True and False Prophecy"). More recently, E. Eynikel focuses his article titled "Prophecy and Fulfillment in the Deuteronomistic History, 1 Kgs 13; 2 Kgs 23,16-18" (1990) on reconstructing the pre-Deuteronomistic, original, prophetic legend behind the present form of 1 Kings 13.³⁰ Basically, he accepts Martin Rehm's view that "While the first part [vv. 1-10] could independently stand alone, the second [vv. 11-32] would be incomprehensible without it."³¹ He argues, "The most logical conclusion . . . is then, that 1 Kgs 13,1-10 existed first and that vv. 11-32 were added afterwards by a redactor, who made ample use of the motifs of the older legend (איש אלהים, דרך, שוב) and elaborated upon it to a certain extent."³²

Lastly, Gary Knoppers published two volumes of monographs under the title, *Two Nations under God: the Deuteronomistic History of Solomon and the Dual Monarchies, The Reign of Jeroboam, the Fall of Israel, and the Reign of Josiah* in 1993 and 1994, respectively.³³ In the two volumes Solomon and Jeroboam are focused on respectively. He analyzes the text through a combination of different methods: textual criticism, source criticism, literary criticism, form criticism, and redaction criticism. Like many others, he ascribes the insertion of stories in 1 Kings 13 to the Josianic Deuteronomist (Dtr¹).³⁴ The Deuteronomist, who is responsible for the inclusion of 1 Kings 13 in the Jeroboam narrative, however, has not "heavily edited the prophetic legends themselves (vv. 1-10, 11-31)," except in a few verses (e.g., part of 1 Kgs 13:1-2 and of 13:32, and 13:33-34).³⁵ He argues that the

---

29. Dozeman, "Way of the Man," 379.

30. Eynikel, "Prophecy and Fulfillment," 227-37.

31. My own translation of the recited quotation in Eynikel's article ("Prophecy and Fulfillment," 228) from Rehm, *1 Könige*, 142: "Der erste Teil könnte zwar selbständig für sich allein stehen, der zweite dagegen wäre ohne ihn unverständlich."

32. Eynikel, "Prophecy and Fulfillment," 228. He concludes that "the first legend consisted of 1 Kgs 13,1a. 3.4.8a.9aab.10; a redactor added 1 Kgs 13,1b.2.8b.9ab.11-32; 2 Kgs 23,16-18" ("Prophecy and Fulfillment," 237). This view is similar to that of Klopfenstein.

33. Knoppers, *Two Nations under God* 1, 2.

34. Knoppers, *Two Nations under God*, 2:50-56. He rejects the view that the prophetic legends were inserted by a later editor who is not a Deuteronomist.

35. Knoppers, *Two Nations under God*, 2:55. In this respect, Knoppers does not agree with Lemke who argued that the hand of the Deuteronomist is visible throughout the whole chapter. Knoppers says, "If the Deuteronomist did write 1 Kings 13, one would expect few incongruities between 1 Kings 13:2 and 32 and between 1 Kings 13 and 2 Kings 23:16-18. These tensions are sometimes resolved by attributing problematic verses

Deuteronomist "recontextualized" his sources to "underscore the ultimate demise of the Bethel sanctuary,"[36] and the theme or intention behind the "recontextualization" is to show that "the triumph of the divine word in the lives of southern and northern prophets points toward the triumph of the divine word in the reign of Josiah."[37] He asserts that the function of 1 Kings 13 is to show "the prospects for the new cult."[38]

This view, shared by Richard Nelson,[39] that 1 Kings 13 mainly addresses the judgment on the Bethel altar while 1 Kings 14 addresses Jeroboam's kingdom (house) is evaluated in chapter 2. Unlike Dozeman who made it a goal of his exegesis to find the theme of the original, pre-Deuteronomistic state of the narrative, Knoppers seeks to discover the purpose of the Deuteronomist's reuse or reworking of the original prophetic legends in 1 Kings 13.[40] He asserts, similar to the view of Crenshaw, "Whatever the original function of the prophetic traditions included in 1 Kings 13, the Deuteronomist reworks them as forewarnings to Jeroboam, accentuating the gravity of his transgressions and the centrality of divine reprisal."[41]

Historical-Critical Topics Related to 1 Kings 13

I have so far reviewed the approaches taken by some of major historical critics who have studied 1 Kings 13. Now I will turn to some of the topics that have been addressed by historical critics in relation to the study of 1 Kings 13 and show their limitations as the theme of the chapter.

---

to later editors, but I think it is more likely that most of these tensions result from the Deuteronomist's practice of editing, but not effacing, his sources (Wilson 1980:188)" (*Two Nations under God* 2, 55).

36. Knoppers, *Two Nations under God*, 2:46.
37. Knoppers, *Two Nations under God*, 2:46.
38. Knoppers, *Two Nations under God*, 2:45. Knoppers partly agrees with Simon that the theme of 1 Kings 13 "is the triumph of YHWH's word over both its subjects and its adversaries" (*Two Nations under God*, 2:58).
39. Nelson, *First and Second Kings*, 88.
40. Knoppers, *Two Nations under God*, 2:50.
41. Knoppers, *Two Nations under God*, 2:63. Sweeney has a similar view and argues that the Josianic Deuteronomist reworked "an older tradition concerning the etiology of the tomb of the prophets in the vicinity of Beth El" to condemn "Jeroboam, the altar at Beth El, and even the city itself as the home of a lying prophet" (*I & II Kings*, 179–80).

A Survey of Modern Scholarship on 1 Kings 13 and Hermeneutical Suggestions

The Theme of True and False Prophecy

The story in 1 Kings 13 (vv. 11–32) draws the immediate attention of the reader for the strange unfolding of events happening between two prophetic figures. The man of God from Judah proclaims the genuine word of Yahweh to Jeroboam and is met by an old prophet from Bethel. This old prophet lies to him and then leads him to disobey the command from Yahweh and as a punishment to be killed by a lion. The motif of two conflicting prophetic voices is discernible, and hence the story seems to describe the conflicts between the true prophet and the false. The similarity in motifs of this story to other parts of the Hebrew Bible led scholars to seek any possible thematic connections with other stories.[42] The theme of true and false prophecy is to be found throughout the Hebrew Bible; Deuteronomy 18:15–22, as one of the most significant passages on this theme, offers a criterion for judging prophets.[43]

The second part of the chapter (vv. 11–32) thus has been analyzed by some scholars, among whom are, as briefly mentioned above, Thomas Dozeman and, more recently, Terence Fretheim, in an effort to demonstrate that it addresses the issue of true and false prophecy.[44] Dozeman argues in his article, "The legend uses this turn of events to draw us into the central questions of the story: When is a prophet authentically speaking in the word of Yahweh (*bidbar Yhwh*)? And what criteria are to be used in assessing prophecy?—the very questions that the prophet from Judah failed to discern in the *nabi*'s test."[45] According to Dozeman, the old prophet of Bethel was uncertain about whether the oracle of the man of God from

---

42. For example, the conflict between four hundred prophets and Micaiah in 1 Kings 22, and a debate between Amaziah and prophet Amos in Amos 7.

43. See Crenshaw, *Prophetic Conflict*, 124. Crenshaw provides a full bibliography of studies through the end of the 1960s (124). Subsequent to that, see Hossfeld and Meyer, *Prophet gegen Prophet*, 113–43; Meyer, *Jeremía und der falsche Propheten* (1977); Sanders, "Hermeneutics in True and False Prophecy," 21–41; Childs, *Old Testament Theology*, 133–44; Sheppard, "True and False Prophecy," 262–81. More recently, R. W. L. Moberly discusses this issue in his book (*Prophecy and Discernment*, 100–9).

44. Fretheim, *First and Second Kings*, 77–82. Fretheim follows Dozeman on the broad scale, whether openly or coincidentally in major points and interprets 1 Kings 13 (especially vv. 11–32) to be addressing the issue of true and false prophecy. He, like Dozeman, states that "ironically, the death of the man of God confirms that his prophecy was true," but does not explain the old prophet's receiving the genuine word of Yahweh (*First and Second Kings*, 80).

45. Dozeman, "Way of the Man," 380. The theme of false prophecy appears elsewhere (e.g., Deut 13:1–5; 18:21–22; 1 Kgs 22:24; Jer. 23:9–40; 28:1–17).

THE FATE OF THE MAN OF GOD FROM JUDAH

Judah was authentic and tested him, and at the end of the story, the old prophet from Bethel affirmed the truthfulness of the man of God's word against the altar (v. 32). According to him, the man of God's failure in the test paradoxically proved the authenticity of his oracle against the altar in Bethel, "for Yahweh certainly would not punish the prophet from Judah for breaking a commandment which he never received."[46]

Such a view, however, has been subjected to many criticisms. B. S. Childs, for example, argues that the theme of the story has to do with the fulfillment of the word of Yahweh and refutes the view that the story is about true and false prophecy. He says,

> All the ethical issues are simply by-passes. The story has to do with the fulfillment of God's word of judgment which will not tolerate any softening or compromise. In a real sense, the narrative marks the furthest extreme possible from an existentialist interpretation of prophecy. Timing and hermeneutics have nothing to do with the true and the false. The distinction is unrelated to the ethical sensitivity of an alert prophet but measured completely by the effect of the word of God.[47]

As Childs asserts, it does not seem that the story is presenting criteria by which the reader can tell true prophecy from false, and the focus of the story is rather on the power of the word of Yahweh. Also, contrary to Dozeman's reading, neither the old prophet from Bethel nor the reader becomes doubtful as to the authenticity of the oracle of the man of God from Judah, because that he came and spoke "by the word of Yahweh" is emphasized through the story (vv. 1, 2, 5, 32). The doubt of the old prophet is not obvious in the text, either. The old prophet lied to the man of God and thus appears to be a false prophet, but he also spoke the true word of Yahweh later. A clear criterion for judging prophets is not present in the story, and the story seems to be saying something else, which will be discussed in full detail in the next chapter. In other words, in my judgment, any attempts to extract from the text any principles whereby to identify a true prophet or a false are unpromising.

Thus, Crenshaw concludes, "This passage deals the death knell to every attempt to specify absolute criteria by which to differentiate the true

---

46. Dozeman, "Way of the Man," 392. Nelson argues that the death of the man of God ironically validates his oracle, because it "demonstrates that the prohibitions which accompanied the Bethel oracle rally were from God" (*First and Second Kings*, 87).

47. Childs, *Old Testament Theology*, 142.

from the false prophet, for the ultimate criterion to which contemporary scholarship appeals (the charismatic intuition of a true prophet) fails in this instance."[48] Knoppers also states, "If the story offers lessons for distinguishing between true and false prophecy, they are not apparent," and he adds, "Dozeman (1982:392) suggests the criteria of fulfillment, prophetic confirmation, and prophetic character, but it is unclear to me how the story communicates these values."[49]

1 KINGS 13 IN ITS RELATION WITH 2 KINGS 23

In addition to the theme of true and false prophecy, scholars have often brought 2 Kings 23 into the discussion of the theme of 1 Kings 13. There exist clear connections between 1 Kings 13 and 2 Kings 23 that cannot be ignored by the reader. The Judean man of God's oracle against the altar in Bethel (v.2) is fulfilled with precision in 2 Kings 23:15–20. Moreover, the old Bethelite prophet's request to his sons that he be buried in the grave where the man of God is buried (1 Kgs 13:31–32) proves itself a wise move to preserve his own bones (2 Kgs 23:18). It seems as if he foresaw that Josiah would destroy the tombs on the mount in Bethel with the exception of the tomb of the man of God from Judah. These connections led scholars to look further into the Deuteronomist's (or an editor's) hand in the arrangement of these materials and the possibility of these two materials originating from the same tradition.

Jepsen, for example, argued in his article "Gottesmann und Prophet" that 1 Kings 13:1–32a and 2 Kings 23:16–18 form a coherent unit and that 1 Kings 13 should be read in light of 1 Kings 23:16–18.[50] He pays attention to the conclusion of the narrative, that is, the old prophet's request that his

---

48. Crenshaw, *Prophetic Conflict*, 47–48.

49. Knoppers, *Two Nations under God*, 2:61. Also see Moberly, *Prophecy and Discernment*, where Moberly comments, though only in passing, that 1 Kings 13, along with Amos 7:10–17, is about "conflict but not about discernment," so he agrees with Crenshaw and Knoppers on that 1 Kings 13 is not providing criteria for discerning between true and false prophecy (105). In his monograph, Moberly asks how one evaluates the statements of those who claim to speak for God, and through the examination of texts from both the Old Testament and the New Testament (i.e., 1 Thess 2:13; Deut 5:22–33; Jeremiah; Micaiah ben Imlah; Elisha; Balaam; 1 John; Paul), he suggests the following criteria for discerning true prophets: the integrity their lives display, their lack of self-serving interests, their message's challenge to the facile prevalence of conventional wisdom, and the capacity to recognize God's presence.

50. Jepsen, "Gottesmann und Prophet," 171–82.

bones be buried beside those of the man of God from Judah (1 Kg 13:31),[51] and asks, "He [the listener] had to ask: why did the prophet then want to lie united with the man of God in death? What has the prophecy against the altar of Bethel to do with the common grave?"[52] He concludes, "That is, 1 Kings 13 is not understandable without 2 King 23:16-18, but only in connection with these verses. Then, this of course leads to the conclusion that the story in the existing present form originated, at the earliest, in the days of Josiah."[53]

Jepsen's conclusion that the present form of the story (1 Kgs 13) most likely came into being either during the time of Josiah or a later time is agreeable, but his statement that 1 King 13 cannot be understood apart from 2 Kings 23:16-20 may need some qualifications. Like Jepsen, Knoppers also argues that 1 Kings 13 should be interpreted in light of 2 Kings 23. He argues that the Deuteronomist who is responsible for 2 Kings 17:24-28 and 23:19 "has rewritten and supplemented 1 Kgs 13:2 and 1 Kgs 13:32."[54] In other words, "the Deuteronomist seems to have largely integrated the prophetic legends into his narrative by rewriting their introduction (vv. 1-3) and conclusion (v. 32) and by adding his own commentary on their significance."[55] Reading 1 Kings 13 in light of 2 Kings 23 led Knoppers to conclude, regarding the theme of 1 Kings 13, that it addresses the prospect of the Bethel cultus. This is a similar conclusion to that of Jepsen, who understands the narratives to be describing the negation of the Bethel altar as a locus of divine worship.

It seems that there is no doubt that the Deuteronomist has these two incidents—1 Kings 13 and Josiah's reformation in 2 Kings 23—in mind as he was narrating 1 Kings 13. Jepsen's view, however, that 1 Kings 13 cannot be understood apart from 2 Kings 23 might disregard the literary function of 1 Kings 13 within its immediate literary context (the Jeroboam

---

51. Jepsen, "Gottesmann und Prophet," 171.

52. My own translation of "Er [ein Hörer] mußte sich fragen: warum wollte denn der Prophet im Tode mit dem Gottesmann vereint liegen? Was hatte die weissagung gegen den Altar von Bethel mit dem gemeinsamen Grab zu tun?" in Jepsen, "Gottesmann und Prophet," 171.

53. My own translation of "Dh 1 Könige 13 ist ohne 2 König 23,16-18 nicht, ondern vielmehr nur in Verbinung mit ien Versen verstandlich. Das führt dann freilich zu der Folgerung, das die Erzählung in der gegenwärtig vorliegenden Form frühestens in der Zeit Josias entstanden ist" in Jepsen, "Gottesmann und Prophet," 172.

54. Knoppers, *Two Nations under God*, 2:54.

55. Knoppers, *Two Nations under God*, 2:54.

narrative). 1 Kings 13 does certainly more than justify and commend Josiah's reformation. Also, the view that 1 Kings 13 addresses mainly the prospect of the Bethel cultus seems to overemphasize one element of the story and consequently subordinate other elements to this one. In other words, the function and theme of the narrative is simplified, and its literary context is disregarded. Consequently, 1 Kings 13 embedded in the Jeroboam narrative is not read on its own.

Simon's criticism seems appropriate here: "Jepsen's attempt to find the key to the meaning of the story outside its confines, that is, by an historical reconstruction of the time and circumstances of its composition, seems to me illegitimate."[56] 1 Kings 13 is certainly about more than negating the Bethel cultus as the locus of a divine worship. Simon continues, "Moreover, the fact that the prophecy of the destruction of the altar uttered by the man of God (13:2) is presented without supporting reason or explanation proves sufficiently that the guilt of Beth-el is not the theme of the story but is merely its background."[57] In sum, though 2 Kings 23 might have been in the mind of the narrator of 1 Kings 13, the theme of the latter does not necessarily depend on the former. Rather, 1 Kings 13 seems to serve its literary function in its immediate literary context.

1 Kings 13 and the Book of Amos

In addition to the connection of 1 Kings 13 and 2 Kings 23, scholars have also seen possible connections between 1 Kings 13 and the Book of Amos, more specifically Amos 7:10-17.[58] It was Wellhausen who suggested a possible link between 1 Kings 13 and Amos,[59] and Eisfeldt[60] and Dietrich[61] fol-

---

56. Simon, "Prophetic Sign," 85.
57. Simon, "Prophetic Sign," 85.
58. Fretheim gives some of the examples of how Kings is in dialogue with other biblical literature: 2 Kgs 18:17—20:19 and Isa 36–39; 2 Kgs 24:18—25:30 and Jer 52; 1 Kgs 22:28 and Mic 1:2; 1 Kgs 12:28 and Exod 32:4; the stories of Elijah and the traditions of Moses and Sinai (*First and Second Kings*, 8).
59. J. Wellhausen, *Die Composition des Hexateuchs*, 277–8.
60. Eissfeldt, "Amos und Jona," 137–42.
61. Dietrich, *Prophetie und Geschichte*, 118.

THE FATE OF THE MAN OF GOD FROM JUDAH

lowed and developed his idea. Though the idea was denied by Jepsen[62] and Lemke,[63] there have been a few adherents of it.[64]

The similarities that have been pointed out between these two parts of the Hebrew Bible are as follows:[65] (1) Both the man of God from Judah in 1 Kings 13 and Amos are from Judah and come to Bethel in obedience to the word of Yahweh (cf. Amos 7:14-15). (2) Both proclaim the destruction of the altar at Bethel (cf. Amos 3:13-15. Also, a prophecy of the destruction of the house of Jeroboam is found in Amos 7:9). (3) Both come into conflict with the leader of Bethel (cf. Amos 7:10-13). (4) Both come to Bethel during the reign of "King Jeroboam." In addition to these, other points of possible correspondence may be noted: (1) the motif of "eating bread" appears in both accounts (cf. Amos 7:12). (2) A lion plays a part in both accounts (cf. Amos 3:4, 8, 12; 5:19). (3) Both do not fit in the category of professional prophets: the man of God in 1 Kings 13 is consistently called "the man of God" throughout the chapter, possibly with the exception of v. 23 (and also v. 18, where the man of God silently agrees to be called a prophet), and Amos refuses to be counted among prophets (cf. Amos 7:14-15).

On the other hand, despite these similarities, some obvious differences have also been noted: (1) The story in 1 Kings 13 is dated to the time of Jeroboam I, whereas that of Amos is dated to the time of Jeroboam II. (2) Amos, as Crenshaw points out, was urged to eat bread in Judah, that is, to earn his living or stay alive, whereas the man of God was commanded not to eat bread.[66] (3) Amos was opposed by a priest, whereas the man of God was opposed by a king. King Jeroboam is only "in the background in the book of Amos."[67] (4) Some key elements of 1 Kings 13 are absent in the

---

62. Jepsen, "Gottesmann und Prophet," 171-82.

63. Lemke, "The Way of Obedience," 315-6. After a detailed discussion on the issue, Lemke concludes, "the similarities between these traditions are sufficiently general and diffuse so as not to allow us to elevate the possibility of a connection into a certainty or even strong probability, and for this reason we would be inclined to go along with most commentators who deny or seriously question the thesis that the antecedents of our story lie in the Amos tradition" (316), but at the same time, he does not completely shut off this possibility, saying, "It is possible, however, that while our story did not originate in the Amos tradition, it may have been partly influenced by the latter" (325, note 95).

64. For example, Crenshaw still believes that Amos is behind the narrative in 1 Kings 13 (*Prophetic Conflict*, 42).

65. Wolff, "Das Ende des Heiligtums," 287-98; Lemke, "The Way of Obedience," 315-6; Crenshaw, *Prophetic Conflict*, 41-42.

66. Crenshaw, *Prophetic Conflict*, 42.

67. Crenshaw, *Prophetic Conflict*, 42.

A Survey of Modern Scholarship on 1 Kings 13 and Hermeneutical Suggestions

book of Amos: for example, as John Gray notes, the withering and healing of the king's hand and the subsequent death of the prophet are unknown in the Amos tradition.[68]

If the connections between the two accounts could be established, it might lead to further discussion on the motif of true and false prophecy. The issue of conflict between true and false prophets might require further investigations,[69] in which case, the old prophet from Bethel in 1 Kings 13 could be construed as someone corresponding to Amaziah in Amos 7, as someone who opposed the genuine word of Yahweh.[70] In my judgment, however, the differences between the two accounts of the Hebrew Bible are more obvious than the similarities. It seems hard to conclude that the connections are intentional. The motifs of a Judean prophet proclaiming judgment against the altar at Bethel are discernible in the two accounts, but the linkage is not strong.[71] Also, it is not likely that a story from the time of Jeroboam II was transposed to the time of Jeroboam I only because of the same name.[72] As Jepsen points out, 1 Kings 13 is "reminiscent" of

---

68. Gray, *I & II Kings*, 295.

69. Dozeman, "Way of the Man," 380. Jörg Jeremias in his article, "The Interrelationship between Amos and Hosea," discusses Amos 7:10-17. Though his focus in the discussion is on the Hoseanic influence on the words of Amos (cf. 7:9), Jeremias clarifies the purpose of the narrative (7:10-17) placed in between the visions (7:1-8; 8:1-2). He asserts that the narrative has been placed in its present location to show that "God's patience ends where the state represented by the priest tries to decide when and where God may speak through his prophet" (179). The motif of conflict "between priest and prophet, between the faithful servant of the king and the faithful servant of Yahweh" is clearly visible here (179), and the narrative along with the surrounding visions visualizes that silencing a prophet from God leads inevitably to God's judgment. In connection with this, we see a thematic resemblance between Amos 7:10-17 and 1 Kings 13. Though we cannot be certain whether this thematic resemblance indicates literary dependence between the two accounts, it is certainly a topic which is worth further investigation. See Jeremias, "The Interrelationship," 171-86.

70. For a comparison of the legend of 1 Kings 13 and Amos, see Crenshaw, *Prophetic Conflict*, 41-42. H. G. M. Williamson also notes connections between Amos 7:9-17 and 1 Kgs. 13 in the following article (119-21): Williamson, "The Prophet and the Plumb-Line," 453-77.

71. Lemke, "The Way of Obedience," 315-6.

72. Brian Peckham argues that the editor of the Book of Amos, who had a special interest in the altar at Bethel, "describes the encounter between Amos and Amaziah (7:10-17) in terms of the Deuteronomistic story (1 Kgs 13) in which the altar of Bethel figured so prominently (1 Kgs 13:1-5)" (*History and Prophecy*, 233, footnote 184). Even when the connection is established, however, the matter of dependence is another issue yet to be considered.

THE FATE OF THE MAN OF GOD FROM JUDAH

the account in the book of Amos, but to go any further than that is to go beyond what is visible to us.[73]

Conclusion

The above review of various approaches taken by historical-critical scholarship of 1 Kings 13 shows that many scholars have invested their efforts in figuring out sources, the provenance of the sources, the pre-history of the text, the date of composition, redactional intentions, and so forth. These investigations contribute to the understanding of the prehistory of the text and the redactional intentions behind the inclusion of the story in the present position. These analyses shed light on the original setting and processes old traditions might have gone through to reach the present form of the text.

On the other hand, this survey reveals that the reconstruction of the pre-Deuteronomistic form of the text remains hypothetical and even, sometimes, arbitrary, as is shown by the different or even conflicting results of those analyses, depending on the methods and their assumptions. Perhaps more importantly, the historical-critical methods have not been very fruitful in revealing the meaning of 1 Kings 13 in its literary or theological context.

As Bosworth correctly points out, historical critics "have concerned themselves with the history of composition more than the result of the compositional process."[74] Consequently, there has been little appreciation of 1 Kings 13 in relation to its immediate context. Source and redaction criticism have by and large considered 1 Kings 13 separately from its immediate context and failed to understand 1 Kings 13 in the context of the Jeroboam narrative and also in the context of the Book of Kings.

Reconstructing and analyzing the pre-Deuteronomistic sources of the story in 1 Kings 13, commentators, with the exception of a few scholars (e.g., Crenshaw and Knoppers) have largely ignored the function of the story in both its immediate and a broader context. Redaction critics have shown their interest in the context of the passage, but as Bosworth pointed out, they are less interested in its content and more concerned with "elucidating the process by which Deuteronomy—2 Kings was composed rather

---

73. Jepsen, "Gottesmann und Prophet," 180, note 15.
74. Bosworth, *Story within a Story*, 120.

than examining the result of the composition."⁷⁵ Consequently, they have not elucidated literary aspects of 1 Kings 13. The theme and function of the text in the Book of Kings as well as in the larger context of the Jeroboam narrative are yet to be more clearly articulated. In sum, the historical-critical approaches have severed our story from its surrounding context, highlighting the *"disconnectedness* within the history,"⁷⁶ and hence failed to see its place and function as it stands in its setting in the completed history.

Also, the theological aspect of the story has been largely ignored by historical-critical scholarship. The absence of theological exegesis is a big gap in the study of our text, especially when we consider that the Book of Kings, as most scholars would agree, is a theological book rather than a mere report of historical events or a collection of historical accounts through which we could restore the historical reality behind the text. Now, it is time to move on to the next category, that is, a theological/literary reading of 1 Kings 13.

Karl Barth: A Theological Reading

So far, I have examined various approaches that historical critics have applied to the study of 1 Kings 13 in the past few decades and some topics related to it. Now, in this part of our discussion, I will turn to more holistic interpretations of 1 Kings 13, an approach generally absent in the previous scholarship. I will review and critique Karl Barth's theological exegesis of 1 Kings 13⁷⁷ and David Bosworth's article and monograph on the chapter.⁷⁸

Karl Barth: A Theological Reading

Karl Barth's exegesis on 1 Kings 13 appears in his massive thirteen-volume work, *Church Dogmatics*, which was published over the span of 35 years from 1932 to 1967. His treatment of 1 Kings 13 is found in *The Doctrine of God, Part 2*. Barth's exegesis predates many of the historical critics we have reviewed above, but his exegesis fits in this part of this current chapter, because it came out in contrast to, and against the background of, the era

75. Bosworth, "Revisiting Karl Barth's Exegesis," 376.
76. Beal, *The Deuteronomist's Prophet*, 41.
77. Barth, *Church Dogmatics* 2/2, 393–409.
78. Bosworth, "Revisiting Karl Barth's Exegesis," 360–83; and Bosworth, *Story within a Story*, 118–57.

in which historical criticism dominated. Through his theological reading of biblical texts, Barth thus filled a lacuna caused by the trend.

Karl Barth reads 1 Kings 13 through the theological lens of God's election and rejection. His main idea is that the man of God from Judah and the old prophet of Bethel represent the Southern and the Northern Kingdom respectively, and the interactions between these two characters prefigure the relationship between the two kingdoms. Barth summarizes the theme of the chapter as follows: "The peculiar theme of the chapter is the manner in which the man of God and the [old] prophet belong together, do not belong together, and eventually and finally do belong together; and how the same is true of Judah and Israel."[79] The man of God's condemnation of the cult at Bethel and the prophecy that a descendant of David will destroy it indicate that the Northern Kingdom is rejected by God. Jeroboam's invitation indicates the possibility of compromise, but the man of God's refusal shows that God will allow no compromise. Thus, the old prophet's invitation is a continuation of the Northern Kingdom's attempt to bring out "the fellowship between Jerusalem and Bethel, the toleration and compromise, which had been the goal of Jeroboam's invitation."[80]

Barth's exegesis has been criticized by many scholars as an example of reading into biblical texts the interpreter's theological perspective. Noth criticizes Barth's exegesis as follows:

> When K. Barth sees in the transaction between the man of God and the prophet a dialectical game of a multiple role reversal between "the elected" and "the rejected," he goes far beyond that which the story really says or can say or even gives to understand in a background sense. It does not at all correspond with the intention of the story to apply the concepts "election" and "rejection" to the two (anonymous) main actors. Also, the fact that according to vv. 20b–22 Yhwh makes use of the prophet as proclaimer of his word is to be understood not as an act of 'election' according to the Old Testament perspective (in this respect we cannot even speak of as a role reversal in this case). Yhwh is free to use from time to time this or that representative. In the course of the eventful story both main actors, the man of God and the prophet, recognize the 'rejection' of Bethel (and the 'election' of Jerusalem).[81]

---

79. Barth, *Church Dogmatics* 2/2, 393.
80. Barth, *Church Dogmatics* 2/2, 395.
81. Noth, *Könige*, 306–7.

It might be a legitimate criticism that Barth's reading does not "correspond with the intention of the story" and in this sense, Barth brings the theology of election and rejection into the story of the two prophets;[82] thus, to many biblical scholars Barth's exegesis appears to be "eisegesis" rather than "exegesis." Crenshaw says of Barth's exegesis, "Barth's interpretation was only a pointer to the way . . . for the narrative is not really concerned with election and rejection."[83]

On the other hand, Barth's typological understanding of the story seems to deserve continued attention. Admittedly, the repeated designation "the man of God *from Judah*" and this *Judean* man of God's coming to Bethel and proclaiming Yahweh's judgment on the altar, which symbolizes Israel's religious departure from Judah,[84] make it hard to believe that the story is only about Yahweh's judgment on the altar at Bethel. Also, there is no doubt that Yahweh's judgment on the Northern Kingdom was in the mind of the narrator, who has witnessed the end of the kingdom in history. Therefore, though the events described in the story have been configured primarily to show Yahweh's judgment on the house of Jeroboam, it seems that the element of God's election of Judah and rejection of Israel might exist in the story.

In conclusion, despite the overall rejection by modern commentators, Barth's exegesis is a good example of the theological reading of the biblical text that was scarce in the early twentieth century, so it deserves much acclaim. Importantly, unlike many other thematic reading of biblical texts, his exegesis displays a careful attention to the details of the events described in the text, and one of the merits of his exegesis is that it gives much interest and consideration to the contexts in which the story is embedded.

David Bosworth: A Literary-Critical Approach

David Bosworth (2002, 2008) is another scholar who is noteworthy in this discussion. He takes Karl Barth's insights as a starting point of his

---

82. Find more criticisms in the following works: Walsh, "The Contexts," 367–8; Lemke, "The Way of Obedience," 317–18; Simon, "Prophetic Sign," 3.

83. Crenshaw, *Prophetic Conflict*, 41.

84. Though through a different prophet, Yahweh's judgment on the house of Jeroboam is extended to the entire Northern Kingdom (1 Kgs 14:15–16). This supports the view that in the narrator's perspective the man of God's prophecy against the altar at Bethel is looking ahead to the destruction of not only the house of Jeroboam but also that of Israel.

interpretation of 1 Kings 13 and takes one step further. Though his literary-critical approach is different from Barth's theological interpretation, it might be suitable to include him in this section since he takes one of his main ideas from Barth's exegesis. Bosworth attends to Barth's point that the relationship and interactions between the man of God and the old prophet of Bethel reflects those between the two kingdoms. The idea is well expressed in the following quote from Barth's exegesis:

> The very significant position which is assigned, even externally, to the story of 1 K. 13 in relation to the historical record of the Old Testament must not pass unobserved. It comes directly after the account of the disruption under Rehoboam and Jeroboam, and in some sense explains it. But it also constitutes a kind of heading, not only for the whole ensuing history of the two separated kingdoms of Israel, but at the same time for the history of the conflict which now begins between professional and original prophets on the one hand, and false and true prophets on the other. All that follows is already announced and prefigured in this story.[85]

From this observation of Barth's, Bosworth argues that 1 Kings 13 should be read as a kind of political allegory that prefigures what will happen between the two kingdoms described in 1 Kings 11 through 2 Kings 23. He states, "Although Barth sees the history of the divided kingdom played out in this story, he does not specifically spell out the relationship between 1 Kings 13 and the history of the divided monarchy in 1 and 2 Kings. Although some scholars have borrowed this central insight from Barth, none has developed it in detail."[86] He reads the events described in 1 Kings 13 and 2 Kings 23:15–20 "as a *mise-en-abyme* in the History of the Divided Kingdom."[87] He argues that the relationship that unfolds between the man of God from Judah and an old prophet of Bethel "adumbrates the relationship that unfolds between their nations during the History of the Divided Kingdom."[88] He argues that there exist *parallels* between the relationship between the two

---

85. Barth, *Church Dogmatics* 2/2, 403.

86. Bosworth, "Revisiting Karl Barth's Exegesis," 372.

87. Bosworth, *Story within a Story*, 118. *Mise-en-abyme* is a term which was used to describe art and literally means 'placement in abyss.' In literature it refers to a literary device in which "an internal text provides a miniature model of the framing text" (Emery, "Figures Taken for Signs," 339–55). Bosworth defines the term as "any internal mirror that reflects the whole of the narrative by simple, repeated, or 'specious' (paradoxical) duplication" (3).

88. Bosworth, *Story within a Story*, 119.

prophetic figures and the relationship between the two kingdoms in five aspects: 1) mutual hostility (1 Kgs 13:11–18; 1 Kgs 11–21), 2) friendship (1 Kgs 13:19; 1 Kgs 22–2 Kings 8), 3) role-reversal (1 Kgs 13:20–23; 2 Kgs 9–11), 4) resumption of hostility (1 Kgs 13:24–34; 2 Kgs 12–17), and 5) southern partner saves northern one (2 Kgs 23:15–20; 2 Kgs 22–23).

It is generally agreed that 1 Kings 13 possesses a strategic position in the history of the Divided Kingdom, and "the passage includes political and prophetic motifs that connect it to its wider context," for example, the motifs of the royal sanctuary at Bethel and the sin of Jeroboam.[89] Also, as mentioned (in the previous section on Barth's exegesis), typological elements seem to be present in the text. It is questionable, however, whether Bosworth's five thematic elements are actually to be found in 1 Kings 13 and 2 Kings 23:15–20. More importantly, the parallels between 1 Kings 13 and the rest of the history of the Divided Kingdom are not as clear. Marvin Sweeney notes "the fundamental conflict [is] between Judah and northern Israel" in the reference to the origins of the man of God as the man of God from Judah.[90] There is no doubt that the text betrays or even intentionally displays the tension between Judah and Israel, but it is to the end of condemning the Bethel cultus rather than implying conflict or hostility between the two kingdoms. Also, as will be argued later, whereas Jeroboam's hostility toward the man of God was clearly expressed, the old prophet's hostility toward the man of God is not clear. The connections thus seem to be imposed upon the texts rather than obviously recognized. David Cotter's question may be legitimate: "Questions remain, of course. Foremost among these must be the question of whether the device is in the text or in the eyes of the reader."[91] In my judgment, it is not likely that the "device" is in the text, and it is hard to believe that the Deuteronomist intended such parallels.

Lastly, on a methodological level, despite Bosworth's claim that he would focus on the context of 1 Kings 13, Bosworth severs 1 Kings 13:11–32 from its more immediate context (1 Kgs 12:26—13:10) and from the rest of the Jeroboam narrative. In sum, Bosworth's thesis that the prophetic conflict mirrors the political division may have some truth in it, but the attempt to read 1 Kings 13 and 2 Kings 23:15–20 as a *mise-en-abyme* in the unfolding events in the history of the Divided Kingdom is not convincing.

---

89. Bosworth, *Story within a Story*, 122.
90. Sweeney, *I & II Kings*, 180.
91. Cotter, Review of David A. Bosworth, 561–3.

Overall, the historical details displayed in the history of the Divided kingdom do not harmonize with the picture that Bosworth draws from 1 Kings 13.

Narrative Criticism

Lastly, I will take a look at literary approaches taken to 1 Kings 13. Narrative critics of biblical texts concerned themselves with interpreting the existing text, or the final form of the text, in terms primarily of its own story world rather than "understanding the text by attempting to reconstruct its sources and editorial history, its original setting and audience, and its author's or editor's intention in writing."[92] This criticism is generally based on the assumption that the text is "an interpretable entity independent of both author and interpreter."[93] Due to such emphasis on the text, narrative criticism is "particularly well suited for enhancing one's appreciation of the artistic side of the composition process."[94] Narrative critics find the meaning by means of "close reading that identifies formal and conventional structures of the narrative, determines plot, develops characterization, distinguishes point of view, exposes language play, and relates all to some overarching, encapsulating theme."[95]

It is relatively recently that scholars started to pay more attention to the mechanics or artistry of the literary construction of 1 Kings 13. What Gary Knoppers said of 1 Kings 1–11 may hold true of 1 Kings 13: "The very heterogeneity of Kings, which leads some interpreters to posit multiple redactions, may appear differently when viewed from the perspective of literary criticism."[96] Recently, more and more scholars approach 1 Kings 13 with increased attention to the literary aspects of the text. Among them Robert L. Cohn (1985) stands out, as in his article titled "Literary Technique in the Jeroboam Narrative" he showed the artistic design by which the Jeroboam Narrative had been constructed.[97] His focus is on analyzing "the strategies through which it [the Jeroboam narrative] manipulates our

---

92. Gunn, "Narrative Criticism," 171.
93. Gunn, "Narrative Criticism," 171.
94. Bodner, *Royal Drama*, 144.
95. Gunn, "Narrative Criticism," 171.
96. Knoppers, *Two Nations under God*, 2:4.
97. Cohn, "Literary Technique," 23–35.

A Survey of Modern Scholarship on 1 Kings 13 and Hermeneutical Suggestions

reactions to Jeroboam and his kingship."[98] His treatment provides an excellent literary reading of the whole Jeroboam narrative. He does touch on, if briefly, the prehistory of the text and also acknowledges that multiple sources might have existed behind the present text of the Jeroboam narrative, but his emphasis is on demonstrating "how the Jeroboam narrative, despite its multiple sources, functions as an integrated literary whole shaped to explain and justify the rise and fall of the man responsible for the division of the kingdom."[99] For him, "the tale of the two prophets" (vv. 11–32) has not "simply been included without any integral relation to the larger Jeroboam story."[100] He suggests a more constructive literary analysis as to the placement and purpose of the story in 1 Kings 13. He says,

> It is possible that this placement is more purposeful, that the fate of the man of God is meant to shed light on the destiny of Jeroboam. After all, the man of God occupies more space in the narrative than does the report of Jeroboam's activities as king! I see this tale as a kind of parable, a story within a story,[101] that sets into relief the theological dynamics of the larger narrative. The story of the man of God illustrates how God's agent can become God's victim if he does not remain true to his calling ... Like the man of God, Jeroboam, through his own actions, becomes the object of God's wrath. Repeating the key word šûb ("return") eleven times in the tale, the author drives home the idea that the man of God's physical reversal of direction was the cause of his downfall. Climatically, the word šûb ("return") appears for the final time predicated of Jeroboam at the conclusion of the tale: "After this thing Jeroboam did not return from his evil way (lo'-šāb yårāb'ām middarkô)." Whereas the sin of the man of God lay in his physical return by the way, the sin of Jeroboam was his refusal to turn back, metaphorically, from his "way."[102]

Cohn's insight as to the function of the story in the Jeroboam narrative is especially helpful. He recognizes the parallels between the man of God from Judah and Jeroboam: "The transformation of the man of God from

---

98. Cohn, "Literary Technique," 25.

99. Cohn, "Literary Technique," 35.

100. Cohn, "Literary Technique," 32.

101. It is obvious that Cohn uses the phrase "a story within a story" in a different way from the way Bosworth uses it. Cohn views 1 Kings 13 as a story within a story (the Jeroboam narrative) that illustrates the rise and fall of Jeroboam, so the larger narrative for Cohn is the Jeroboam narrative.

102. Cohn, "Literary Technique," 32–33.

THE FATE OF THE MAN OF GOD FROM JUDAH

God's ally to his enemy mirrors the fate of Jeroboam himself."[103] This explains why the story of the man of God from Judah has been placed in the Jeroboam narrative. His attention to the repeated use of key words in the story brings light to the narrator's intention behind it.

On the other hand, since Cohn's article treats the whole Jeroboam narrative, he does not explain some important details of 1 Kings 13; for example, the old prophet's lie and his receiving the true oracle from Yahweh remain to be explained. Also, his view that the old prophet's attitude toward the man of God changes and "acknowledges the truth of the man of God's prophecy" only after the death of the man of God is, in my judgment, to be weighed against the details of the text. The genre of the narrative as a parable might not be precise. I will discuss these matters in more detail in the next chapter.

Nelson in his commentary *First and Second Kings* (1987) reads the narrative mostly in its final form.[104] Nelson understands the story of the two prophets to be describing the transformation of the old prophet's position from "an opponent of the word to a supporter"; the transformation was enabled by the death of the man of God which validated the truthfulness of the oracle of the man of God. Nelson shares a similar view to that of Cohn that what happened to the man of God "illustrates" what will happen to the king. He writes, "Not being buried with one's fathers will also be a factor in the punishment of Jeroboam (14:13), so this present story illustrates what will soon happen to the king who has disobeyed."[105] For Nelson, 1 Kings 13 is not a story about true and false prophecy, but about the word of God. It is "a story about the word's power to get itself done (Isa. 55:10–11; Mark 4:26–29). The word of God changes adversaries into supporters who end up unconsciously fulfilling it (John 11:49–52)."[106]

Fretheim's commentary, *First and Second Kings* (1999), also takes the approach of "viewing the text in its present (final) form" and provides a literary and theological reading of the story, without completely excluding the issues of the date and composition of the story.[107] His diachronic observation concurs in broad outlines with the conclusions of the past scholarship:

---

103. Cohn, "Literary Technique," 35.
104. Nelson, *First and Second Kings*, 82–90.
105. Nelson, *First and Second Kings*, 88.
106. Nelson, *First and Second Kings*, 89.
107. Fretheim, *First and Second Kings*, 8.

> This chapter consists of two originally independent stories about prophets (vv. 1–10; 11–32) that have been integrated to provide a dual prophetic judgment on Jeroboam's religious activity; the chapter ends with a Deuteronomistic judgment of indictment and disaster for his house (vv. 33–34). This narrative also provides an occasion to refer prophetically to Josiah (v. 2), whose reform three hundred years later reversed these actions of Jeroboam (2 Kgs 23:15–20). As such, this chapter anticipates Josiah's reign and is concerned to establish his reforms as a God-given corrective to Jeroboam's condemned idolatrous religion.[108]

In his view, the text reflects the view of a narrator (the Deuteronomist) at the time of Josiah.[109] Yet Fretheim's focus is more on the literary and theological aspects of the story. He contends that the second segment of the story "turns on a specific case of true and false prophecy, that is, on the identification of the truth of the word of the man of God on the part of the prophet from Bethel."[110] The whole story is about Jeroboam's receiving "a *double* witness" against himself from "the leadership of both kingdoms,"[111] and the two parts of the story are conjoined in doubly witnessing against Jeroboam through the leadership of both kingdoms.[112] Therefore, for Fretheim, "the focus of the story must not be placed on the obedience or disobedience of the man of God or prophet"[113] but on a double prophetic witness against Jeroboam.

Lastly, Keith Bodner in his monograph on the Jeroboam narrative, *Jeroboam's Royal Drama* (2012), approaches the Jeroboam narrative from the narrative critical perspective. Without disregarding historical-critical

---

108. Fretheim, *First and Second Kings*, 77.

109. Fretheim, *First and Second Kings*, 78.

110. Fretheim, *First and Second Kings*, 79. I do not share Fretheim's view that the old prophet from Bethel is a false prophet and that he was "convinced by a remarkable series of events (including a prophet's death and God's use of him to utter a genuine word vv. 21–22) that the man of God from Judah was indeed a true prophet and, by implication, that he himself had been a false prophet" (81). He continues, "a false prophet has been convinced by events that the man of God was a true prophet and he himself becomes a true prophet, first by mediating the word to the man of God (vv. 21–22) and then by reiterating his word about Jeroboam" (81). This view that he had been a false prophet and became a true prophet by mediating and reiterating the word to the man of God may need a careful evaluation against the text. The text is clear that the word of Yahweh was *given* to the old prophet by Yahweh.

111. Fretheim, *First and Second Kings*, 81.

112. Fretheim, *First and Second Kings*, 81.

113. Fretheim, *First and Second Kings*, 81.

issues (i.e., redactional processes), Bodner pays heightened attention to "the development of Jeroboam's character over the course of his career."[114] By attending to the tools of narrative devices employed in the Jeroboam narrative such as "telescoped interior discourse, intertextuality, temporal sequencing, ironic reversal, structural analogy, spatial settings, and deliberate ambiguity," Bodner describes how the character of Jeroboam is transformed "from legitimate rebel to a king under the cloud of judgment."[115] Bodner also asks why 1 Kings 13:11–32 "is placed in the midst of the account of Jeroboam's reign, or how it contributes to the larger storyline."[116] Then, he reads the two parts of the chapter together in the way they relate to Jeroboam's characterization.[117] Especially, he understands 1 Kings 13:11–32 as a "play-within-a-play, a type of political allegory that functions as a subtle reflection on the fate of Jeroboam's kingship."[118] His basic idea is that the man of God is used to prefigure King Jeroboam, and the man of God becomes an illustration of King Jeroboam. On this point, he stands in line with J. K. Mead and Walsh[119] as well as the above scholars (Cohn, Nelson, and Fretheim). My reading of 1 Kings 13 owes much to that of Bodner, and he will be cited frequently in the second chapter.

The contributions that the narrative critics have made are clear. One of their contributions is that they read 1 Kings 13 in its immediate literary context. They pay attention to the literary devices that have been employed by the narrator, which shed light on the narrator's intention. Also, the function and theme of the story in its literary context becomes clearer. On the other hand, some narrative critics tend to read too much into the biblical text, which leads us to the issue of the reader's role in the process of interpretation, one of the hermeneutical issues of Narrative Criticism. When it comes to the study of 1 King 13, the narrative critics have contributed to the analysis of the artistry and poetics of the text, making the message of the final form of the text come alive.

---

114. Bodner, *Royal Drama*, 8.
115. Bodner, *Royal Drama*, 9.
116. Bodner, *Royal Drama*, 97.
117. Bodner, *Royal Drama*, 97.
118. Bodner, *Royal Drama*, 97–98.
119. Mead, "Kings and Prophets," 192–205, and Walsh, "The Context," 365.

HERMENEUTICAL SUGGESTIONS FOR THE INTERPRETATION OF 1 KINGS 13

I have so far reviewed various approaches and methodologies that have been taken to 1 Kings 13. Though this review is not comprehensive, it covers most, if not all, of the key interpreters of 1 Kings 13, and leads to the following observations. Scholars have reached a rough consensus as to the date and composition of 1 Kings 13 that it is the work of the Josianic Deuteronomist, while this view does not rule out the possibility that the exilic editor's hand is also present in the final form of the text. The theme of the story is still debatable, while the following themes are among the most favored ones: the importance of obedience to the word of Yahweh, the true and false prophecy, and the triumph of the word of Yahweh.

The function of the story is generally agreed upon among scholars, especially among narrative critics, that the story in its final form has been placed in its present location to describe why God's judgment on Jeroboam was inevitable, though such a view still awaits clearer explanations. The nature or genre of the story is also among the issues yet to be resolved. Many scholars consider our story a prophetic legend. This categorization, however, is not very helpful to the interpreting of the story, because the prophetic legend as a genre is somewhat generic and comprehensive.[120] Besides these issues, this story has aroused many ethical, moral, and theological questions throughout the history of interpretation. The God in the story has been perceived to be incomprehensible or even bizarre.[121] The behavior of the characters remains enigmatic, and the motives behind them have been subject to much speculation.

To contribute to the interpretation of 1 Kings 13 and to resolve some of the vexing interpretive difficulties with the chapter, this study will look at 1 Kings 13 and the Jeroboam narrative from a literary and theological perspective, which I believe has been somewhat neglected in the past studies of this literary unit. Through this study, the theme and function of the story will become clearer, and its nature and genre, which I believe is the key to the interpretation of the story, will be discussed in detail. The theology of the story will become clear against the background of the Deuteronomistic History.

---

120. Long, *1 Kings*, 257–58.

121. For a review of the ethical and theological problems regarding 1 Kings 13 raised by various scholars, see Gross, "Lying Prophet," 108–10.

First, I will pay heightened attention to the literary devices and the artistry of the text. In my judgment, the text of 1 Kings 13 itself demands such an approach, because it features a number of literary devices—the unusually frequent repetitions of key motifs and expressions, parallels, and literary connections with its surrounding narrative. The repeated expressions betray the narrator's emphases, and the parallels contribute to forming the structure of the story. I argue that ignoring these literary features results in a failure to grasp the messages the narrator intended to deliver to his intended reader and thus in rather arbitrary interpretations that are not based on the text. In this respect, this study will approach the text synchronically, without excluding the diachronic aspects of the text completely.

In my study, it is presumed that the text is the product of a narrator who was responsible for the final form of the text and that the narrator employed various literary devices to make his message as clearly as possible, so close attention is paid to reveal the narrator's probable intention.[122] At the same time, we admit that every interpretation is subject to some degree of subjectivity, and it would be a naïve claim that a sound methodology can firmly establish the *true* or *authentic* meaning of a given text, intended by its narrator. Admittedly, "no interpretation is absolute; each interpretation is inherently hypothetical."[123] I believe, however, that the formal features of the biblical text provide the reader with some guidelines to get the message(s) that the narrator intended to convey. Frolov states, "Polyvalence does not equal omnivalence; there may be an infinite number of legitimate interpretations, but not every interpretation is legitimate. Above

---

122. Throughout the dissertation the term "narrator" is used frequently. I use the term to refer to the one who is responsible for the final form of the Hebrew text of the Book of Kings. It is assumed that the narrator used the materials in his possession and shaped them for his purpose so as to deliver his message to the intended reader. The narrator is responsible for the inclusion of 1 Kings 13 and other materials in the Jeroboam narrative and for the arrangement of them in their present order. Though some of the motifs and expressions in the present text may have been in original materials, they have been reused or reworked by the hand of the narrator, so the key motifs and other various literary devices that contribute to forming the theme of the text are attributed to the narrator. In this sense, the narrator may be identified with the final editor of the Book of Kings, or the Deuteronomistic editor. In chapter 4 I use the term "Deuteronomist" more frequently than "narrator" only because it is more convenient for my purpose, which is to discuss the theology of the Book of Kings and of the entire Deuteronomistic History.

123. Van Leeuwen, "Form Criticism," 65–84.

all, exegesis is constrained by formal features of the biblical text because without a foothold in this text the interpretation becomes something else."[124]

To this end, I will first turn to the structure of the narrative. A well-executed analysis of the structural form will help to avoid the mistake of raising up individual features to the status of the primary message of the story.[125] Though we do not rule out the possibility of the presence of more than one idea in the story, we believe that most parts, if not all, have been arranged by the narrator to contribute to the primary message that the structure of the final form of the story betrays to the reader. And the proper way of outlining the structure of the narrative is by means of finding the literary devices that the narrator has employed in designing the narrative.

Secondly, I will argue that identifying the genre/form of the story is a key to the correct interpretation of 1 Kings 13. Understanding the primary characteristics of a certain form of narrative—prophetic symbolic actions in our case—will resolve some difficult problems raised regarding 1 Kings 13 (i.e., ethical or theological problems of the text, and speculations about characters' motives of their actions). With a view to identifying the genre of the story, our study will involve the methodology that is commonly called "form criticism." Though it is originally known to be a diachronic analysis of texts that is focused on reconstructing the oral traditions in a particular, original setting (i.e., Hermann Gunkel, Gressmann, and Sigmund Mowinckel), form criticism has undergone some fundamental changes in the past few decades. As Frolov notes, though the form criticism of Gunkel and Gressmann was profoundly diachronic, "form criticism is not inherently diachronic, and subsequent theoretical advances have massively shifted its emphasis towards the final form of the HB."[126]

In the volume they co-edited titled *The Changing Face of Form Criticism for the Twenty-First Century*, Marvin A. Sweeney and Ehud Ben Zvi note this shift in the form-critical studies in the past decades and draw

---

124. Frolov, *Judges*, 9.

125. For example, Barth and Klopfenstein saw a role reversal between the man of God and the old prophet of Bethel as a key to interpreting the story (see Barth, *Church Dogmatics* 2/2, 393–409, and Klopfenstein, "1 Könige 13," 668), whereas Gray saw the contrast between the disobedient man of God and the obedient beast (*I & II Kings*, 302). The analysis of the structure of 1 Kings 13 will show that a role reversal between the man of God and the old prophet of Bethel (Barth and Klopfenstein) and the contract between the man of God and the lion do not receive as much emphasis in the text and that the scholars read oppositions into the text that do not exist in the text.

126. Frolov, *Judges*, 3.

attention to how the study of form criticism could co-operate with other methods of criticisms. They state, "Many, if not most, form-critical scholars will no longer restrict themselves to the presumed authors of texts or the reconstructions of their presumed sociohistorical settings and intentions."[127] They continue,

> Many, if not most, form-critical scholars will engage fully the literary dimensions of texts. These dimensions include the larger literary patterns that unite the smaller units that comprise larger literary compositions, such as historical works or prophetic books; their interrelationships with other literary works, whether by citation, imitation, or debate; and their aesthetics or artistic dimensions that contribute to the expression of ideas.[128]

Also, while the genres have been understood to be fixed or static in the past, it is now viewed that the genres can be "transformed to meet the needs of the particular communicative situation of the text."[129]

With this "changing face of form criticism" in mind, my analysis of the text of 1 Kings 13 will pay more attention to *the narrator's role* in shaping the narrative in a particular genre. In other words, I will argue that the story in our text has been *shaped by the narrator* into a prophetic symbolic action. The role of the narrator in shaping a narrative into a specific literary genre, I would argue, is discernible in other passages in the Book of Kings, and this particular point may demand a revision of "the long-held form-critical assumption that originally oral forms of texts were incorporated without substantive change into the present forms of biblical literature."[130] Michael H. Floyd, in his article titled "Basic Trends in the Form-Critical Study of Prophetic Texts," argues that form criticism is now undergoing a shift "from a primarily historical to a primarily literary orientation,[131] and that "prophetic literature appears not in the form of transcribed original oral speech acts, but in the form of a specific type of narrative literature, which displays its own rhetorical patterns and presupposes the settings and concerns of their much later redactors."[132] I hope this approach will provide

---

127. Sweeney and Ben Zvi, "Introduction," 10.
128. Sweeney and Ben Zvi, "Introduction," 9.
129. Sweeney and Ben Zvi, "Introduction," 9–10.
130. Sweeney and Ben Zvi, "Introduction," 7.
131. Floyd, "Basic Trends," 311.
132. Sweeney and Ben Zvi, "Introduction," 8.

a fresh look at the story in 1 Kings 13 and also will contribute to an understanding of the narrator's view of the prophets' role in the history of Israel.

Lastly, I will read 1 Kings 13 against the larger theological background of the Deuteronomistic History. 1 Kings 13, I would argue, takes an important position in the formation of the theology of the Deuteronomistic History. The comparison of our text with other key Deuteronomistic texts shows that our text is very "Deuteronomistic," as is also indicated by the narrator's frequent employment of significant Deuteronomistic expressions and themes in the story,[133] and therefore, our story is in a theological dialogue with other parts of the Deuteronomistic History. Viewing our text along with other related Deuteronomistic texts may also help us to read between the lines or fill in the gaps that may exist in the text, when necessary.[134] All this evidence will indicate that 1 Kings 13 is an integral part of the Deuteronomistic History and serves its role in forming the Deuteronomistic theology.

---

133. I believe that the narrator's (or the Deuteronomist's) theology of the history of Israel has been smeared throughout the text. The term "narrator" is used in this study interchangeably with the term "Deuteronomist," and though we will deal with the issue of composition of the Book of Kings briefly, it is suffice to say, at this point, that the narrator is best understood as the implied author.

134. Sternberg, *Biblical Narrative*, 186–229, esp. 189.

2

Exegesis of 1 Kings 13

INTRODUCTION

In the previous chapter, I located the current status of the studies on 1 Kings 13 by reviewing past scholarship, and then I suggested some hermeneutical guidelines for the interpretation of the chapter. In this chapter, I will analyze the text of 1 Kings 13 with a view to identifying the theme, function, and genre of the story in 1 Kings 13. This analysis attempts to demonstrate that reading the story attending to the nature/genre of the story resolves and clears away some difficult interpretive problems.

EXEGESIS OF 1 KINGS 13

The Goal of Exegesis

In this section, I will first attempt to delineate the structure of the story. It is assumed in this study that the intention of the text is conveyed by the structure and details of the text and that it can be identified through a careful reading of the text. Thus, analyzing the structure of 1 Kings 13 will help to identify the theme of the story. In the course of exegesis, the genre of the story will also become evident, which will in turn reveal the nature of the story. By the "nature" of the story I mean a particular aspect of the story, that is, the narrator's—or the implied author's—role in shaping

Exegesis of 1 Kings 13

the narrative into a particular literary form/genre. Through this exegesis, I will attempt to present a coherent reading that attends to various literary features of the text.

The Scope of Our Study

This current study will focus on analyzing the present form of the text, though the historical or diachronic aspects of the text will also be touched on occasionally. Also, the text that I will be using in our analysis is mainly the Hebrew text (MT). It has been well noted that there exist differences between the Hebrew text (MT) and LXX of the Jeroboam narrative, especially in 1 Kings 12 and 14, which have been treated by some scholars.[1] This matter, however, is beyond the scope of this study and deserves a separate study in a different kind of research.[2] In this chapter, I will study the story in 1 Kings 13, and in the next chapter, the scope of our study will be extended to the entire Jeroboam narrative (1 Kgs 11:26—14:20).

Delimitation of the Text

It has been subject to much debate where the story in 1 Kings 13 begins, while the ending of the unit is more obvious (13:33–34). Some scholars argue that the beginning of the original story was eliminated when the story was inserted into the present location.[3] In the present form of the text, however, the setting of 1 Kings 13:1 is continued from chapter 12. Also, 13:1 is seamlessly connected to 1 Kings 12:33,[4] as the former continues to describe the scene of Jeroboam's burning incense: "And he instituted a feast for the sons of Israel, and *he went up to the altar* to burn incense. And

---

1. For this, see Sweeney, "Reassessment," 165–95; Schenker, "Jeroboam's Rise and Fall," 367–73; Schenker's earlier study, "Jeroboam and the Division," 214–57. Schenker views that the LXX version may have been based on an old, pre-deuteronomistic source "resembling the books of Judges and Samuel" (256). See also Galpaz-Feller, "The Reign of Jeroboam," 13–19.

2. In chapter 3, where I discuss the larger literary context of 1 Kings 13, that is, the Jeroboam narrative, we will briefly examine the differences between the Hebrew text and LXX in 1 Kings 12 with a view to identifying the Hebrew narrator's intention in the characterization of Jeroboam.

3. For example, Dozeman argues that "the original introduction has been eliminated in order to weave the legend into the life of Jeroboam" ("Way of the Man," 381).

4. Blum, "Die Lüge des Propheten," 40.

THE FATE OF THE MAN OF GOD FROM JUDAH

behold, a man of God came out of Judah by the word of Yahweh to Bethel. And *Jeroboam was standing by the altar* to burn incense" (italics added) (12:33b—13:1). It seems that they were intended to be read together, and for this reason, I will read them together as parts of a literary unit.

It still remains for us to determine where the literary unit begins. I argue that it is reasonable to take 1 Kings 12:32 as the beginning of the story for the following reasons:[5] First, the proper noun "Jeroboam" appears in 12:32 and disrupts the flow of the narrative that began at 12:26, where the proper noun "Jeroboam" also appears and disrupts the narrative. This "unnecessarily repeated subject" seems to indicate the beginning of a new literary unit.[6] Second, the repeated use of the phrase אשר־עשה, "which he had made," in vv. 32–33a creates some temporal distance between Jeroboam's earlier actions in vv. 26–31 and his later actions in vv. 32–33a. Verses 26–31 describe Jeroboam's initial cultic inventions (note the repeated use of עשה in vv. 28, 31[x2]), whereas vv. 32–33 describe his later actions through the repeated use of אשר־עשה:

> and he went up to the altar, *which he had made* (אשר־עשה)[7] in Bethel, sacrificing to the calves *which he had made* (אשר־עשה). And he placed in Bethel the priests of the high places *which he had made* (אשר־עשה). And he went up to the altar *which he had made* (אשר־עשה) in Bethel in the fifteenth day of the seventh month, in the month *which he had devised* (אשר־עשה) in his own heart.[8] (32b–33; italics added)

Third, vv. 32 and 33a form a concentric structure, and thus it seems more reasonable not to separate the two verses but rather to keep them together. The concentric parallels are discernible as follows (1 Kgs 12:32–33a):

---

5. Among those who suggest 1 Kgs 12:32 as the beginning of the narrative are Noth (*Könige*, 291), Montgomery (*The Books of Kings*, 259), Gressmann (*Die älteste Geschichtsschreibung*, 247), and Klopfenstein ("1 Könige 13," 652). But Gray (*I and II Kings*, 324) and Šanda (*Die Bücher der Könige Erster*, 351) argue for 1 Kgs 12:33 as the beginning of the narrative.

6 The name "Jeroboam" is mentioned in 1 Kings 12:25; 12:26; 12:32. See Walsh, *1 Kings*, 169–71, and Sweeney, *I & II Kings*, 175–6.

7. Following the BHS editor's suggestion, we accept אשר־עשה as original instead of כן עשה. The former is more plausible when it is compared with v. 33:. וַיַּעַל עַל־הַמִּזְבֵּחַ אֲשֶׁר־עָשָׂה בְּבֵית־אֵל.

8. Qere; the Kethib form is מִלְבַּד.

A. And Jeroboam instituted *a feast* (חג) in the eighth month on the fifteenth day of the month, like the feast which is in Judah,

    B. and he *went up to the altar* (ויעל על־המזבח) that he had made[9] in Bethel, sacrificing to the calves which he had made.

        C. And he placed in Bethel *the priests of the high places* (את־כהני הבמות) which he had made.

    B'. And he *went up to the altar* (ויעל על־המזבח) that he had made in Bethel on the fifteenth day in the eighth month, even in the month which he had devised in his own heart.[10]

A'. And he instituted *a feast* (חג) for the sons of Israel. (italics added)

Lastly, vv. 26–31 describe Jeroboam's invention of two golden calves (vv. 26–30) and other cultic inventions (high places, non-Levite priests, v. 31). From v. 32, the narrator narrows his perspective to *Bethel* and prepares the reader for the ensuing events in Bethel. For these reasons, I will take 12:32 as the beginning and 13:34 as the end of our narrative.[11]

Structural Analysis of 1 Kings 13

Our exegesis begins with an examination of the structure of the text. Outlining the structure of a biblical text is sometimes considered a rather subjective process whereby one can impose his or her understanding of the text on the structure. The structure of the passage, however, should not be underestimated as a means the interpreter employs to make his or her points. Frolov contends, "Although the form of the communication is by no means reducible to its structure, the importance of the latter is difficult to overestimate: no form-critical investigation (and indeed no other exegetical project) can proceed until the studied fragment is positioned vis-à-vis the hierarchy of the literary units that make up the received HB."[12] Thus the purpose of structural outlining is to *listen* to the text, rather than to *speak* to the text. Subjectivity can be minimized when careful attention is paid

---

9. See n. 168.
10. See n. 169.
11. Though I take 12:32 as the beginning of the narrative in our study, I do not completely rule out other views, and I do not believe that where the narrative begins affects the interpretation of the narrative significantly.
12. Frolov, *Judges*, 4.

THE FATE OF THE MAN OF GOD FROM JUDAH

to the literary devices in the text, such as parallelism and repetitions. The expected outcome of our structural analysis is to bring the emphases of the narrator into sharp relief.

Structure of the Story

The structure of 1 Kings 12:32—13:34 can be delineated as follows:

A. *Opening Exposition* (vv. 12:32–33a)

   B. *The Prophecy against the Altar at Bethel by the Man of God from Judah* (12:33b–13:2)

      i. The Man of God Comes from Judah "by the Word of Yahweh" (vv. 12:33b–13:1)

      ii. The man of God's Cries against the Altar "by the Word of Yahweh" (v. 2)

      C. *The First Set of "Word" and Fulfillment* (vv. 13:3–6)

         i. "The Sign Which Yahweh Has Spoken" is Given to Jeroboam (v. 3)

         ii. Jeroboam's Initial Reaction to the "Word" of the Man of God, and His Hand Becomes Withered (v. 4)

         i'. "The Sign that the Man of God Had Given by the Word of Yahweh" Is Fulfilled (v. 5)

         ii'. Jeroboam's Appeal to the Man of God for His Prayer for Healing (v. 6)

         D. *The Man of God's Obedience* (vv. 7–10)

            i. Jeroboam's Invites the Man of God to His House (v. 7)

            ii. The Man of God Refuses the Invitation Because of the Command Given Him "by the Word of Yahweh" (vv. 8–9)

            iii. Obedience: The Man of God Returns by Another "Way" (v. 10)

            E. *Transition: Introduction of the Old Prophet of Bethel* (vv. 11–14)

        i. The Old Prophet Hears of the Man of God's Deeds and Words (v. 11)

        ii. The Old Prophet Asks Which "Way" the Man of God Went (v. 12)

        iii. The Old Prophet Goes After the Man of God and Finds Him (vv. 13–14)

    D'. *The Man of God's Disobedience* (vv. 15–19)

        i. The Old Prophet Invites the Man of God to His House (v. 15)

        ii. The Man of God Refuses the Invitation Because of the "Word" Spoken to Him "by the Word of Yahweh" (vv. 16–17)

        iii. The Old Prophet Lies to Him (v. 18)

        iv. Disobedience: The Man of God Returns to Bethel, Eats, and Drinks (v. 19)

  C'. *The Second Set of "Word" and Fulfillment* (vv. 20–26)

        i. "The Word of Yahweh" Comes to the Old Prophet (v. 20)

        ii. The Old Prophet "Cries" against the Man of God from Judah (21–22)

        iii. The Old Prophet's Prophecy is Fulfilled (vv. 23–24)

        iv. The Old Prophet Pronounces that the Death of the Man of God Was Done "According to the Word of Yahweh" (vv. 25–26)

B'. *The Man of God's Prophecy against the Altar at Bethel Is Confirmed by the Old Prophet* (vv. 27–32)

    i. The Old Prophet Retrieves and Buries the Body and Laments over Him (vv. 27–30)

    ii. The Old Prophet Confirms that the Man of God's Prophecy against the Altar Will Certainly Come True (vv. 31–32)

A'. *Ending: The Narrator's Comment* (vv. 33–34)

THE FATE OF THE MAN OF GOD FROM JUDAH

Notes on the Structure

Many scholars have the view that 1 Kings 13 may have been composed of two different stories (vv. 1–10, 11–32). The reasons for such a view include the following: First, Jeroboam does not appear in the second part (vv. 11–32). Second, the tale of the two prophetic figures "has no obvious connection to the surrounding context which concerns the political separation of Israel and Judah after Solomon's death."[13] For those scholars, the prophetic story seems to be an interruption with no clear intention behind it. Nevertheless, the text in its present form seems to constitute a whole literary unit that displays rich coherence and parallels between different parts of the story.

The coherence of the narrative in its present form has been recognized even by some historical critics.[14] Some of their observations have been submitted in support of the unity of the story as follows:

a. The man of God from Judah remains the main character in both parts, though he changes his partners, from King Jeroboam to the old prophet of Bethel.

b. Quite a few motifs are repeatedly used throughout the narrative: בדבר יהוה "by the word of Yahweh," (vv. 1, 2, 5, 9, 17, 18, 32),[15] the divine directives to the man of God from Judah (vv. 8–9, 16–17, 21–22), שוב "turn/return," (vv. 4, 6[x2], 9, 10, 16, 17, 18, 19, 20, 22, 23, 26, 29, 33[x2]),[16] and דרך "way" (vv. 9, 10, 12, 17, 24, 25, 26, 28, 33), "the altar" (vv. 1, 2[x3], 3, 4[x2], 5[x2], 32).

c. The "use of adjectival definitions (the man of God, an old prophet), instead of proper names," also links major sections of the narrative.[17]

---

13. Bosworth, *Story within a Story*, 118.

14. Gray, *I & II Kings*, 321, Gross, "Lying Prophet," 97–135, and Long, *1 Kings*, 145.

15. The fact that the expression, "by the word of Yahweh," occurs seven times in this chapter is significant because it occurs only once more elsewhere in the Book of Kings (1 Kgs 20:35). What may be even more significant is that, as Beal notes, it is a motif that is voiced not only by the characters of the story but also by the narrator (Beal, *1 & 2 Kings*, 190). This motif gives the unity to the narrative where two different stories appear to have been combined together (vv. 1–10, 11–32).

16. It is notable that, despite the negative meaning of the uses of the "turning back" throughout the narrative, the narrator uses the verb in a positive sense in v. 33.

17. Eynikel, "Prophecy and Fulfillment," 227.

These features suggest the coherence of the present form of the text and hence should not be overlooked. As Burke Long says, "Certainly from the standpoint of style, vv. 1–32 stand closely linked together,"[18] which justifies our reading the whole story as a coherent unity. It is also notable that the repeated phrases and parallels throughout the story not only bind the narrative into a coherent whole but also contribute to forming the concentric structure of the narrative.[19] First, the man of God from Judah proclaims against the altar (B, vv. 1–2), and the old prophet of Bethel confirms that the prophecy will certainly come true (B', vv. 31–32). This parallel is strengthened by the common phrase "he cried against the altar by the word of Yahweh," which appears only in vv. 2 (וַיִּקְרָא עַל־הַמִּזְבֵּחַ בִּדְבַר יְהוָה) and v. 32 (קָרָא בִּדְבַר יְהוָה עַל־הַמִּזְבֵּחַ) in the narrative.

Second, another parallel is clearly visible in the second pair (C and C'); the spoken word of Yahweh and its fulfillment appear in both vv. 3–6 and vv. 20–26. In vv. 3–6 (C), a sign "which Yahweh has spoken" (דִּבֶּר יְהוָה) is given (v. 3), and its fulfillment is reported with the oracle fulfillment formula (v. 5): "according to (כְּ) the sign that the man of God had given by the word of Yahweh." Likewise, in vv. 20–26 (C'), Yahweh's punishment which is proclaimed by the old prophet in the form of "the word of Yahweh" (דְּבַר־יְהוָה) is fulfilled again with the oracle fulfillment formula: "according to (כְּ) the word that Yahweh spoke to him." (See the table below.)

Table 1: Parallels between 1 Kings 13:3–6 and 1 Kings 13:20–26

1 Kings 13:3–6	1 Kings 13:20–26
[3] Then he gave a sign the same day, saying, "This is the sign which *Yahweh has spoken* (דבר יהוה), 'Behold . . .'"	[20] And as they were sitting down at the table, *the word of Yahweh* (דבר־יהוה) came to the prophet who had brought him back;
[4] And when the king heard the saying of the man of God, which he *cried* (קרא) against the altar in Bethel . . .	[21] and *he cried* (ויקרא) to the man of God who came from Judah, saying . . .

18. Long, *1 Kings*, 145.

19. Knoppers also notes that two parallels are to be found in 1 Kings 12 and 1 Kings 13: the closing verses of 1 Kings 12 and 1 Kings 13, and 1 Kings 13:1–3 and 1 Kings 13:32 (*Two Nations under God* 2, 47). Knoppers agrees with Noth (Könige, 292–3), Simon ("Prophetic Sign," 88), de Vaux (The Bible and the Ancient Near East, 109), and Dozeman ("Way of the Man," 383) that v. 3a ("and he gave on that day a sign, saying") is a late insertion [not by the Deuteronomist] into the text. He views it as "a gloss, which attempts to harmonize the prophecy of vv. 2–3 with the actions of Josiah in 2 Kgs 23:15, 17" (48).

THE FATE OF THE MAN OF GOD FROM JUDAH

| ⁵ The altar also was split apart and the ashes were poured out from the altar, *according to* the sign which the man of God had given *by the word of Yahweh* (כמופת אשר נתן איש האלהים בדבר יהוה). | ²⁶ Now when the prophet who brought him back from the way heard it, he said, "... therefore Yahweh has given him to the lion, which has torn him and killed him, *according to the word of Yahweh* which He spoke to him (כדבר יהוה אשר דבר־לו). |

Third, the parallels between vv. 7–10 (D) and 15–19 (D') are even more conspicuous than the ones in the other pairs. Invitations (v. 7 and v. 15) and the man of God's initial refusals (vv. 8–9 and vv. 16–17) are nearly identical in their use of the same phrases. The only difference between the two sections is the old prophet's lying part (v. 18):

Table 2: Parallels between 1 Kings 13:7–10 and 1 Kings 13:15–19

	Verses 7–10	Verses 15–19
Invitation	King's invitation (v. 7)	The old prophet's invitation (v. 15)
Refusal	The man of God's refusal (vv. 8–9)	The man of God's refusal (vv. 16–17)
Lying		The old prophet's deception (v. 18)
Response	The man of God's obedience (v. 10)	The man of God's disobedience (v. 19)

It is noteworthy that the old prophet of Bethel succeeds in deceiving the man of God by means of the phrase "by the word of Yahweh." This is significant because it serves to reinforce the narrator's emphasis on the power of the word of Yahweh. The outcome is the opposite: the man of God obeys God's command the first time (v. 10), but he fails the second (v. 19).

From this structural analysis we can gain insight into the narrator's literary strategies. The most significant action and event in the story are initiated by the word of Yahweh. The man of God is bound by the command given "by the word of Yahweh," and nothing can change his commitment to the command, until one unexpected factor appears on the scene (the old prophet of Bethel—the transitional part, vv. 11–14). In addition to this, the two sets of Yahweh's word and its fulfillment seem to underscore the narrator's emphasis on the fulfilling power of the word of Yahweh. Thus, the structural analysis shows that the word of Yahweh is emphasized throughout the narrative more than in almost all other passages in the entire Hebrew Bible.

Exegesis of the Story

The exegesis of the story will proceed in the order of the headings provided in the structure.

Opening Exposition (12:32–33a)

First Kings 12:32–33a functions as a kind of hinge between 1 Kings 12:26–31 and 12:33b—13:32 in the sense that it continues with the "sin of Jeroboam" but, at the same time, prepares the reader for the events at Bethel. While 12:26–31 describes the beginning of the downfall of King Jeroboam, by depicting his making and setting up of the two golden calves in Bethel *and* Dan and his building of shrines on high places and appointing non-Levitical priests, the focus in 1 Kings 12:32–33a is narrowed down to the altar at *Bethel*—in vv. 32–33a Bethel alone is mentioned three times—which becomes the main setting for the events in the story that follows. Thus, the focus is shifted from an overall summary of Jeroboam's cultic inventions to the altar at Bethel. In this respect, these two verses serve their purpose as the exposition of a biblical narrative; they detach "the readers from the materials they had been dealing with and introduce[s] them to a new or different story world without losing their place in the sequence."[20]

This opening exposition is paired up with the ending (13:33–34). In the ending framework, the narrator comes back to where he was before, that is, Jeroboam's installing non-Levitical priests for the high places, and more importantly, to the sin of Jeroboam (cf. 12:30).[21] However, Jeroboam

---

20. Amit, *Reading Biblical Narratives*, 35.

21. The narrative in 1 Kings 13 fits well into Amit's description of a typical narrative unit. In other words, it is composed of exposition (12:32–33a), the body of the story (13:1–32), and an ending (13:33–34). She says, "We may conclude that the exposition contains different kinds of details from those that appear in the body of the story, which describes the events. While the events are dynamic, the opening is descriptive, meaning that it is static, while the ending marks the exit of the personae and returns the reader to the static condition of the opening. Nevertheless, in a story with a concentric ending, the hero or heroes only seem to return to the condition from which they had set out, because the events have affected them—and the reader with them. The reality to which they return is not the same as it was" (*Reading Biblical Narratives*, 36).

did not go back to the status quo after the events described in the body of the story but to a far harsher reality, because he "did not turn from his evil way" even "after this thing" (v. 33). Therefore, what we see in the body of the story is how the events described in the story affected the fate of King Jeroboam. This structure demands that the whole story, though Jeroboam does not appear in the second half of the story, be read in relation to Jeroboam and his "house" or "dynasty."

The altar at Bethel receives special attention in the story that unfolds. Verse 32 provides a general description of Jeroboam's inventions (a feast on the fifteenth day of the eighth month that was modelled after the feast that was in Judah, his sacrificing to the calves that he had made, and his setting up priests of the high places in Bethel). The summary-like overview may suggest that it is a list of what Jeroboam had been doing regularly or on a yearly basis, whereas v. 33a seems to be describing Jeroboam's actions that lead right up to the event that is now developing (12:33b—13:10).

The Prophecy against the Altar at Bethel by the Man of God from Judah (12:33b—13:2)

Now Jeroboam goes up to the altar to burn incense, and he is surprised to meet an unexpected guest from Judah (12:33b). The man of God appears with הִנֵּה which announces a new development of events. Jeroboam, who "went up to the altar to burn incense" (v. 33b), "is [still] standing by the altar to burn incense" as the man of God arrives at the scene from Judah. As seen above, this pericope is supposed to be read with the previous one.[22] The man of God's oracle presupposes Jeroboam's cultic inventions. Bodner notices the connection and says that Jeroboam's motive of making golden calves (12:26–32) "provides a vivid backdrop for the confrontation at the beginning of chapter 13."[23] Otherwise, Yahweh's judgment against the altar, which the man of God proclaims, would hardly make sense. In other words, the man of God's address would lack "any statement of the grounds for the punishment," because "the grounds for the announcement have already been laid out in 1 Kgs 12:32–33 . . ."[24] For this reason, although some scholars argue that the original heading of the narrative is missing,[25] it is

---

22. Knoppers, *Two Nations under God*, 2:58.
23. Bodner, *Royal Drama*, 100.
24. Sweeney, *I & II Kings*, 180.
25. Knoppers believe that the connections of 13:1 with 12:26–33 (e.g., וירבעם עמד

very obvious that the narrator intended the two parts to be read together. The clause that follows the demonstrative הנה is to be seen as dependent upon 12:33.[26]

The narrator's emphasis on the word of Yahweh is apparent in this pericope. First, the man of God arrives in Bethel "by the word of Yahweh" (v. 1) and utters an oracle against the altar "by the word of Yahweh" (v. 2). In other words, the first two actions of the man of God—"came" (בָּא) and "cried" (וַיִּקְרָא)—have been directed or commanded by the word of Yahweh. The repetition of the phrase "by the word of Yahweh" in two consecutive verses (v. 1. and 2) catches the eyes of the reader. Though the meaning of the phrase "by [or in] the word of Yahweh" is not clear, it is likely to signify that the man of God has acted under the authority of Yahweh. Remarkably, the phrase "by the word of Yahweh" (בדבר יהוה) is almost exclusive to this narrative (seven occurrences), appearing only five times elsewhere in the rest of the entire Hebrew Bible: twice in Deuteronomistic History (1 Sam 3:21; 1 Kgs 20:35) and three times outside the history (2 Chr 30:12; Ps 33:6; Jer 8:9), and then the phrase in Psalm 33:6 and Jeremiah 8:9 is used with a different meaning.[27] It is also worth noting that the word of Yahweh is a motif voiced by the narrator (vv. 1, 2, 5), the man of God (vv. 9, 17), and the old prophet (vv. 18, 32).[28] The fact that the same motif is given by three different voices (the narrator, the man of God, and the old prophet of Bethel) indicates the narrator's literary hand in the story and his emphasis on the word of Yahweh.

Second, the appearance of the name King Josiah is even more unique. Bosworth observes, "The prophecy is unique within the prophecy-fulfillment schema because the person who fulfills the prediction is identified by name. In all other cases, the person who fulfills the prediction is named in the fulfillment notice, if at all."[29] This prophecy remains unfulfilled within the story and only looks forward to its fulfillment in some three hundred years (2 Kgs 23), but the function of this prophecy and the mention of the name King Josiah is, as Bodner says, "perhaps to underscore the reality of

על־המזבח להקטיר, והנה) are deuteronomistic, and hence "the original beginning of the prophetic narratives can no longer be recovered" (*Two Nations under God*, 2:52).

26. Frolov, *Judges*, 6. Also, see Gross, "Lying Prophet," 101. Gross sees 1 Kgs 13:1a as a continuation of 12:33c, "להקטיר ויעל על־המזבח."

27. Beal, *1 & 2 Kings*, 191.

28. Beal, *1 & 2 Kings*, 190.

29. Bosworth, *Story within a Story*, 126.

THE FATE OF THE MAN OF GOD FROM JUDAH

the prophetic word."[30] Most likely, the intended reader of the book was also aware of King Josiah, and thus the prophecy of King Josiah's defilement of the altar might have had the reader anticipate the fulfillment of the prophecy in the later history.[31] This reveals the narrator's theological perspective operating in the text. Brueggemann remarks, "This pivotal reference to Josiah suggests the artistic and deliberate way in which the entire narrative of Kings is arranged with great theological self-consciousness."[32] For the Deuteronomistic narrator, the "word" uttered through prophets is the means by which God advances the history of Israel. The prophetic formula, "Thus says Yahweh," also serves to heighten the authority of the oracle by the man of God.

All this is supposed, in my judgment, to show that the prophecy proclaimed against the altar is the genuine will of Yahweh. Contrary to the view of some scholars (e.g., Dozeman), the narrator does not leave room for doubt as to the authenticity of the man of God's proclamation. Instead, it is presented with great clarity that the man of God spoke the authentic word of Yahweh. In this regard, the designation "the man of God" is also notable. Many scholars believe that the designation has been used in the narrative only for the purpose of distinguishing between the prophet from Judah and the prophet of Bethel. That may be partially true, but it is noteworthy that the designation "the man of God" was used in the Hebrew Bible only in the positive sense to refer to an authoritative prophetic figure or someone who deserved great respect.[33] Thus the title does contribute to the perception of both the genuineness and authority of his oracle.

30. Bodner, *Royal Drama*, 104.

31. Cross, *Canaanite Myth and Hebrew Epic*, 280.

32. Brueggemann, *1 & 2 Kings*, 168.

33. The people designated "man of God" in the Hebrew Bible include Moses (ex. Deut 33:1; Josh 14:6; 1 Chr 23:14; 2 Chr 30:16; Ezra 3:2; Ps 90:1), an angel (Judg 13:8), Samuel (1 Sam 9:6–10), Shemaiah (1 Kgs 12:22; 2 Chr 11:2), the man of God in 1 Kings 13 (and 2 Kgs 23:16–17), Elisha (2 Kgs 4–8; 13:19), David (2 Chr 8:14; Neh 12:24, 36), an anonymous man of God (2 Chr 25:9) and lastly, Igdaliah (Jer 35:4). Since the list includes King David, the term does not seem to have been limited only to someone in the prophetic office, though most of the time it refers to someone with a prophetic office. The usage in the Hebrew Bible seems to indicate that it was an honorary epithet rather than a title used to refer to a certain group of people. The man of God in 1 Kings 12:22 and another man of God in 1 Kings 13 seem to be from Judah, but the term is more frequently used of Northern figures (cf. Elijah [1 Kgs 17:18; 18:22] and Elisha [2 Kgs 19:2; 20:1,11,14]. Also, see Sweeney, *I & II Kings*, 172), so it is not distinctively used for the prophets from the North, but the term itself may indicate its origin in the Northern prophetical circles. Bosworth argues, "The biblical evidence does not support a geographical

The focus of the prophecy is on the altar at Bethel, as it pronounces the desecration of the altar at Bethel by King Josiah. Brueggemann says, "At the outset we may surmise that this is a Judah-David polemic against the Northern establishment that serves primarily to detract from the claims of Jerusalem."[34] Notably, the man of God's oracle is addressed to the altar, which is rather unusual, because "The double vocative normally seeks to capture the attention of a human listener (Gen 22:11; 46:2; Exod 3:4; 1 Sam 3:4, 10)."[35] With this, the adjectival phrase that follows the man of God, "from Judah" (vv. 1, 12, 14, 21), also deserves our attention. That is, the altar at Bethel in the Northern Kingdom is denounced by the man of God "from Judah." Jeroboam's cultic inventions for the Northern Kingdom are condemned, because they signify the kingdom's religious departure from Judah or Jeroboam's apostasy from Yahweh, especially in the eyes of the Judean historian. In that sense, the adjectival phrase "from Judah" may betray the narrator's view that Yahweh approves of the Judean temple but not of the separate cultic center in the Northern Kingdom.

The First Set of "Word" and Fulfillment (13:3–6)

This pericope describes the sign given by the man of God followed by its fulfillment (vv. 3, 5), and Jeroboam's response to the sign followed by its consequence and his request to the man of God for his prayer for healing (vv. 4, 6). The emphasis on the "word" continues in this pericope: the man of God gives "the sign which Yahweh has spoken (דִּבֶּר יְהוָה)" (v. 3); Jeroboam hears "the word (דְּבַר) of the man of God" and attempts to get him arrested (v. 4). The altar is split, and its ashes pour out according to the sign that the man of God had given "by the word of Yahweh (בִּדְבַר יְהוָה)."

---

distinction between these two terms" (Bosworth, *Story within a Story*, 126). Wilson says, "it is possible that the characteristics of the man of God were originally different for those of the prophet . . . but it is now impossible to separate the two figures" (Wilson, *Prophecy and Society*, 140). The epithet was never used negatively in the Hebrew Bible for someone respectable (see Blum, "Die Lüge des Propheten," 34–36). It is natural to expect from the outset of the narrative that the man of God from Judah was a man with divine authority, which contributes to the overall message of the story (Gray, *I & II Kings*, 299). A similar view is shared by Karl Barth. See Barth, *Exegese von 1. Könige 13*, 12–56, esp. 15.

34. Brueggemann, *1 & 2 Kings*, 167.

35. Bosworth, *Story within a Story*, 124. David Marcus understands the address to the altar, an inanimate object to be constituting a ridicule, "a slight to the royal presence" ("Elements of Ridicule and Parody," 67–74).

THE FATE OF THE MAN OF GOD FROM JUDAH

Some scholars have contended that vv. 3 and 5 did not belong originally in the story and were secondarily inserted later.[36] For example, Uriel Simon does not regard the two verses as belonging to the original story and thus ignores them in his analysis of the narrative,[37] while Walsh argues that vv. 3 and 5 should be read with parenthesis.[38] This view is supported by the fact that *waw* + the perfect form of the verb נתן (וְנָתַן) disrupts the narrative and that the flow of the narrative seems natural without the two verses. Fretheim suggests the possibility that v. 5 was "an aside by the narrator that the sign was fulfilled in his own day by Josiah," based on the assumption that "prophetic signs do not always take place immediately."[39] These views do not, however, explain why then v. 3 and v. 5 have not been put together, one after another, and more importantly, why these verses have been put in the current location in the first place. At any rate, whether or not vv. 3 and 5 are original, I am more interested in the literary effect of the present form of the story than in distinguishing between the original and later insertions. In the present form of the text, the motif of "ripping" in vv. 3 and 5 (נִקְרָע) links this narrative with other parts of the Jeroboam narrative (cf. 1 Kgs 11:11–13; 11:30–31; 14:8),[40] which seems to demand that the reader pay more attention to the narrator's intention in shaping the story and the Jeroboam narrative than we now have.[41]

The narrator deliberately emphasizes that the sign had been given "by the word of Yahweh" (בדבר יהוה, v. 5). By employing the same phrase "by the word of Yahweh" as he did for the man of God's oracle against the altar (v. 2) and reporting that the sign has now been fulfilled, the narrator convinces the reader that the fulfillment of the man of God's oracle is also

---

36. See Noth, *Könige*, 292–3; Simon, "Prophetic Sign," 88; de Vaux, *The Bible and the Ancient Near East*, 109. Knoppers considers only 1 Kings 13:3a (ונתן ביום ההוא מופת לאמר, "and he shall give on that day a sign, saying") as a gloss. De Vaux's argument that 13:2 and 3a, 5b and 32 should be considered as additions is not compelling, as Knoppers argues in *Two Nations under God* 2, 56.

37. Simon, "Prophetic Sign," 88. Though Simon ignores vv. 3 and 5 in his analysis, he still comments on the function of the verses: "... this portent is not merely formal; the demolition of the altar on that day patently demonstrates the fate that awaits it in the future" (88).

38. Walsh, *1 Kings*, 178.

39. Fretheim, *First and Second Kings*, 78.

40. Bodner, *Royal Drama*, 104.

41. The withering of the hand of Jeroboam is also very symbolic, indicating the weakening of the power of Jeroboam (for Bodner's observation of the word "hand" in 1 Kings 11–12, see Bodner, *Royal Drama*, 105).

certain. This serves as "a sign of the veracity" to authenticate the prophecy that is given in v. 2.[42] Knoppers asserts, "At the hand of the Deuteronomist, the immediate fulfillment of this sign accentuates the oracle's validity and, hence, the surety of divine retribution through Josiah."[43] The sign proves to Jeroboam and everyone present beside the altar (and also the reader) that the man of God from Judah had spoken a genuine word from Yahweh, so there is no confusion as to the authenticity of the man of God and his message (contra Dozeman and Fretheim;[44] see the section titled "The Prophecy against the Altar at Bethel by the Man of God from Judah" in chapter 2).

Here in this pericope we find the first set of a prophetic word and fulfillment in the narrative, which is clearly expressed in the narrator's comment that the sign ("the word of Yahweh") was fulfilled *"according to the sign* which the man of God had given *by the word of Yahweh"* (v. 5, italics added). This clear emphasis on the word of Yahweh is followed by a detailed description of King Jeroboam's response to the word. His initial response is negative; he attempts to have the man of God arrested, only to find his stretched-out hand withered. The king's withered hand is "a sign of God's judgment and a sign of prophetic power over royal power."[45] At the sight of his withered hand (v. 4) and the fulfilled sign (v. 5), he suddenly changes his attitude toward the man of God. Then he asks the man of God to pray for him. To our surprise, the man of God does pray for the healing of the hand, and his hand is restored (וַתָּשָׁב). God listens to the prayer for Jeroboam!

The text is silent about the inner motive of the king. However, a careful reader notes the significant phrase here (v. 6): "Pray for me!" (וְהִתְפַּלֵּל בַּעֲדִי), which may be a reminder of the theme that recurs through the Deuteronomistic History, the theme of "returning" or "repenting." Jeroboam's request for the intercessory prayer of the man of God is reminiscent of the Israelites' request to Samuel for his prayer for them (1 Sam 12:19, 23). Especially, the construct of the verb "to pray" (the Hithpael form of פלל) and "on behalf of" (בַּעַד) is notable. It is employed somewhat frequently by

---

42. Lindblom, *Prophecy in Ancient Israel*, 53; Fretheim, *First and Second Kings*, 78.

43. Knoppers, *Two Nations under God*, 2:59.

44. Fretheim argues that the king's initial response (anger and attempt to arrest him) shows he failed to "recognize that this was a true prophet" (*First and Second Kings*, 78). The issue at here, however, is not whether or not he recognized the man of God as a true prophet. It was apparent that he was a true prophet, and Jeroboam did not turn because he failed to recognize that he was a true prophet, but because he was stubborn.

45. Fretheim, *First and Second Kings*, 78.

the Deuteronomist; it occurs thirteen times in the Hebrew Bible,[46] three of which are found in the Book of Samuel (twice in 1 Sam 12:19; 12:23) and the Book of Kings (1 Kgs 13:6; see the section titled "The Story's Literary Effects on the Reader" in chapter 4).

The basic tone of both passages (1 Sam 12 and 1 Kgs 13:6) is similar. In both passages a prophet prays for the people (or a king) who have sinned and therefore are in desperate need of God's mercy. With this intertextual linkage and with the occurrence of the motif of "turning" (vv. 4 and 6), I would argue that the reader is *led* to have the suspicion that King Jeroboam might have changed his stance toward the man of God and, more importantly, toward the word of Yahweh. The fact that the king asked for the man of God's prayer and that he received the healing of his hand seems to signal that the king may have repented from his evil ways, drawing the reader's attention to the rest of the story. The king's invitation to the man of God to his house in the next pericope (vv. 7–10) adds more plausibility to such a hope. We will not be able to find out, though, whether he genuinely "repented" from his evil way until the end of the story. Bodner puts it this way, "Still, later episodes may suggest that the king's repentance—if that is the best label—will be more of a fleeting affair."[47]

The Man of God's Obedience (vv. 7–10)

In this part we find the king's invitation to the man of God to his house: "Come with me to the house and rest. And I will give you a gift" (v. 7). The man of God rejects the invitation, informing the king of the prohibition that he has received (vv. 8–9). Then he leaves Bethel, taking another way, as was commanded (v. 10).

Many scholars speculate on the motive of the king's invitation. It could be "gratitude, an effort to come into contact with a person of blessing, or an attempt to bribe the prophet and defuse the threat of his oracle."[48] Dozeman thinks it was from his gratitude,[49] whereas Simon argues that it was from

---

46. Gen 20:7; Num 21:7; Deut 9:20; 1 Sam 12:19, 23; 1 Kgs 13:6; Job 42:10; Ps 72:15; Jer 7:16; 14:11; 29:7; 37:3; 42:20; cf. Jer 11:14.

47. Bodner, *Royal Drama*, 106–7.

48. Nelson, *First and Second Kings*, 86.

49. Dozeman, "Way of the Man," 384–5; Würthwein, "Die Erzählung," 181–9, esp. 182.

Exegesis of 1 Kings 13

hostility.⁵⁰ Similarly, Noth and Walsh contend that the king is attempting to disarm the prophetic threat against his altar.⁵¹ The text is, however, silent about the king's motive for the invitation. The fact that it goes unstated may imply that it is outside the concern of the narrator. Rather, the emphasis seems to be on introducing the prohibition from God into the narrative, which will remain an important literary element throughout the rest of the narrative.⁵² The man of God obeys God's command by rejecting the king's invitation this time (vv. 8b–9).

As is the case with the king's motive for the invitation, no reason is given for God's prohibition, either. Knoppers says, "That the man of God is not to eat, drink or travel by the same route by which he came (1 Kgs 13:8–9) underscores the gravity of the divine judgment against Bethel."⁵³ The rationale behind the prohibition may have to do with coming back (שׁוּב) to *Bethel*, as is shown in the emphasis in v. 8: "If you give me half your house, I will not go in with you. And I will not eat bread or drink water *in this place*" (בַּמָּקוֹם הַזֶּה)—also, note that "this place" receives emphasis in vv. 16 and 22. If there is a reason for the prohibition, it would be to demonstrate that Bethel is unfit for worship of God.

With that said, however, it seems that the content of the prohibition is not as important as the prohibition itself. In other words, the prohibition is important as a command from Yahweh, and why he was prohibited from "eating, drinking, and returning" is less important, as is indicated by the silence of the text. Though we can guess that returning by the way he came may be regarded as "a sign of an unfulfilled mission"⁵⁴ or as voiding the mission and forfeiting the goal,⁵⁵ the emphasis is clearly on whether or not the man of God will obey the command. The statement in v. 10 that "he went another way and did not return by the way that he had come to Bethel" also seems to support this view. Van Seters notes the subtle difference in emphasis between the prohibition being against not returning to

---

50. Simon, "Prophetic Sign," 88.

51. Noth, *Könige*, 298; Walsh, "The Contexts," 360.

52. Nelson sees the king's offer as "a literary necessity to permit the man of God to turn it down" (*First and Second Kings*, 86). Dozeman has the same view and says, "The king's request provides the context for a necessary progression in the narrative. It allows the prophet from Judah to state the accompanying restrictions of his call" ("Way of the Man," 384–5).

53. Knoppers, *Two Nations under God*, 2:59.

54. Fretheim, *First and Second Kings*, 79.

55. Simon, "Prophetic Sign," 88.

Bethel and it being simply not taking the same route.⁵⁶ For Van Seters, the narrator's statement (v. 10) does not harmonize with the text's emphasis on "this place." Thus, for him, it is an example of "a lack of literary skill by the author."⁵⁷ It probably did not, however, bother the ancient reader as much as it does the modern reader. The statement seems to simply mean that the man of God obeyed the command. Thus, the emphasis is on keeping the command; there is nothing inherently wrong with eating bread, drinking water, and going back by the same way he came. The narrator is interested in showing that "he" (v. 9)—it is not clear who "he" is (cf. v. 21)—commanded (צִוָּה) the man of God "by the word of Yahweh" (בדבר יהוה), and that the man of God is now put to a test of obedience. The man of God passes the test this time (v. 10).

The function of this pericope is to introduce the command of Yahweh imposed on the man of God and to show that he obeyed the command in the first test. This motif is important for the rest of the story, since whether or not he would stay obedient to this command remains the focus of the story. In connection with this, two other key motifs surface in this pericope: the "way" (דֶּרֶךְ) and "to turn" (שׁוּב). Dozeman observes, "The constant repetition of 'the way' (*derek*) is a literary device meant to prepare the reader for a motif which becomes central to the remainder of the narrative."⁵⁸ From this pericope on, the reader is invited to pay attention to these key words.⁵⁹ In this regard, this pericope links with vv. 11–32 "insofar as G-d's stipulations become the basis upon which the man of G-d ultimately dies."⁶⁰

Transition: Introduction of the Old Prophet of Bethel (vv. 11–14)

This pericope serves to provide a transition to the story. The disruptive clause that begins with a *waw* + a noun (וְנָבִיא) announces the transition. The old prophet will change the fate of the man of God from Judah. The man of God who passed the first test successfully will face another through the more experienced prophet in the following section (vv. 15–19).

The new character is introduced as "an old prophet living (יֹשֵׁב) in Bethel" (v. 11). This description is brief and neutral, and it is not clear yet

---

56. Van Seters, "Reading the Story," 225–34, esp. 228.
57. Van Seters, "Reading the Story," 233.
58. Dozeman, "Way of the Man," 387.
59. Nelson, *First and Second Kings*, 86.
60. Sweeney, *I & II Kings*, 181.

how the prophet is portrayed. His sons come and tell him of the "deeds which the man of God had done on that day in Bethel" and "the words which he had spoken to the king" (v. 11). Upon hearing of the man of God, the old prophet responds in an unexpected way; he asks his sons, "Where is the way by which he went?" The old prophet, who has been shown "the way by which the man of God had gone," tells his sons to saddle a donkey for him, and he rides on the donkey and goes after the man of God. He finds him "sitting" (יֹשֵׁב) under an oak tree (v. 14).

Once again, the text keeps silent about the reason or motive for the old prophet's actions. Many commentators assume that the old prophet of Bethel might have been a professional cultic prophet employed by Jeroboam (e.g., Karl Barth), but this view remains a speculation.[61] Fretheim's argument that "the explicit reference to Bethel may mean that he [the old prophet of Bethel] is associated with Jeroboam's religious leadership" is not convincing, either,[62] given that he was old and stayed at home and that even the news of the man of God had to be delivered to him by his sons. The description that he was an *old* prophet seems to play some important role in the story, though the opinions as to its significance vary among commentators. For Bodner, his old age suggests that "he is *not* a significant player in Jeroboam's administration. If he is a marginalized figure like Ahijah, it could immediately enhance the old prophet's credibility."[63] Though the significance of his old age is not clear at this point, his old age is reminiscent of the elders (הַזְּקֵנִים) who provided wise counsel for King Rehoboam in the previous chapter (1 Kgs 12:1–17).

The description of saddling a donkey and the old prophet's riding it in v. 13 is somewhat tedious, and a similarly detailed description is also found in the later parts of the narrative (v. 27). As some scholars have suggested, it may be functional rather than just creating a dramatic delay. In my judgment, the frequent mentions of saddling or riding donkeys serves to emphasize the agedness of the old prophet (vv. 13, 23, 27, 29). Riding a donkey in this narrative indicates physical (and later, spiritual) weakness, in which the man of God joins the old prophet later (vv. 13, 27), when he was struck by the word of Yahweh (v. 23) and then when he died (v. 29). The process of weakening whereby the man of God joins the old prophet in weakness may be insinuated in v. 14, where the man of God is described to be sitting

---

61. Crenshaw, *Prophetic Conflict*, 44.
62. Fretheim, *First and Second Kings*, 79.
63. Bodner, *Royal Drama*, 108–9.

under an oak tree: the man of God was "sitting" (יֹשֵׁב) under an oak tree, just as the old prophet was "dwelling" (יֹשֵׁב) in Bethel, and then later they both are described to be "sitting" (יֹשְׁבִים) at the table together (v. 20).

The old prophet's question to his sons is significant: "Where is the way (הַדֶּרֶךְ) by which he went?" And his sons show him "the way" (הַדֶּרֶךְ) by which the man of God went (v. 12). The use of the word "way" here is clearly intentional, drawing the reader's attention to the threefold prohibition that the man of God spoke of to King Jeroboam (vv. 9–10). Will the man of God "return" (שׁוּב) to Bethel? It is the question that the reader now asks and will soon find out the answer to in the following story.

The Man of God's Disobedience (vv. 15–19)

This pericope is composed of the old prophet's invitation to the man of God (v. 15), the man of God's rejection (vv. 16–17), the old prophet's lie (v. 18), and the man of God's disobedience to the word of Yahweh (v. 19). As we saw in the structure analysis, this section is paralleled with the first set of invitation and rejection (vv. 7–10), except for the old prophet's lie (v. 18). The prophet's lie changes the "way" of the man of God; the man of God, who obeyed the command of Yahweh before, changes the direction of his way.

John Gray speculates that the old prophet of Bethel lied to the man of God from Judah out of a sinister motive because he regarded the man of God's rejection of the invitation of Jeroboam as "an insult to the king and patron of the shrine to which he was attached" and thus he wished to "test the genuineness of the word of God."[64] Eynikel refutes this view and says, "He does not do so because he wants to test his veracity or because he is a state prophet connected with the sanctuary of Bethel, as some propose, for then there would be no explanation for his desire to be buried in the same grave as his 'enemy.'"[65]

Given that the old prophet's lie is a very significant factor whereby the direction of the whole story as well as the fate of the man of God is completely changed, the text's silence about the old prophet's motive for his lie is surprising. Moreover, it is noticeable that the narrator is not passing any judgment on the old prophet for his deception. If the old prophet's lying was intended to be perceived to be "wrong" and if it was the direction

---

64. Gray, *I & II Kings*, 300.
65. Eynikel, "Prophecy and Fulfillment," 234.

Exegesis of 1 Kings 13

in which the narrator is leading the story, what follows in the rest of the story hardly makes sense. It does not seem that the narrator was interested in passing judgment on the old prophet's lie or even addressing the ethical aspect of the story. The old prophet is not criticized for his behavior at all. Instead, as we will discover in the next pericope, the word of Yahweh comes to him, and Yahweh speaks through him to proclaim judgment on the man of God who disobeyed his command (v. 20–21).

The reader of the Micaiah ben Imlah story in 1 Kings 22 may be reminded of the old prophet's lie in 1 Kings 13 and wonder about possible links between the two stories. The theme of "true and false prophecy" seems to be operating in the Micaiah ben Imlah story in 1 Kings 22 (cf. Deut 13:1–3 and Jer 28). I have argued and shown in the previous chapter that the story in 1 Kings 13 in its present form is not *mainly* dealing with the issue of true and false prophecy.

With that said, however, the concept of the "lying spirit" of 1 Kings 22 could shed light on interpreting the old prophet's lie in 1 Kgs 13. The Hebrew words used in each text are different: "a lying spirit" (רוּחַ שֶׁקֶר) in 1 Kgs 22:22, 23, and "He lied to him" (כִּחֶשׁ לוֹ) in 1 Kgs 13:18. For this reason, a close literary connection is not clear. The concept of "lie," however, is still worth a further consideration. In 1 Kgs 22, a true prophet, Micaiah, tells a lie (v. 15), and more importantly, God himself recruits a "spirit" (רוּחַ) who will "entice" (פָּתָה) Ahab to go up and fall at Ramoth-gilead (v. 20), and the spirit becomes "a lying spirit" in the mouths of all Ahab's prophets (vv. 21–23). This story is peculiar in that Yahweh himself is portrayed to be sending out "a lying spirit" for the purpose of accomplishing his plan of judgment.[66] What is also noticeable here is that no ethical judgment is made about Yahweh's action, or, at least, the ethical issue is not in the theological concern of the narrator here. This can be illuminating for the story in 1 Kings 13 in two ways. First, the fact alone that the old prophet "lied" does not make him a false prophet. Second, the narrator is not likely to be dealing with an ethical issue regarding the old prophet's lie. The study of the

---

66. Divine deception is not a concept foreign to the Hebrew Bible. Robert P. Carroll states, "Deuteronomy, Jeremiah, Ezekiel and the deuteronomists all recognized that Yahweh could and did deceive communities and individuals" (*When Prophecy Failed*, 198). In Samuel 16:2, Yahweh devises the deception for the safety of Samuel. Brueggemann takes the deception in 1 Kings 13 as "plain old deception." He states, making note of 1 Kings 22:19–23 and 1 Samuel 16:2, "The cases are enough to make clear that the cunning of divine purpose cannot be held to our belated ethical norms" (*1 & 2 Kings*, 169).

word "to lie" (כחש) shows that lying is in general not a commendable thing, but any ethical judgment is not the focus of the story.

Clearly, the emphasis is on the man of God's disobedience to the command that had been given him, and from a literary perspective the old prophet's lie is just an instrument by which the man of God's disobedience was brought about. The narrator does not describe the old prophet's psychological motive for his lie, but only the man of God's failure in keeping the command and how the failure came about. Therefore, interpretive movements toward speculating about the old prophet's motive for his lying or basing the interpretation of the theme of the story on it, I would argue, may not be necessary for grasping the narrator's intention or emphasis. The phrase "by the word of Yahweh" is used twice in the short dialogue between the man of God and the old prophet (v. 17 and v. 18). The man of God rejects the old prophet's invitation, "because a word came to me 'by the word of Yahweh'" not to eat, drink, and return by the way he came (v. 17), and the only way for the old prophet to bring the man of God back was also by means of the old prophet's employment of the phrase "by the word of Yahweh." Thus, the emphasis on the word of Yahweh continues here, and the man of God's disobedience to the word receives special attention.

The reference to an angel by the old prophet has caught some scholars' attention. As Bosworth comments, "The angel remains a curious detail" in the text.[67] Alexander Rofé argues that the story reflects a polemic against angels.[68] In his view, the features regarding the man of God in 1 Kgs 13 are typical of the "angel of God" texts in the Hebrew Bible (cf. Judg 6, 13). The similarities are found in the motifs of the communal meal ("eating" and "drinking" in 1 Kgs 13) and the angel's sudden disappearing from the scene (the man of God's departure from Bethel to go back to Judah in 1 Kings 13). Because of the anti-angelological tendency, the man of God was substituted for the angel of God in 1 Kings 13. This view is based on the assumption that "the struggle against the popular belief in angels may take on the literary form of describing a messenger of God as a person of flesh and blood and angelic properties (to refrain from eating and drinking and to disappear mysteriously at the end of his utterance)."[69] Also, Rofé argues that the man of God's failure is due to his belief in angels. In other words, the

---

67. Bosworth, *Story within a Story*, 138.

68. Rofé, "Classes in the Prophetical Stories," 143–64. For more discussion on this, also see Rofé, *The Prophetic Stories*, 170–82.

69. Simon, "Prophetic Sign," 84.

old prophet's words that an angel had spoken to him should have signaled to him that it was a lie. His view has been generally rejected by scholars. Mordechai Cogan, for example, contends that the reference to an angel in v. 18 "was not a signal, missed by the man of God, that he was lying, for it would not have been considered unusual for an angel to do YHWH's bidding, even when a man of God was the recipient of the act or message (e.g., I Kgs 19:5–7)."[70] Also, Blum points out,

> Sieht man von der Frage der Plausibilität des angenommenen antiangelologischen Skopus zunächst einmal ab, bleiben bei dieser originellen Deutung aber doch spezifische Details der Erzählung unerklärt: Das Verbot der Mahlgemeinschaft ist nicht an ein bestimmtes Auftreten gebunden, sondern (sehr betont) an einen bestimmten Ort (V. 8.16 und 22), und die Anweisung für den Rückweg impliziert—nach dem Fortgang der Erzählung zu urteilen—kein unbemerktes Verschwinden des Judäers.[71]

Then, why has the reference to the angel been made in our narrative? Would there be any significance of the reference to an angel here? Throughout the Deuteronomistic History, we find, besides 1 Kings 13:18, five texts where an angel speaks to a prophet or to the people: an angel of Yahweh to all the people of Israel (Judg 2:1–4), an angel of Yahweh to Gideon (Judg 6), an angel of Yahweh to Samson's parents (Judg 13), an angel to Elijah in the wilderness (1 Kgs 19:5, 7), and an angel of Yahweh to Elijah (2 Kgs 1:3, 15). Thus, it should not surprise the reader to find a reference to an angel in the text, though it is not clear what the significance of the reference would be. Was the reference to an angel meant to raise questions in the mind of the man of God about veracity, as Rofé understands? If so, it did not work; the man of God did not get it. As with other parts, the text is ambiguous. This issue, however, may deserve more investigation in relation with other texts in the Hebrew Bible. With that said, the reference may reveal the narrator's assumption that it was through an angel that the word of Yahweh had been delivered to the man of God earlier in vv. 9 and 17. This also explains why the man of God believed the old prophet's lie so readily.

On the other hand, the narrator's brief judgment ("He lied") is interesting and demands some careful thought. As argued above, clarifying the motive of the old prophet may not be essential to grasping the narrator's message, but the insertion of the judgment in the story remains an

---

70. Cogan, *I Kings*, 370.
71. Blum, "Die Lüge des Propheten," 30.

THE FATE OF THE MAN OF GOD FROM JUDAH

interesting detail. This omniscient judgment by the narrator might represent the old prophet's conscious intention. Though it is impossible to know why the old prophet lied, it is likely to be a test; the old prophet lied so as to have the man of God reject his invitation. He was testing the man of God to see if he would stay faithful to God's original word and not take any lateral detours. If the text is registering something about a larger problem of discerning true prophecy in some way, the lesson might be something like this: True prophets do not adjust what they have been told even when given plausible lateral counsel, parading as divine word. If the man of God had passed the test, it would have confirmed his oracle against the altar. Even when he failed the test, however, his disobedience, in a mysterious way, also confirmed his message for Jeroboam, because it served as a "sign" for him.

The narrator ends this pericope in v. 19 as follows: "Then, he returned (וַיָּשָׁב) with him and ate bread in his house and drank water." The man of God did what he was commanded not to do. Dozeman writes of the man of God's returning, "The word of Yahweh is at the center of the prophet's response. Although that word includes a prohibition against eating and drinking, the command concerning the prophet's direction envelopes his response and acquires special emphasis. He must take care to be in the proper way. The way of the prophet becomes a central concern."[72] The consequence of his "returning" is described in the next pericope.

The Second Set of "Word" and Fulfillment (vv. 20–26)

This section describes God's judgment on the man of God and its fulfillment. God's judgment is proclaimed in the form of "the word of Yahweh" (דְּבַר־יְהוָה), and the following events happen "according to the word of Yahweh" (כִּדְבַר יְהוָה). When the man of God turned back from his way, the word of Yahweh arrived with no delay at the scene of his disobedience, that is, while "they were sitting (יֹשְׁבִים) at the table" (v. 20).[73] What perplexes the reader the most may be that the word of Yahweh now comes to the old prophet, "the prophet who has brought him back" (v. 20).

There is no question, however, that the word that came to the old prophet is a genuine word of Yahweh. He "cried" (וַיִּקְרָא) to the man of God from Judah, saying, "Thus says Yahweh (כֹּה אָמַר יְהוָה), because you

---

72. Dozeman, "Way of the Man," 386.

73. The man of God gradually joins the old prophet in his sedentariness until he becomes completely immobile, and his body must be carried by a donkey (v. 29).

disobeyed the mouth of Yahweh (פִּי יְהוָה) and did not keep the commandment which Yahweh your God had commanded you . . ." (vv. 21–22). The vocabulary employed in v. 21 connects this part with the man of God's oracle against the altar in v. 2, where the man of God "cried" against the altar, and the messenger formula, "Thus says Yahweh," was also used. The man of God, who had proclaimed God's judgment against the altar (the object that symbolizes the sin of Jeroboam), has now become the object of God's judgment himself. Here is formed a parallel between Jeroboam and the man of God. In this respect, God's punishment of the man of God for his disobedience becomes a sign or a warning that Jeroboam will also be punished for his disobedience.[74] Furthermore, the accusation that the man of God "did not *keep the commandment* which Yahweh your God had commanded you" (וְלֹא שָׁמַרְתָּ אֶת־הַמִּצְוָה אֲשֶׁר צִוְּךָ יְהוָה אֱלֹהֶיךָ) is reminiscent of the narrator's comment on Solomon's apostasy and Yahweh's subsequent words to Solomon (11:10, 11), and more importantly, Ahijah's oracle regarding Jeroboam (11:34, 38; cf. 14:8): "who *kept my commandments* and statutes" (אֲשֶׁר שָׁמַר מִצְוֹתַי וְחֻקֹּתָי, v. 34).

The rest of this pericope describes the fulfillment of the word of Yahweh that the old prophet has spoken. After the eating and drinking, the old prophet saddles a donkey for him, "for the prophet[75] whom he had brought back" (v. 23). We notice the change in the appellation for the old prophet of Bethel here. Dozeman notes, "The appellative for the old *nabi* changes immediately after the test to 'the *nabi* who caused him to return' (*hannābî ʾăšer hăšîbô*, v. 20). This title is repeated once more in the second scene (v. 23c). The complete form of the appellative occurs in the final scene when the nabi is identified as 'the *nabi* who caused him to return from the way' (*hannābî ʾăšer hăšîbô min-hadderek*, v. 26)."[76] Here the narrator's emphasis is betrayed; he depicts the old prophet as the one who had brought the man of God from the "way," which can be understood both literally and metaphorically.[77] The man of God turned away from the road, but also he turned away from the way, or the mission, of obeying Yahweh's command.

---

74. Leithart, *1 & 2 Kings*, 100.

75. The prophet in the phrase "for the prophet whom he had brought" in v. 23 must refer to the man of God from Judah. That this is the only place where the man of God is called "the prophet" is not a problem, because the man of God did not object to being identified as a prophet in the old prophet's self-introduction in v. 18.

76. Dozeman, "Way of the Man," 389.

77. For a discussion on the range of meaning and the different ways in which the words "to turn" and "way" have been used in 1 Kings 13, see Lemke, "The Way of

THE FATE OF THE MAN OF GOD FROM JUDAH

Interestingly, here we find no hint of animosity between the man of God and the old prophet—at least, it is not depicted in the text. Bodner points this out and says, "Any expected animosity between these two characters—in light of the negative judgment just pronounced on the one by the other—is not apparent as the old prophet saddles his donkey for the guest to depart."[78] Would the old prophet have done this as an apology for his deception? The text keeps silent. And the man of God is silent as well, which gives the reader the impression that he is ready to quietly receive God's punishment.

It is worth noting that the man of God now rides on a donkey, whereas nowhere in the previous text is the man of God found riding on a donkey. Riding a donkey signifies that the man of God has now become completely feeble. The man of God rides on a donkey for the first time, after he has heard the word of Yahweh proclaimed against him (vv. 23–24), which shows that the man of God has now been pounded by the word of Yahweh and has been totally weakened. I would argue that this symbolizes and prefigures what will happen to Jeroboam.

The man of God's death is described rather simply and with no emotion attached to the description (v. 24). As he went, "a lion found him on the way" (וַיִּמְצָאֵהוּ אַרְיֵה בַּדֶּרֶךְ), just as the prophet Ahijah had found Jeroboam on the way in 11:29 (וַיִּמְצָא אֹתוֹ אֲחִיָּה הַשִּׁילֹנִי הַנָּבִיא בַּדֶּרֶךְ).[79] The parallel between the man of God and Jeroboam may be implied here as well, though Ahijah announced Jeroboam's ascension to kingship, whereas now the lion has executed God's judgment on the man of God.

The narrator ensures that the lion's killing was the fulfillment of the word of Yahweh, and not a haphazard tragic event. The lion stood beside the body of the man of God and ate neither the body of the man of God nor the donkey, which shows that the lion was an agent of divine punishment and that this incident was brought about by Yahweh.[80] The words of the old prophet confirm this one more time: "He is the man of God who disobeyed the command of Yahweh, and Yahweh gave him over to the lion, and it has

---

Obedience," 310–2.

78. Bodner, *Royal Drama*, 111.

79. Bodner links this account with 2 Kings 2:23–5 where two female bears tore up forty-two little lads who had taunted Elisha and argues that the "geographical symbolism" is at work, noting that both events happen in Bethel (*Elisha's Profile in the Book of Kings*, 3).

80. For a discussion on the word נְבֵלָה "corpse," see Marcus, "Lying Prophet," 70.

torn him and killed him according to the word of Yahweh which he had spoken to him" (v. 26b). Bodner correctly observes,

> While the narrator refrains from mentioning any direct causation, the old prophet is quick to interpret the dramatic events as divine judgment. But the tone is far from triumphal gloating, and his next actions seem pastoral: he orders his sons to (again) saddle the donkey, and he sets out to recover the body of his deceased colleague, in the process gaining a firsthand glimpse of the unmolested donkey standing beside the self-controlled lion.[81]

On the other hand, Nelson argues that the lion's unnatural act (not eating the body of the man of God) gave the old prophet a proof that "the outrageous word against his home town is true, because its attendant prohibition has been validated by the fulfillment of a revelation he himself transmitted (v. 32)" and that through the realization the old prophet "has been transformed from an opponent of the word to a supporter."[82] In my judgment, however, it is not the psychological change in the old prophet's mind toward the man of God that the narrator describes here. The old prophet already knew that the oracle by the man of God was authentic, since he heard everything that had happened at the altar site (v. 11). The old prophet of Bethel's declaration in v. 26 is just a confirmation that the word of Yahweh that had been proclaimed came true. What is emphasized is the fulfillment of the word of Yahweh, not the old prophet's realization of the genuineness of the oracle of the man of God. The sole focus is placed on the man of God's disobedience and God's judgment on him.

Thus, in this section (vv. 20–26) is found another set of a prophetic word and its fulfillment, forming a concentric parallel with the first set of a prophetic word and fulfillment (vv. 3–6). These two sets of prophecy and fulfillment carry out a particular function in the narrative; the narrator's emphasis on the fulfilling power of the spoken word of Yahweh shows the reader that the word against the altar at Bethel will be certainly fulfilled. Burke Long puts it this way: "The fulfillment of the Bethelite's word of Judgment in the death of the Judahite man of God is another 'sign,' the means to affirm the oracle against Bethel."[83] God's judgment on the man of God who failed to keep his commandment is sharp and firm. Likewise, God's

---

81. Bodner, *Royal Drama*, 113.

82. Nelson, *First and Second Kings*, 88. For a similar view, see Cohn, "Literary Technique," 34.

83. Long, *1 Kings*, 148.

judgment on the altar (hence on Jeroboam) will also be executed with certainty.

The Man of God's Prophecy against the Altar at Bethel Is Confirmed by the Old Prophet (vv. 27–32)

The body of the man of God is retrieved and buried by the old prophet. This time his sons saddle the donkey for the old prophet (v. 27), and he goes and finds the body flung on the way, with the donkey and the lion standing beside the body. The lion did not eat the body; nor did it "break" (שָׁבַר) the donkey (v. 28), through which the narrator confirms once again that the death of the man of God by the lion was a punishment from God, not an accident.

The old prophet lifts up the body of the man of God and puts it on the donkey and "brings it back" (שׁוּב), but this time the man of God "returns" (שׁוּב) as a dead body, being carried by a donkey. The old prophet places the body in his own grave and laments over it, "Alas, my brother!" (v. 30). This lamentation does not harmonize with a negative characterization of the old prophet. He calls him "my brother" (אָחִי), which seems to be referring to the office of prophet that they share in common. It seems that he deplores the fate of the man of God, who had to die a tragic death in the course of performing his prophetic commission.

After he has buried the man of God, he says to his sons, "When I die, bury me in the grave where the man of God is buried. Beside his bones shall you lay my bones" (v. 31). He gives the reason for his request: "for the word shall surely come to pass which he cried by the word of Yahweh against the altar which is in Bethel and against all the houses of the high places which are in the cities of Samaria."[84] At least, two things deserve mentioning here: First, he confirms that, though the man of God was killed because of his disobedience to the command of Yahweh, the word that he has proclaimed against the altar will certainly be fulfilled.[85] Second, the old

---

84. As many commentators have pointed out, the name "Samaria" appears here for the first time in the Book of Kings. Considering that the "the reference to Samaria as a province obviously dates from at least after 734," which is more than 150 years after this event (Gray, *I & II Kings*, 303), we can conclude that the narrator is narrating the words of the old prophet from his own perspective. Bethel and the cities of the Northern Kingdom are identified as "the cities of Samaria" here.

85. It seems that the narrator has in mind the events described in 2 Kings 23:15–20, but I argue that the narrative in 1 Kings 13 is to be read and interpreted in its immediate

prophet's request that he, when he dies, be buried beside the man of God in the same grave does not have to be understood as from a selfish or evil motive.[86] Rather, it describes the old prophet's conviction of the certainty of the man of God's oracle against the Bethel altar, which betrays the narrator's emphasis. It is not the old prophet's interest in his personal wellbeing after death that the narrator describes here.

Thus, this section is linked with the initial oracle by the man of God (vv. 1–2). Bodner comments on the literary link between 13:1-2 and 13:30–32,

> There are two items in the old prophet's words of 13:30–32 that are of principal interest here. First, the apostrophic utterance ("Alas, O my brother!") in 13:30 parallels the man of God's utterance to the altar. In both cases, an inanimate object is addressed (altar and corpse respectively), and the irony is deadly: the man of God unleashes an apostrophic excoriation of Jeroboam's altar, and now his corpse is given an apostrophic address by the old prophet of Bethel and other attendees ("they lamented" is plural in Hebrew, most likely the sons of the old prophet). The two parts of 1 Kings 13 are thus powerfully linked, and the fall of the altar in Bethel anticipates the fall of Jeroboam (soon to be announced). The funeral oration of the man of God becomes a virtual eulogy for the king.[87]

The parallel between Jeroboam and the man of God becomes obvious and clear: (1) the word of Yahweh was declared to both. (2) They both obeyed it first, but later they both turned away from it and disobeyed it. (3) Therefore, God's judgment on both King Jeroboam and the man of God is final. Thus, the fate of the man of God reflects the looming destiny of Jeroboam.

Ending: The Narrator's Comment (vv. 33–34)

The narrator's editorial comment in the ending framework clarifies the purpose of the story for the reader. "The short paragraph that concludes the chapter is often seen as an appendix, but these words are best read as the culmination of the entire chapter and the conclusion to the allegorical second part."[88] Without this comment, the inclusion of the story in the context.

86. Marcus, "Lying Prophet," 71.
87. Bodner, *Royal Drama*, 114.
88. Bodner, *Royal Drama*, 116.

Jeroboam narrative would not have been as clear. Jeroboam did not "turn away" from his evil "way." The motifs of "turning" (שׁוּב) and "way" (דֶּרֶךְ) connect the editorial comment to the body of the narrative. The phrase "after this thing" may refer to the whole event through which Jeroboam should have received enough warning and changed the direction of his life. Through the encounter with the man of God and through the tragic event that had happened to the man of God, Jeroboam was given one more chance to turn away from his evil, but even "after this thing," he did not turn away from his evil way, but he "turned and stayed" in his disregard for God's command.

The "sin" of Jeroboam was mentioned in 1 Kings 12:30 and is mentioned here again. In 1 Kings 12:30, it was mentioned in relation to Jeroboam's setting up two golden calves in Bethel and Dan, and in 1 Kings 13:33–34, the "sin" is mentioned in relation to his establishing illegitimate priests. Distinguishing between these two, however, is meaningless. Rather, they describe one sin, Jeroboam's apostasy.

From this comment, we learn the favor that Jeroboam showed to the man of God after his hand was restored did not last and the experience did not make him genuinely repent. Bodner puts it clearly,

> With the altar having imploded and his own hand dried and healed, a reader may have expected some revision in his domestic policy, perhaps even with some public support in Bethel (many citizens, after all, would have witnessed the events and heard the proclamation). Such inflexibility carries a high price, as articulated in 13:34, the final sentence of this incomparable chapter: "This thing became a sin to the house of Jeroboam, so as to make it desolate (כחד) and to destroy it (שׁמד) from the face of the earth."[89]

Now, God's judgment on the house of Jeroboam is firm and irrevocable.

THE THEME OF THE STORY

Up until this point, I have analyzed the structure and constituent parts of the narrative. Now I am moving forward to finalize the theme of the narrative. Numerous suggestions have been submitted for the theme of 1 Kings 13: the importance of obedience (e.g., Walter Gross, Lemke), the

---

89. Bodner, *Royal Drama*, 118.

relationship of Judah and Israel (e.g., Karl Barth, Roland Boer,[90] Bosworth), true and false prophecy (e.g., Dozeman, D. W. Van Winkle,[91] Fretheim), judgment against Bethel (e.g., Walter Brueggemann,[92] Gary Knoppers), the triumph of the word of Yahweh (e.g., B. S. Childs, Richard Nelson), a satire directed against the prophets (e.g., David Marcus).[93]

The plethora of the proposed themes indicates that many different ideas exist in the narrative. Thus, the task of finding the theme of the narrative involves sorting out various ideas and finding one idea that encompasses other ideas without making it too general. It also involves figuring out how smaller parts form a meaningful whole and contribute together to the theme of the whole narrative, not only within the narrative but also in the broader context of the Jeroboam narrative.

Altar: A Metonym for the Sin of Jeroboam

In the narrative the altar is one of motifs that bind different parts of the narrative together, appearing in both parts of the story (12:32, 33; 13:1, 2, 3, 4, 5, 32). Clearly, the narrator intended to show that the prophecy against the altar would certainly be fulfilled. There is no doubt that Josiah's purification work (2 Kgs 23:15–20) was in the mind of the narrator. Bosworth states, "The altar becomes again the specific focus of the fulfillment in 2 Kgs 23:15–20 and is mentioned four times (23:15, 16 bis, 17). The altar thereby stands at the center of this example of the prophecy-fulfillment schema in the Deuteronomistic History."[94]

Considering the special attention given to the altar, we must admit the altar is an important element of the narrative. For this reason, Knoppers

90. Boer, "National Allegory," 95–116.

91. Van Winkle, "1 Kings XIII," 31–43.

92. Brueggemann, *1 & 2 Kings*, 167.

93. Marcus, "Lying Prophet," 67–74. Marcus interprets the narrative by the two concepts, ridicule and parody, and concludes that the story is a satire. He says, "The principle concern of the story is to satirize its targets, the man of God and the prophet of Bethel. They are satirized because of their behavior: for stupidity, and concern with petty values." In his understanding, the man of God is portrayed as a stupid prophet who disobeyed God, and the old prophet as being only concerned about his own remains, hence being purely selfish. Marcus does not analyze the literary context or explain how the story fits within the larger Jeroboam narrative. Thus, his assessment does not provide a coherent and integrated reading of the story.

94. Bosworth, *Story within a Story*, 124–25.

concludes 1 Kings 13 is about "the prospects for this new cult."⁹⁵ He argues 1 Kings 13 shows the prospects for the Bethel altar and 1 Kings 14 the prospects for the house of Jeroboam. Simon contends, however, that "the fact that the prophecy of the destruction of the altar uttered by the man of God (13:2) is presented without supporting reason or explanation proves sufficiently that the guilt of Beth-el is not the theme of the story but is merely its background."⁹⁶ In my judgment, a close reading of the narrative supports Simon's view. At any rate, the altar disappears in most of the story (vv. 7–30). It is not likely that the whole narrative is simply about the prospects for the Bethel altar, but rather, the altar seems to be a *metonym* for the "sin of Jeroboam" (cf. 12:30; 13:34). God's judgment on the altar constitutes part of and contributes to the theme of God's judgment on the house of Jeroboam.

Obedience and Disobedience

The key motifs found in the narrative hold the different parts of the narrative together and move the plot of the story forward. Thus, the interpretation that does not take into consideration this aspect of the narrative does not do justice to the narrative.⁹⁷ As we have discussed, the motif of "the word of Yahweh" is significant and essential to the shaping of the theme. Walsh states,

> Insofar as 1 Kings 13 is an exemplar of what it means to be a "man of God" it is really at its deepest level a story of the word of God itself. The motif phrase "by the word of Yahweh" (the Hebrew is, literally, "in the word of Yahweh") means something like "in the power of/by the authority of the word of Yahweh." The word is not simply something passive, entrusted by Yahweh to the man of God and delivered by the man of God like an inert message. It is active; it is power and authority.⁹⁸

The powerful and authoritative word of Yahweh, then, demands obedience from those who receive it. As the plot of our narrative proceeds, whether

---

95. Knoppers, *Two Nations under God*, 2:45.

96. Simon, "Prophetic Sign," 85.

97. For example, Marvin Sweeney's commentary (*I & II Kings* [2007]) provides a close reading of the text by means of intertextuality and the historical and archeological data, but he ignores the literary structure indicated by repeated important motifs.

98. Walsh, *1 Kings*, 191.

the man of God would stay obedient to the word remains the sole focus of the story. Which "way" (דֶּרֶךְ) is he going? Will he "turn" (שׁוּב) to go back to Bethel? Sadly and unfortunately, the man of God does not walk in the "way" of obedience but "turns" away from it. Thus, we see that the theme of obedience and disobedience is clearly discernible in the text. This theme, however, cannot be the main theme of the narrative in its present shape, mainly because it does not explain why the story has been included in the Jeroboam narrative or why the narrator shaped the narrative the way it is. As we saw above, the narrator's intention is presented most clearly in his comment at the end of the narrative. The comment shows that even "after this matter Jeroboam did not turn from his evil way," and thus it justifies God's judgment on his "house." Of the narrator's comment, Walsh states,

> By repeating after the events of chapter 13 the same information and almost the same words about Jeroboam's cultic evils, the narrator implies that the intervening events make no lasting impression on the king. He has heard the man of God's condemnation of the altar and felt the power of that condemnation in his own flesh, withered and then restored. He has heard, surely, of the man of God's violent death and miraculous honor guard, and of the Bethel prophet's confirmation of the original oracle. Yet he perseveres, apparently unperturbed, in his evil ways. To the offenses of idolatrous sanctuaries and illicit priests, Jeroboam adds obduracy.[99]

In a similar tone, Cohn also comments on the formation of the chapter. He says the narrator "could have made this declaration [v. 34] as the immediate conclusion to the initial recitation of Jeroboam's cultic reforms in 12,26–33 and then reported Ahijah's prophecy of destruction [14:1–20]. Instead he chose to separate the sin from its consequences with the oracle of and the story about the man of God. At first glance, this material appears to be secondary. However, because it constitutes the very center of the chiastic structure of the Jeroboam narrative, we must attempt to ascertain its literary purpose."[100] Cohn's point is insightful. Though it may seem that, because of the similarity between the opening exposition (12:32–33 and more broadly 12:26–33) and the ending (13:33–34), Jeroboam has returned to the condition from which he set out, in effect "the reality to which they [Jeroboam] return is not the same as it was."[101]

99. Walsh, *1 Kings*, 191–2.
100. Cohn, "Literary Technique," 31.
101. Amit, *Reading Biblical Narratives*, 36.

THE FATE OF THE MAN OF GOD FROM JUDAH

The Certainty of God's Judgment on the House of Jeroboam

In this regard, we conclude that the narrator shaped and designed the whole narrative to be an illustration or explanation of why the house (dynasty) of Jeroboam had to be destroyed completely. Jeroboam did not go back to the status quo but to a far harsher reality. Therefore, the reader is led to believe the story was about the house of Jeroboam, and why Jeroboam, despite his great privilege as God's chosen for the ten tribes (cf. 11:29–40), had to be condemned and rejected. The anonymity—the non-naming of the two protagonists, the man of God and the old prophet—serves to allow attention to fall on the only named figure: Jeroboam. Thus, we conclude that the theme of 1 Kings 13 in its present form has to reflect this aspect.

All the constituent parts of the story work together, and various ideas co-operate for this purpose. The motif of obedience and disobedience becomes important because it is concerned with *Jeroboam's* initial obedience and later disobedience to the command he had received (cf. 11:38). The motifs of "turning" and "way" also become significant because they dramatize *Jeroboam's* not "turning away from his evil way." The motif of prophecy and fulfillment (vv. 3–6, 20–26) is important, because the word of Yahweh that has been proclaimed against the altar at Bethel, a metonym of the sin of Jeroboam, will certainly be fulfilled. The theme of a polemic against the Bethel cultus and the theme of obedience and disobedience are therefore woven together by the hand of the narrator who has made the story into a story about Jeroboam[102] and a sign for God's judgment on Jeroboam.

We conclude that the theme of the narrative is the certainty of God's judgment on the house of Jeroboam, and the function of the narrative is to justify God's judgment on Jeroboam, who turned away from the way of Yahweh and continued in his evil way. God's special favor toward Jeroboam had required him to "listen to all that I command you," "walk in my ways," and "do what is right in my eyes by keeping my statutes and my commandments" (1 Kgs 11:38). Jeroboam, however, failed to walk in God's ways and instead chose the way of apostasy in his effort to ensure his kingship by building golden calves in Bethel and Dan. In addition to his apostasy, Jeroboam rejected the word of Yahweh that the man of God brought to the altar, refusing to turn away from his evil way. Hence, God's judgment on him is now inevitable and final.

---

102. Lemke, "The Way of Obedience," 306.

1 KINGS 13:11-32 AS PROPHETIC SYMBOLIC ACTIONS

The parallels between the man of God and Jeroboam are the key to understanding the symbolic nature of the narrative. In the rest of this chapter, based on this observation, I will argue that 1 Kings 13 was intended to be read as an account of prophetic symbolic actions that dramatizes the rise and fall of King Jeroboam. The narrative as prophetic symbolic actions shows some deviations from typical ones, but I will try to demonstrate that the deviations are due to the unique nature of the narrative. This analysis will show that the narrator designed the story in a particular way so that what transpires between the two prophets dramatizes and has symbolic meanings for the reality about Jeroboam.

More scholars in recent years have pointed out the symbolic or parabolic nature of our text. J. K. Mead remarks, "A growing number of recent scholars contend that the portrait of the man of God is also used to picture King Jeroboam, and the chapter is organized to highlight 'what is central for the narrator, namely the way in which the man of God becomes an example of the king himself.'"[103] Cohn and Walsh also share the view that "the man of God is a paradigm for Jeroboam: the chosen instrument of Yahweh's will can, through disobedience, come to a bad end."[104]

Other scholars see symbolic aspects only in some elements of the narrative. For example, Uriel Simon sees the triple prohibition given to the man of God as a typical prophetic sign, which is "intended to concretize the prophecy about the total rejection of the Beth-el altar and to initiate, *as of this day*, the process of its consummation."[105] Burke Long also finds some symbolic elements in the story. He says, "If the Judahite somehow in obedience was a 'sign,' in disobedience he becomes merely ordinary."[106] Here we notice that Long sees a sign in the man of God's obedience only, but not in his disobedience. Keith Bodner takes one step further and argues that the two parts of 1 Kings 13, not only vv. 1-10 but also vv. 11-32, have been shaped to *characterize* Jeroboam. The second part of the story (vv. 11-32), which describes transpirations mainly between the two prophets, "has a number of implications for both Jeroboam's portrait and some of

---

103. Mead, "Kings and Prophets," 197.
104. Walsh, "The Contexts," 365, citing Cohn, "Literary Technique," 32-34.
105. Simon, "Prophetic Sign," 88.
106. Long, *1 Kings*, 148.

THE FATE OF THE MAN OF GOD FROM JUDAH

the larger thematic contours of the narrative."[107] He argues that just as "the fall of the altar in Bethel anticipates the fall of Jeroboam," so "the funeral oration of the man of God [v. 30] becomes a virtual eulogy for the king."[108] I agree with these scholars in broad lines and build more arguments to demonstrate 1 Kings 13 contains prophetic symbolic actions.

The Man of God from Judah Symbolizing King Jeroboam

From the parallels delineated so far, it has become clear that the man of God from Judah inside the narrative (or the text) is symbolizing Jeroboam. The reader recognizes the literary connections that the narrator intended in the texts as follows: First, both Jeroboam and the man of God are tested on keeping the word of Yahweh. "Both Jeroboam and the man of God are tested—albeit in different ways and for different reasons—and both stumble. Jeroboam's test is internal, as revealed in his soliloquy, while the man of God is tested externally by the old prophet's ruse."[109] Second, for their failure in the test, the word of judgment is proclaimed against both of them on the site of their disobedience: God's judgment is proclaimed to Jeroboam while he is *standing on the altar* (vv. 1–2), and the word of God is spoken against the man of God while he is *sitting at the table* (vv. 20–22). Both of the judgment proclamations (v. 2 and v. 20–21) contain the motif of "(by) the word of Yahweh" and the same vocabulary such as "he cried" (ויקרא) and the messenger formula "Thus says Yahweh" (כה אמר יהוה)—this messenger formula occurs only twice in v. 2 and v. 21 in this chapter.

Third, the man of God is portrayed as a man who first walked in obedience to God's command and then later turned away from the "way" he was commanded to walk in. Likewise, Jeroboam's beginning is portrayed positively (11:26—12:25—I discussed this in greater detail in chapter 3), but later in his life he undergoes a sudden change in his "heart" toward God (12:26–31). The fate of the man of God is closely paralleled with that of King Jeroboam: Jeroboam's rise (1 Kgs 11:26—12:25) and fall (1 Kgs 12:26—14:18), and the man of God's obedience (1 Kgs 13:1–10) and disobedience (1 Kgs 13:15–32). Lastly, they share similar punishments: "The man of God's punishment is one of disinheritance: he will not be buried

---

107. Bodner, *Royal Drama*, 98.
108. Bodner, *Royal Drama*, 114.
109. Bodner, *Royal Drama*, 109–10.

in his ancestral tomb, and thus foreshadows the similar fate of Jeroboam's house."[110] These parallels are summarized by Bodner:

> Both figures, after all, are the recipients of a word from God that, for modulated reasons, they abandon in pursuit of a different way. In spatial terms, both depart from the road and venture to Bethel—the man of God returns to Bethel, the city Jeroboam has consecrated (for political security). Both are raised up to counter illicit cultic activity, and both survive attempts at arrest by formidable monarchs. Yet both Jeroboam and the man of God detour from their mandates, and are penalized with a violent, premature demise.[111]

These parallels clearly show that the man of God from Judah played the role of Jeroboam in this prophetic drama to show how Jeroboam went from obedience to disobedience and as a consequence what his end will be. The narrator portrays the man of God as someone sent from God to illustrate how God's judgment on Jeroboam became irrevocable. Therefore, it seems that there are two "signs" in the narrative; the first and more obvious one is the sign (מוֹפֵת) in vv. 3–6. This sign is a visual demonstration of God's judgment on Jeroboam's cultic innovations. The second sign, the more complicated one, is the man of God himself who obeyed, disobeyed, and then was penalized for disobedience, which is described in the rest of the narrative (vv. 7–32).

On the other hand, there are some differences between the man of God and Jeroboam, the most prominent of which may be that the man of God is a servant of God's word and he does what he is called to do; the word is proclaimed, and Jeroboam is the recipient of God's judgment in consequence. There is no parallel here with Jeroboam; the man of God was obedient vis-à-vis the king, Jeroboam. Though the man of God is paralleled with Jeroboam in many aspects, he, as a prophet from God, is differentiated from Jeroboam. Thus, he receives sympathy both from the reader and from the old prophet. The man of God, in his obedience, was honorable, and he has given his life (via his disobedience) so that God's word could be proclaimed. This explains the positive desire of the old prophet to be buried with him.

---

110. Bodner, *Royal Drama*, 145.
111. Bodner, *Royal Drama*, 113.

THE FATE OF THE MAN OF GOD FROM JUDAH

Prophetic Symbolic Actions in the Hebrew Bible

Now, I have established the parallels between Jeroboam and the man of God. Before we move further, it is necessary to discuss briefly on the genre/form of prophetic symbolic actions in the Hebrew Bible.

Since World War II, major advances in understanding the genres of prophetic speech and literature have been made. During the following decades, "Form-critical work has been considerable, contributing to other developments such as traditio-historical research, the question of the background and origin of prophecy, and the issue of the prophetic role."[112] We do not need to review the research that has been done in the last half a century in the form-critical study of the prophetic literature, since it is to be found in other works.[113] Instead, I will focus here on the studies of the genre of the report of the prophetic symbolic (sign) actions.

In the Hebrew Bible we not infrequently see prophets receiving commands or instructions "in visions and by other means to perform some action as symbol of God's intentions toward his people."[114] A few examples include Hosea 1 and 3; Isaiah 7:3; 8:1–4; 20:1–6; Jeremiah 13:1–11; 16:1–4, 5–7, 8–9; 32:1–15; Ezekiel 4. George Fohrer, who has made the extensive study of the reports of prophetic symbolic actions in the early 1950s, suggested three essential elements of the literary genre: (1) a command to perform the prophetic symbolic action, (2) the report that the prophet performed the action, and (3) the interpretation of the symbolic action. Along with these essential elements, he added other occasional ("unselbständigen") features, such as eyewitnesses who were present, Yahweh's assurance that the symbolized action would be realized, and explanations of the relationship between symbol and reality.[115]

Fohrer's criteria for the genre has been largely successful and followed by later scholars, but at the same time it also has been modified to some degree. Stacey, for example, noted that "[the] occasional features are often as important as the definitive ones, and any tidy arrangement that excludes them or makes them appear marginal would not help the understanding

---

112. Tucker, "Prophecy and Prophetic Literature," 325–68, esp. 335.

113. For this see House, *Beyond Form Criticism*, and Sweeney and Ben Zvi, *The Changing Face*.

114. March, "Prophecy," 172.

115. Fohrer, "Die Gattung der Berichte," 101–20.

of the whole phenomenon."¹¹⁶ He also modified the essential elements of Fohrer's criteria, stating, "In the early prophetic narratives, the command from Yahweh to perform the action hardly appears at all, and in Ezekiel, more often than not, command and explanation are entangled together and an account of the action being performed is lacking."¹¹⁷ Tucker also has pointed out some variation from the Fohrer's criteria and said, "However, one also finds only two of these elements (command and interpretation, Isa 8:1–4; Jer 16:2–4; or report and interpretation, 1 Kgs 11:29–31; Jer 28:10–11), and sometimes only one element (command, Isa 7:3; report, 1 Kgs 19:19–21; explanation, Isa 20:1–6) (1953:18)."¹¹⁸ These conclusions have revised the previous understanding of the genre quite significantly and marks that the formal features of this category vary to a significant degree.¹¹⁹ Viberg asserts that using the scheme as "a test as to whether an act is a proper prophetic symbolic act" is "going too far in the form-critical agenda."¹²⁰

The scholarly discussion on the reports of prophetic symbolic actions continued to the topic of the function of the genre. Stacey argues that "prophetic dramas" are not necessarily "communicative" in the sense that the acts were performed for the purpose of conveying a message.¹²¹ Rather, they "stand over against reality in the sense of representing, interpreting and revealing its inner nature and manifesting its totality."¹²² Viberg, as opposed to the view of Stacey, argues for a more communicative aspect of prophetic symbolic actions. Prophetic symbolic acts, according to Viberg, are more rhetorical communication devices. He says, "What is lacking in Stacey's study, beside a sufficient theoretical basis, is an explanation of the function

---

116. Stacey, *Prophetic Drama*, 63.

117. Stacey, *Prophetic Drama*, 63.

118. Tucker, "Prophecy and the Prophetic Literature," 342.

119. Walther Zimmerli notes that there was "a clear change of form" in the narratives of sign-actions (*Ezekiel: A Commentary*, 156). Martin Rösel applies a form-critical theory to the study of inscriptional material from ancient Israel and its surrounding cultures and demonstrates "inscriptional texts exhibit far greater fluidity in the use of generic elements known from the Bible" (Sweeney and Ben Zvi, "Introduction," 7). Also, see Rösel, "Inscriptional Evidence," 107–21.

120. Viberg, *Prophets in Action*, 15.

121. Stacey, *Prophetic Drama*, 265–66.

122. Viberg, *Prophets in Action*, 16.

of the prophetic act. It may mirror reality, but why did the prophets choose to perform them in those particular ways at particular moments?"[123]

Then, what is the prophetic symbolic action?[124] For Stacey, prophetic symbolic actions ("prophetic actions" or "prophetic drama") are actions performed by "men who were recognized, not only in their day but in later times, to be prophets" for the purpose of delivering a divine message.[125] The prophetic sign actions were "usually performed at the specific behest of Yahweh,"[126] which "is so much an essential element of the true form."[127] They were "usually, but not always, accompanied by an oracle or supplied with an explanation which brought out whatever meaning may not have been obvious in the act itself."[128] These observations led Stacey to further clarifications as to the nature of prophetic symbolic actions. He states, "Prophetic actions must, therefore, be seen as a class by themselves. They were specific actions with a specific purpose, carried out by a peculiar kind of person, who believed himself to be, and was generally acknowledged to be, called by God, perhaps even from the womb (Jer 1.5), to this special service."[129]

On the other hand, Viberg in his recent book defined prophetic symbolic actions as follows:

> A prophetic symbolic act is an act whose performance by a prophet has the function of conveying a secondary meaning that transcends the primary meaning related to its physical accomplishment. This meaning forms an inherent part of that prophet's message as a divine messenger, and functions in cooperation with and as an integrated part of his verbal teaching.[130]

Viberg takes a more limited stance, compared to Stacey. For example, Stacey includes the actions performed by someone other than a prophet in the category of prophetic symbolic actions when they are interpreted by the

---

123. Viberg, *Prophets in Action*, 17.

124. For the studies of the literary genre of the reports of prophetic symbolic (sign) actions, see Fohrer, "Die Gattung der Berichte," 101–20; *Die Symbolischen Handlungen*; March, "Prophecy," 141–77; Woodard, "The Form of the Symbolic Acts."

125. Stacey, *Prophetic Drama*, 60.

126. Stacey, *Prophetic Drama*, 61.

127. Stacey, *Prophetic Drama*, 61.

128. Stacey, *Prophetic Drama*, 62.

129. Stacey, *Prophetic Drama*, 62.

130. Viberg, *Prophets in Action*, 27.

prophet to have symbolic meanings (e.g., Jeremiah's visits to the potter's house in Jer. 18:1-4), whereas Viberg considers only the actions taken by prophets as prophetic symbolic actions.[131] Second, Stacey includes acts performed without audience in the prophetic drama, whereas Viberg requires audience for the category. This difference in view is due to the difference in their understanding as to the "rhetorical" function of the actions.

Due to the differences in understanding the characteristic features of the category, different scholars have produced different selections of passages for the genre. Fohrer gives a list of 32 accounts,[132] whereas Stacey has some 48 passages that fall under the category.[133] More recent works include that of Kelvin Friebel, who presents his own list of some 27 prophetic sign actions.[134] Viberg's list is the shortest, naming only 19 passages.[135] Although the totals are close, the lists are not identical. These scholars all provide their own limiting criteria, and only about 20 are common to all. This difference between the lists suggested by different authors indicates that the limiting criteria for the category is not fixed or clear-cut. Scholars generally agree on the function of the accounts of prophetic symbolic actions, except

---

131. Viberg, *Prophets in Action*, 13-54. For example, Viberg considers Jer. 18:1-4 as "a case of prophetic symbolism, but not a prophetic symbolic act" because it was not Jeremiah himself who performed the act and "only interprets the potter's ordinary work in a symbolic manner" (49).

132. 1 Kgs 11:29-39; 19:19-21; 22:11; 2 Kgs 13:14-19; Hos 1; 3; Isa 7:3; 8:1-4; 20; Jer 13:1-11; 16:1-4; 16:5-7; 16:8-9; 19:1-2a, 10-11a; 27:1-3, 12b; 28:10-11; 32:1-15; 43:8-13; 51:59-64; Ezek 4:1-3; 4:4-8; 4:9-17; 5; 12:1-11; 12:17-20; 21:11-12; 21:23-29; 24:1-14; 24:15-24; 3:22-27; 24:25-27; 33:21-22; 37:15-28; Zech 6:9-15. See Fohrer, "Die Gattung der Berichte," 101-20.

133. 1 Sam 15:27f.; 1 Kgs 11:29-31; 18:20-46; 19:19f.; 19:21; 22:1-12 and 2 Chr 18:1-11; 2 Kgs 2:12f.; 13:14-17; 13:18f.; Hos 1:2f.; 1:3-9; 3:1-5; Isa 7:3; 7:10-17; 8:1-4; 20; Mic 1:8; Jer 13:1-11; 16:1-4; 16:5-7; 16:8f.; 18:1-12; 19:1-13; 25:15-29; 27-28; 32:1-15; 35; 36; 43:8-13; 51:59-64; Ezek 2:8—3:3; 3:22-27; 24:25-27; 33:21f.; 4:1-3, 7; 4:4-6; 4:9-17; 5:1-4; 6:11-14; 12:1-16; 12:17-20; 21:6f., 12 [21:11f, 17 in Hebrew]; 21:8-17; 28-32 [21:13-22, 33-37 in Hebrew]; 21:18-22 [21:23-27 in Hebrew]; 24:1f.; 24:3-14; 24:15-24; 37:15-28; Zech 6:9-15; 11:4-17.

134. Friebel, "Hermeneutical Paradigm," 25-45. His list of prophetic sign-actions are as follows: Hos 1:2-9; 3:1-5; Isa 20:1-4; Jer 13:1-11; 16:1-9; 19:1-13; 27:1—28:17; 32:1-44; 35:1-19; 43:8-13; 51:59-64; Ezek 3:26-27; 24:25-27; 33:21-22; 6:11-12; 12:1-16; 12:17-20; 21:11-22 [Eng: vv. 6-17]; 21:23-28 [Eng. vv. 18-23]; 24:15-24; 37:15-28; Zech 6:9-15; 1 Kgs 11:29-37; 2 Kgs 13:14-19; 1 Kgs 22:11 and 2 Chr 18:10; Jer 28:10-11.

135. 1 Kgs 11:30; Isa 20:2; Jer 13:1-11; 19; 27; 28:1-17; 32:1-15; 43:8-13; 51:59-64; Ezek 4:1-3; 4:4-8; 4:9-13; 5:1-4; 12:1-16; 21:18-22; 24:15-24; 37:15-28; Hos 1:1-2; 3:1-2; Zech 6:9-15 (Viberg, *Prophets in Action*, 44-45).

1 Kings 13 and 1 Kings 20:35-36

In the given lists of prophetic symbolic actions proposed by scholars, most of the prophetic symbolic actions are found in the Latter Prophets and only a few in the Former Prophets. The prophetic symbolic actions in the Former Prophets, as presented by the three scholars (Fohrer, Stacey, and Friebel), are seven in total (1 Sam 15:27-29; 1 Kgs 11:29-39; 1 Kgs 18:20-46; 1 Kgs 19:19-21; 1 Kgs 22:1-12; 2 Kgs 2:12-18; 2 Kgs 13:14-19), and the prophetic symbolic actions that are listed by all three scholars are only two: Ahijah's tearing the cloak into twelve parts (1 Kgs 11:29-37)[136] and Elisha's last words to King Joash using the bow and arrows (2 Kgs 13:14-19). In this section, I will take a look at 1 Kings 20:35-43 and weigh the possibility of including the passage in the category of prophetic symbolic actions. This passage has been chosen for its similarities to 1 Kings 13 in many ways and hence is important for my arguments.

In 1 Kings 20, Ben-Hadad the king of Syria attacks Israel and King Ahab. Ahab defeats Ben-Hadad in the two consecutive battles. Although God gives Israel the victory, Ahab releases Ben-Hadad with some conditions. With this release in the background, a strange interaction occurs between two prophetical figures (1 Kgs 20:35-36). A certain man of the sons of the prophets (most likely the disciples) appears on the scene and says to his fellow prophet "by the word of Yahweh" (בִּדְבַר יְהוָה), "Strike me!" (הַכֵּינִי נָא). Confused by this strange command, the fellow prophet refuses to strike him. Then the prophet who has delivered the command says to him, "Because you have not obeyed Yahweh, behold, as soon as you have gone from me, a lion (הָאַרְיֵה) shall strike you down." This word of the prophet was fulfilled. As soon as he had departed from him, a lion *found* (וַיִּמְצָאֵהוּ) him (v. 36; cf. 1 Kgs 13:24) and struck him down.

The rest of the story (vv. 37-43) describes the prophet appearing before King Ahab. He finds another man and tells him to strike him. This time the man strikes him and wounds him. Then the prophet disguises himself with a bandage over his eyes, so that the king cannot recognize him. When the king passes by, the prophet cries to the king and says,

---

136. Viberg has stricter criteria for prophetic symbolic actions, and he finds only one instance of prophetic symbolic actions in the former prophet, which is 1 Kings 11:30.

> Your servant went out into the midst of the battle, and behold, a soldier turned and brought a man to me and said, "Guard this man; if by any means he is missing, your life shall be for his life, or else you shall pay a talent of silver." And as your servant was busy here and there, he was gone (39b-40a).

King Ahab then says to him, "So shall your judgment be; you yourself have decided it." Then, the prophet takes the bandage off from his eyes, and King Ahab recognizes him as one of the prophets. The prophet delivers an oracle: "Thus says Yahweh, 'Because you have let go of your hand the man whom I had devoted to destruction, therefore your life shall be for his life, and your people for his people.'" King Ahab then goes back to his house "vexed and sullen" and goes to Samaria.

Scholars' views are divided on the interpretation of vv. 35-36. Some scholars interpret what took place (vv. 35-36) merely as a preparation for the prophet's confrontation with King Ahab; the prophet had to disguise himself as if he had come from a battlefield, so he needed someone to strike and wound him. This view cannot explain a few details in the text. For example, the prophet commands his fellow to strike him "by the word of Yahweh." This rare form of command required absolute obedience from the receiver of the command. If the command (or request) was merely for the purpose of preparing himself to appear before the king, he would not have needed such a serious command in the first place. Also, the punishment of the fellow prophet for his refusal to strike him is too harsh; he gets killed by a lion. This signifies that the command was more than a preparation for appearing before the king.

The interactions between the two prophets followed by a tragic death of one (vv. 35-36) come right after King Ahab's release of Ben-Hadad (vv. 31-34), which makes the interactions more significant. The fellow prophet's refusal to "strike" resembles King Ahab's leniency to Ben-Hadad, and the punishment that he receives for disobedience to the command ("Strike me!") prefigures God's punishment of King Ahab. In this sense, vv. 35-36 seems to be a prophetic drama or symbolic action—note that these two figures are prophets—that reveals God's decision regarding King Ahab. Burke Long writes,

> The prophet announces punishment for an individual, just as he will do before the king, and in a closely similar manner of speech (cf. vv. 36a and 42). The bizarre scene perfectly mirrors beforehand the divine word aimed at the monarch. Hence, the quick,

THE FATE OF THE MAN OF GOD FROM JUDAH

> effortless fulfillment, the startling death by lion, carries its own ominous quality. This prophetic word comes true, as though inevitable or prescient. And the destiny he will claim as the king's cannot fail to take its due.[137]

Also, Montgomery asserts, "The theatrical parable [was] presented by some one of the sons of the prophets to the king in condemnation of his leniency to Ben-Hadad. The fate of the first comrade, who did not obey the word of YHWH, was an omen of the disaster to befall Ahab."[138] Thus, the actions taken by the two prophets and the measures taken on one of the prophets is, I would argue, a case of prophetic symbolic actions that dramatizes what King Ahab has done and prefigures what will happen to the king as punishment.

It is noteworthy that 1 Kings 20:35–36 shows multiple striking similarities to 1 Kings 13:11–32, not only in terms of milieu and genre, but also in common words and motifs.[139] The connections between the two texts are highlighted by the shared motifs: First, both stories describe what has transpired between two prophetic figures (the old prophet of Bethel and the man of God from Judah in 1 Kings 13, and a certain man of the sons of the prophets and his fellow prophet in 1 Kings 20). Second, a rare expression "by the word of Yahweh" plays an important role in both stories. Given that, other than 1 Kings 13, 1 Kings 20:35 is the only place in the Book of Kings where the phrase occurs, this connection is quite significant. Third, the prophet who has received the command *disobeys* it, just as the man of God did, and as a punishment for the disobedience, the prophet gets killed by a *lion*, just as the man of God was killed by a lion. In the Book of Kings, lions as God's punishing tool for disobedience are found only in three passages: 1 Kings 13, 1 Kings 20, and 2 Kings 17:25–26.[140] These similarities

---

137. Long, *1 Kings*, 220.

138. Montgomery, *The Book of Kings*, 325.

139. Gross, "Lying Prophet," 125. Gross points out the parallel between 1 Kings 13 and 1 Kings 20:35–37, but at the end of his essay, he admits, "Still unresolved at the content level is the question of what criteria one uses to locate convincing parallel texts like 1 Kgs 20:35–37."

140. Second Kings 17 records the fall of the Northern Kingdom, and lions appear in the chapter when the king of Assyria resettled the people from other parts of the empire in the cities of Samaria. The narrator makes it clear that it was Yahweh who sent lions among them, because the peoples settled there did not know "the law of the god of the land" (v. 26). So the king of Assyria sent one of the priests "whom they had carried away from Samaria" to *Bethel* to live there, who taught the peoples "how they should fear Yahweh" (v. 28). Second Kings 17 is generally agreed to be one of the key Deuteronomistic

are not coincidental and point to the connections with 1 Kings 13 in theme and genre.

1 Kings 13 as Prophetic Symbolic Actions

Most scholars put the narrative in 1 King 13 in the literary category of a prophetic legend.[141] The prophetic legend is a genre "which focuses chiefly on the prophet as main character and exemplar of virtue, goodness, piety, and divine favor."[142] One of the primary reasons scholars have included 1 Kings 13 in this category is that the narrative contains miracles and wonders, and also that they read this narrative as a story that is told to generate respect for prophets and their heroic words and deeds.[143] The scholars argue that the original traditions behind the present text were prophetic legends regarding the death and tomb of the man of God, the provenance of which must be sought in Northern prophetic circles.[144]

This categorization, however, is not very helpful for the interpretation of the narrative, because it is somewhat generic and comprehensive. Moreover, our narrative in its present form is not merely about the prophets' heroic words or deeds, nor does it seem to generate respect for the prophets. Our narrative as a whole explains why God's judgment on Jeroboam was irrevocable, and the interactions between the man of God and the prophet dramatize and visualize the sin of Jeroboam and its punishment. In this dramatization, the two prophets play their roles to show God's judgment on Jeroboam. The man of God in 1 Kings 13, as does the fellow prophet in 1 Kings 20, becomes a *victim* in the prophetic symbolic action in that he is punished for his rather innocent inadvertent disobedience to the command given "by the word of Yahweh."

In this sense, both prophets (the man of God in 1 Kings 13 and the fellow prophet in 1 Kings 20) join other prophets, mostly in the Latter Prophets such as Isaiah, Jeremiah, Ezekiel, and Hosea, in their sufferings

---

passages, and the common motifs (lion's killing as Yahweh's punishment and the city Bethel) links it with 1 Kings 13 and 1 Kings 22.

141. For examples, see Bentzen, *Introduction*, 237–40, and Crenshaw, *Prophetic Conflicts*, 41. For a concise definition of prophetic legend, see the list of genres in the "Glossary" section of Long's commentary (*1 Kings*, 257–8).

142. Long, *1 Kings*, 257–8.

143. Long, *1 Kings*, 252, 256. Also, see Nelson, *First and Second Kings*, 83.

144. Long, *1 Kings*, 252. Also, see Lemke, "The Way of Obedience," 314.

for prophetic duties; these prophets had to bear sufferings of different degrees to carry out their prophetic commissions.[145] This aspect of the narrative explains the man of God's rather innocent death, and the same is true of the "fellow" prophet in 1 Kings 20:35-36.

A Few Problems to Consider

Some questions remain to be answered, as we read 1 Kings 13 as prophetic symbolic actions. First, does our narrative still qualify for prophetic symbolic actions when the prophets in the story did not intend to give messages through their actions? Viberg, for example, considers only an action that is "performed with intention of being a prophetic symbolic act" a prophetic symbolic act.[146] Second, where is the audience of the prophetic symbolic actions? Third, it seems that God's command and explanation of the symbolic meanings of the actions are not clearly visible. For these reasons among others, our narrative does not seem to qualify for the category of prophetic symbolic actions. Thus, we need to consider and answer these questions at this point.

First, the matter of intention is worth considering in the discussion of the genre of prophetic symbolic actions; scholars have different views on whether intention is an essential element of prophetic symbolic actions. For example, in Jeremiah 18, a potter does his usual work of making pots, but his making vessels out of clay and reworking the clay into another vessel is interpreted symbolically by Yahweh to be revealing Yahweh's sovereignty over nations. Also, "the tearing of the robe in 1 Sam. 15:27f. was an accident; nevertheless it was interpreted by Samuel as a sign."[147] With that said, our narrative, in my judgment, sheds light on the narrator's role in shaping a narrative into the case of prophetic symbolic actions. It is not likely that the man of God, as depicted in the narrative, intended to play the role of Jeroboam in prophetic symbolic actions, and it is not plausible, either, that the old prophet was aware that he was involved in prophetic symbolic actions.

---

145. For example, Isaiah's walking naked and barefoot for three years "as a sign and a portent against Egypt and Cush" (Isa. 20:2-3), Ezekiel's lying and getting bound for 390 + 40 days (Ezek 4), and Hosea's marriage with Gomel (Hos 1). See chapter 4 for a detailed discussion on the theme of prophets' suffering.

146. Viberg, *Prophets in Action*, 49.

147. Stacey, *Prophetic Drama*, 219.

Exegesis of 1 Kings 13

What is peculiar about our story is that the intention is not clearly discernible in the prophets who did the actions themselves, but it is the narrator who saw the symbolic nature in the story and intended to depict the story as prophetic symbolic actions. Our narrative, in this regard, does not fit in the typical prophetic symbolic actions. I believe, however, we should avoid making a hasty conclusion here. On the contrary, it is necessary to look closely at the narrator's literary role, which I believe may lead us to a new understanding of the Deuteronomistic narrator's literary skills.

Could we find other examples of the narrator's shaping a story into the prophetic symbolic action? We may find an example in a passage that is not far from our narrative, 1 Kings 11:29–30, which is generally agreed to be a report of prophetic symbolic actions. As the narrator begins to narrate the account, he describes the scene: "The prophet Ahijah the Shilonite found Jeroboam on the road. Now Ahijah had dressed himself in a *new* garment, and the two of them were alone in the open country. Then Ahijah laid hold of the *new* garment that was on him and tore it into twelve pieces" (italics added). The narrator emphatically mentions that the garment that Ahijah was wearing was *new*, and that, twice. The "newness" of the garment constitutes an important element of the account, symbolizing the relative newness of the kingdom that is soon to be torn into pieces. Interestingly, Ahijah himself does not mention or specify that the garment was new, and it is only found in the narrator's description. Here the narrator is not merely describing the events, but he understands the symbolic significance of the interactions and adds details into the prophetic symbolic actions to make the message clearer. In other words, he is not just a recorder of a story but an active interpreter of the symbolic actions.

The account in 1 Kings 20:35–36 contains the same literary skill.[148] The phrase "by the word of Yahweh" is voiced not by the prophet but by the narrator (20:35). Given that the phrase plays an important part in the symbolic actions and also that the fellow prophet is severely condemned for not obeying "the voice of Yahweh" (v. 36), the narrator's comment becomes even more significant. Here we witness the narrator's voice actively contributing to the shaping of the story into an account of prophetic symbolic actions. Similarly, as we noted previously in our narrative (1 Kgs 13), the phrase "by the word of Yahweh" is voiced by three different persons (the narrator, the man of God, and the old prophet). These observations

---

148. For a detailed discussion on the similarities between the two passages, see the section titled "1 Kings 13 and 1 Kings 20:35–36" in this chapter.

indicate that the narrator interpreted some actions as having symbolic meanings, and he then shaped the stories into the prophetic symbolic action. This kind of "shaping" is more obvious in our narrative. Though the historical man of God and the historical old prophet in our narrative did not have the intention of delivering messages through their actions, the narrator understood their actions to have symbolic meanings and shaped what happened between the two in a particular way that it became an illustrative presentation of God's will for Jeroboam.

Second, if one decides to go by the criteria of Viberg for prophetic symbolic actions, where is the audience for whom the symbolic actions have been performed?[149] In the case of 1 Kings 13, we could think about the audience at two different levels: inside the story and outside the story. First, inside the story there are witnesses of the events: the sons of the old prophet are witnesses to the man of God's words and deeds at Bethel (v. 11) and, the passersby on the way are the witnesses of his disobedience and God's punishment for it, but more importantly, the old prophet explains the reason for his death to them (vv. 25–26). These witnesses become the audience inside the story.

When we broaden our perspective and consider the symbolic nature of the narrative, we realize that the audience of the prophetic symbolic actions in 1 Kings 13 was intended to be Jeroboam and, more broadly, the intended reader. Since the narrator depicts the actions as prophetic symbolic actions, the symbolic message is directed toward Jeroboam (and toward the intended reader—I will discuss this aspect in more detail in chapter 4). That Jeroboam becomes the first implied audience of these symbolic actions is clear in the editorial comment (vv. 33–34). It is not clear what "this thing" (v. 33) might refer to, but in the present form of the text, "this thing" should include what happened to the man of God (vv. 11–32) as well as his encounter with Jeroboam (vv. 1–10). It is not likely, or at least is not clear in the text, that Jeroboam heard of what had happened to the man of God. The narrator, however, makes Jeroboam the audience of the events and condemns him for not changing his ways even "after this thing." By making Jeroboam the audience of the story, the narrator achieves the literary effect, which is that God's decision on the judgment of Jeroboam is justified and hence becomes final.

---

149. Viberg considers only the prophetic actions performed in front of the audience prophetic symbolic actions. Note, however, that there are no witnesses to the event in 1 Kings 11:29–39, which is an obvious case of prophetic symbolic actions.

Thirdly, where are the command and explanation elements, two of the three essential criteria of prophetic symbolic actions as proposed by Fohrer? I believe that they are to be found in the narrative, though in a slightly different style from typical accounts of prophetic symbolic actions. The element of command does exist in the story: the man of God receives a command from God to go to Bethel and to cry against the altar. He also receives the prohibition (v. 9). As in the case of other prophetic symbolic actions, these commands initiate a series of following events. Based on the command, his obedience and the following disobedience to the command become the prophetic symbolic actions. The explanation element, as I mentioned in the previous section, is brought in through the words of the old prophet from Bethel in vv. 26 and 32 and of the narrator (vv. 33–34):

> And when the prophet who had brought him back from the way heard it, he said, "That is the man of God who disobeyed the mouth of Yahweh. Yahweh gave him over to the lion, which mauled him and killed him in accordance with the word that Yahweh had spoken to him" (v. 26).

In conclusion, based on these observations, I argue that the story of the man of God in 1 Kings 13 is supposed to be read as centered on prophetic symbolic actions for Jeroboam and the intended reader.

On a final note, the identification of 1 Kings 13 as a text containing prophetic symbolic actions may lead to further studies of other similar symbolic actions in the Book of Kings: 1 Kings 11:29–39; 1 Kings 20:35–43; 2 Kings 13:14–19. These stories share insightful affinities. First, all these stories involve two people, at least, one of them being a prophetic figure (two prophets in 1 Kings 13:11–32 and 1 Kings 20:35–36, a prophet and a king [or a king-to-be] in 1 Kings 11:29–39; 1 Kings 20:37–43; 2 Kings 13:14–19). Second, the message is always somehow related to God's decision about or his judgment against the king (or a king-to-be). For example, in 1 Kings 11, Ahijah the prophet comes to Jeroboam and initiates a series of actions that are symbolic of the fate of the new kingdom and of Jeroboam. Likewise, in 2 Kings 13, Elisha the prophet and King Joash perform actions, where how King Joash has responded to Elisha's request (striking the ground with his arrows three times) prefigures what will happen between King Joash and Ben-Hadad. As Stacey observed, this is the case "where a second party is incorporated in the action because he is involved in the fulfillment."[150] Lastly,

---

150. Stacey, *Prophetic Drama*, 222. Stacey provides more cases of this. They include Elijah's wrapping his mantle around Elisha (2 Kgs 19:19–21) and Ahijah's action before

THE FATE OF THE MAN OF GOD FROM JUDAH

in some of the accounts, one of the parties involved in the symbolic actions either does not fully understand what symbolic significance his actions may have, or is not even aware that the actions that he takes have symbolic significance.[151] For example, the fellow prophet in 1 Kings 20:35–36 has no idea of what is going on. Also, King Joash takes the arrows and strikes the ground with them three times, but he does not understand what his actions signify (2 Kgs 13:18). The comparison of these stories may shed light on our view and understanding of the Deuteronomistic narrator's literary skills and strategies.

CONCLUSION

So far, I have endeavored to show that 1 Kings 13 has been designed by the narrator to be read as containing prophetic symbolic actions that dramatize Jeroboam's sin and its entailing judgment. Lastly, I will show how this understanding of the story resolves some difficult problems that have been raised by commentators.

Reading 1 Kings 13 as containing prophetic symbolic actions leads the reader to approach the narrative in a new way. First, it resolves a problem that has been raised almost every reader of the story, which Bosworth articulates as follows: "The problem interpreters have long had with the narrative is the difficulty that the man of God is punished for his gullibility while the prophet who deceived him goes unpunished. Scholars have struggled to locate a didactic lesson in the seemingly unedifying story."[152] As Fretheim puts it, there is "no retributionary scheme" in this narrative.[153] If the old

---

Jeroboam (1 Kgs 11:29–31). There are also cases where "the other person may be present simply because the action requires a second party, as, for example in the purchase of the field at Anathoth, where Hanamel participates in the actions to enable it to happen but is no part of the reality" (222).

151. When a prophetic symbolic action requires a second party, the subject of the significant action varies. For example, as Stacey observes, "In the arrow-shooting in II Kings 13, Joash actually shot the arrow, though it might be argued that Elisha, by laying his hands on the king's hands, made him his surrogate. In the next verse, although Elisha is in charge, it is the king's performance with the arrows that is significant. Similarly, in Jeremiah 35 Jeremiah sets up the incident, but the significant act, the refusal of the wine, is the act of the Rechabites. Again, in the next chapter, Jeremiah receives the command from Yahweh, but the work of writing and reading is done by Baruch" (*Prophetic Drama*, 218).

152. Bosworth, *Story within a Story*, 155.

153. Fretheim, *First and Second Kings*, 80.

prophet's lie was considered a significantly rebellious act against the will of God, he should be punished, but there is no hint of punishment for him from God. Instead, Yahweh speaks through him. On the contrary, Yahweh's punishment of the man of God is hardly to be understood. Thus, it is not strange that Robinson said the following: "The story . . . shows him as applying retributive justice in a narrowly mechanical and impersonal way; the action of a harsh tyrant . . . the view of God's nature underlying this chapter is crude and insensitive."[154] I believe reading our narrative this way does not do justice to the text. Rather, we should understand the narrative this way: the sin of Jeroboam, which made him the archetypal *Unheilsherrscher*, was so great that it required this extreme form of prophetic symbolic actions to be performed. God, as implied in this narrative, is not a crude and insensitive God, but he had to employ this extreme form of prophetic actions at the cost of his own servant, "the man of God," to deliver to Jeroboam and to his people an urgent warning/message.

Second, in the prophetic symbolic actions, the motive of the old prophet for his behaviors is not as important as the actions themselves. The actions have much significance, but asking about the motives of the prophets is meaningless. For example, reading Hosea 1 and 3, the reader does not ask Hosea's motive for marrying the adulterous woman. His action of marrying the woman itself becomes a message, but no psychological explanations for Hosea's actions are necessary, even as readers often seek these. The same principle can be applied to our reading of 1 Kings 13. God's prohibition is necessary in the narrative as an important element of this prophetic symbolic action for the purpose of testing the man of God's obedience. The reader is led to pay more attention to whether the man of God obeys the command than to why those specific prohibitions were given.

The old prophet's motive for his lie is another example. Our text keeps silent about why the old prophet lied. Instead, the text emphasizes that the man of God "turned back" and disobeyed God's command. In the prophetic symbolic action, the old prophet's motive is less important. Nevertheless, numerous commentators speculated on the old prophet's motive for his lie. The easiest solution to the problem was making the old prophet of Bethel a false prophet (Josephus is an old example).[155] Those interpreters understand

---

154. Robinson, *The First Book of Kings*, 162.

155. For Josephus, the old prophet of Bethel is "a certain wicked man" and "a false prophet." Out of fear that the man of God might be more esteemed by the king than he was, the old prophet lies to the man of God, who Josephus identifies as Jadon. Josephus does not explain what the old prophet of Bethel expects to see happen or how bringing

THE FATE OF THE MAN OF GOD FROM JUDAH

that the old prophet of Bethel deceived the man of God from Judah with an evil plan in his mind. This interpretation provides no satisfying answer about the genuine word of Yahweh coming to the old prophet (vv. 20–22) and his lament over the death of the man of God (v. 30). Also, he plays a very significant role in the narrative, especially related to the theme of the narrative; he confirms that the oracle that the man of God proclaimed against the altar in Bethel will surely come true (v. 32). According to my understanding, the old prophet's lie is a part of the prophetic symbolic actions. The action (his lie) is necessary for the prophetic symbolic actions, through which the man of God's obedience was tested. Thus, it is understandable that no ethical judgment is passed on the old prophet's lie or at least it is not the concern of the narrator. The ethical aspect of the narrative is not in the prism of the narrator.

---

him back might damage the man of God's esteem. Josephus avoids answering a difficult question of why the word of Yahweh came to the old prophet, who lies by twisting the story and making Yahweh "appear" to Jadon, the man of God from Judah, at the dinner table, not to the old prophet. He simply makes a mention that the man of God's death was done according to the will of God, and this made Jeroboam not "give heed to the words of Jadon, as of one that had been convicted of lying." Josephus adds extra details to the story frequently. For example, the old prophet of Bethel, "a wicked and impious man," goes to Jeroboam and "by a wicked trick" persuades the king that the sign that the man of God performed on the hand of the king and the altar was a mere coincidence. He "alienated" the king's mind from God and "encouraged him to go on in his impious practices." It seems that Josephus speculated that the old prophet of Bethel tries to nullify the authenticity of the man of God's oracle by making him disobey the word of Yahweh. The problem with Josephus's reading is that the interpretations cannot claim any support for such readings from the text (*Antiquities*, chapter IX, § I).

3

A Literary Analysis of the Jeroboam Narrative

INTRODUCTION

IN CHAPTER 2 I analyzed 1 Kings 13 and came up with the theme, function, and nature of the narrative. Now in this chapter I will turn my focus to the broader context, that is, the Jeroboam Narrative. By and large, most historical-critical scholars have neglected to read 1 Kings 13 in the context of the Jeroboam Narrative. Consequently, historical-critical studies have not considered the Jeroboam narrative as a unified literary unity and the connections among the different parts. Recently, more scholars read the Jeroboam narrative holistically.[1] In the following discussion, I will examine how the different parts of the Jeroboam narrative communicate with one another, and how 1 Kings 13 contributes to the larger storyline of the Jeroboam Narrative. It will come to the fore that the narrator employed literary techniques to deliver the messages efficiently. I will identify literary connections existing between chapter 13 and the surrounding texts in the Jeroboam Narrative and then discuss the location and function of 1 Kings 13 in the Jeroboam narrative.

---

1. Some examples include Cohn, "Literary Techniques," 23–35; Walsh, "The Contexts," 355–70; Knoppers, *Two Nations under God*, 2:1993; Bodner, *Royal Drama*, 2012.

THE FATE OF THE MAN OF GOD FROM JUDAH

A LITERARY ANALYSIS OF THE JEROBOAM NARRATIVE

Delimitation of the Jeroboam Narrative

Scholarly opinion differs on how the materials have been arranged in the Book of Kings. The text of 1 Kings 11:26—14:20 that I refer to as the Jeroboam narrative in this study is often considered to belong to the account of the reign of Solomon.[2] Other scholars understand 11:26—14:20 as the beginning part of the Divided Kingdom account.[3] In this study, I follow Walsh who defines 1 Kings 11:26—14:20 as the Jeroboam narrative, because, as I argue in this chapter, it displays artistic unity and thereby should be considered as a literary unit.[4]

We have many reasons to believe, however, that the present form of the Jeroboam narrative is from the same hand that is responsible for the texts before and after it. For example, Ahijah's words to Jeroboam in 11:31-36 repeat Yahweh's words to Solomon in 11:11-13 almost verbatim. Also, the key motifs found in both texts are found in 1 Kings 15:1-5 (walking in the "sins," "his heart being not wholly true to Yahweh," "as the heart of David his father," "Yahweh God" giving "him a lamp in Jerusalem" "for David's sake," turning aside from anything that he commanded him, etc.). Besides, the judgment which was pronounced against the house of Jeroboam in 14:10 and 14 is fulfilled in 15:29-30. Thus, the section which we refer to as the Jeroboam narrative (11:26—14:20) is set aside from the surrounding texts based mainly on the content rather than on other factors, such as different origins or sources.

---

2. Sweeney, without addressing the reign of Jeroboam separately, places 1 Kings 11:41—14:20 ("the Establishment of Northern Israel") in the "Regnal Account of Solomon ben David" (1 Kgs 2:12—14:20). Sweeney, *I & II Kings*, vii–viii.

3. J. Gray includes 1 Kings 12:25—14:18 in the section of "the Divided Kingdom" (1 Kgs 12–2 Kgs 17). He divides the text into two accounts (12:25-33; 13:1—14:18) and discusses each account under the subheadings of "Significant events of Jeroboam's reign" and "Prophetic tradition of the reign of Jeroboam" respectively (*I & II Kings*, 6). Fretheim places the Jeroboam story it in a section called "The Division of the Kingdom" (1 Kgs 12:1—16:34) (*First and Second Kings*, 70–93). Similarly, R. Nelson includes the Jeroboam narrative in the section called "Shalom Is Broken" (1 Kgs 11–16) (*First and Second Kings*, vii).

4. Walsh, *1 Kings*, v. Knoppers takes 1 Kings 12:21 as the beginning of the Jeroboam narrative and 1 Kings 14:16 as the end (*Two Nations under God* 2, vii–viii). B. Long sets aside 1 Kings 12:1—14:20 as the "reign of Jeroboam" (*1 Kings*, 13).

Overall Structure of the Jeroboam Narrative

Robert Cohn in his article titled "Literary Technique in the Jeroboam Narrative" focuses on the literary artistry employed in the Jeroboam narrative. He defines the Jeroboam narrative as "the account of the rise and fall of king Jeroboam,"[5] and argues that the account (1 Kgs 11:26—14:20) "offers a fine example of such composite artistry. Although the narrative is manifestly a compilation of several sources, it bears the marks of a talented author who, by ordering and editing, created a unified story."[6] Cohn further argues that the sources of the narrative have been structured into "a generally chiastic shape which neatly charts the rise and fall of Jeroboam."[7] The chiastic shape Cohn suggests is as follows:[8]

A Introductory exposition: Jeroboam and Solomon (11:26–28)

  B1 Prophecy of Ahijah (11:29–40)

  B2 Fulfillment of prophecy (11:41—12:24)

    C Jeroboam's sin (12:25–33)

      D Man of God interlude (13:1–32)

    C' Jeroboam's sin (13:33–34)

  B1' Prophecy of Ahijah (14:1–16)

  B2' Fulfillment (in part) of prophecy (14:17–18)

A' Concluding exposition: death of Jeroboam (14:19–20)

Ahijah's prophecy (11:29–39) is reversed almost verbatim in his other prophecy at the end of the Jeroboam narrative (14:1–16); hence the two parts together form a concentric parallel. The sin of Jeroboam is also treated in both 12:25–33 and 13:33–34. In my judgment, however, Cohn's structure needs some adjustments. Jeroboam's sin (C', 13:33–34) is so tightly woven into the story of the man of God (13:1–32) that it seems better not to separate it from the preceding text. Also, the fulfillment of Ahijah's second prophecy (B2', 14:17–18) is considerably short compared to its corresponding part (B2, 11:41—12:24). After all, the fulfillment described in this part (14:17–18) is only partial and most of the prophecy is fulfilled in 1 Kings

---

5. Cohn, "Literary Technique," 24.
6. Cohn, "Literary Technique," 24.
7. Cohn, "Literary Technique," 24.
8. Cohn, "Literary Technique," 24.

15:27–30. For these reasons, I would propose a slightly different outline of the Jeroboam narrative.

Knoppers sees 1 Kings 12:26–33 as the hinge in the Jeroboam narrative, because "All preceding coverage of Jeroboam is positive; all succeeding coverage of Jeroboam is negative."[9] This observation may reflect the arrangement of the narrative better.[10] Thus the Jeroboam narrative can be divided into two parts, with 12:26–31 at the center; the first half (11:26—12:25) depicts the rise of Jeroboam, and the second half (13:1—14:20) the fall of Jeroboam. Each half then can be further divided up into two parts, respectively, as the outline below shows:

A Ahijah's Prophecy Regarding the Rise of Jeroboam (11:26–43)

   B The Rise of Jeroboam and the Secession of the Northern Tribes (12:1–25)

      C The Sin of Jeroboam (12:26–31)

   B' The Fall of Jeroboam Dramatized (12:32—13:34)

A' Ahijah's Prophecy Regarding the Fall of Jeroboam (14:1–20)

Literary Connections among the Constituent Parts of the Jeroboam Narrative

Now I will look into the different parts of the Jeroboam narrative, focusing on the literary connections among them. I will show how different parts connect to each other and how the various connections help the reader grasp the narrator's messages. When necessary, I will rearrange the content of the text for the purpose of clarity. Although the following discussion discusses the development of the plot and pays attention to textual details, the goal of this discussion is not to explain every detail of the text. Rather, I will focus on my purpose, which is to grasp the narrator's literary strategy and emphases. I will proceed in the order of the subunits outlined in the structure above and discuss all of them, except 1 Kings 12:32—13:34, which I have already analyzed in chapter 2. At the end, I will discuss the location and function of 1 Kings 12:32—13:34.

---

9. Knoppers, *Two Nations under God*, 2:7.

10. Walsh also places 1 Kings 12:26–31 at the center of a concentric structure. See Walsh, "The Contexts," 361–62.

A Literary Analysis of the Jeroboam Narrative

Ahijah's Prophecy Regarding the Rise of Jeroboam (11:26–43)

In this part of the narrative, Jeroboam appears on the scene for the first time. The narrator provides the reader with a brief introduction to the main character, Jeroboam, and describes how he became favored by Solomon (vv. 26–28), but the account ends with Solomon seeking to kill Jeroboam (v. 40). Between the two events, Ahijah meets Jeroboam and delivers an oracle concerning him (vv. 29–39). The main purpose of this story, as stated in v. 27, is to show how Jeroboam got to "raise his hand against Solomon," the actual unfolding of which, however, is not described until the next chapter (12:1–25).

INTRODUCTION OF JEROBOAM (11:26–28)

The introduction of Jeroboam is brief, but significant: "Jeroboam son of Nebat, an Ephraimite of Zeredah—and the name of his mother was Zeruah, a widow—was a servant (עֶבֶד) of Solomon, and he raised his hand (יָד) against the king" (v. 26). The initial noun clause that distinguishes the following story from the preceding material announces Jeroboam as "a principle character."[11] Jeroboam appears in the context where Solomon's adversaries are introduced one after another (cf. 11:14, 23). Thus, the accounts of Hadad and Rezon "play a key role in contextualizing the coming rebellion,"[12] but the description of Jeroboam in 11:26 distinguishes him from the first two. As for Hadad and Rezon, they were each called an "adversary" (שָׂטָן, vv. 14, 23) whom God "raised up" (וַיָּקֶם),[13] whereas, in Jeroboam's case, Jeroboam himself "raised (וַיָּרֶם) his hand against the king" (v. 26)[14] and the term "adversary" is not used for him. Cohn is correct in

---

11. Sweeney, *I & II Kings*, 159.
12. Bodner, *Royal Drama*, 38.
13. It is debatable where in the Solomon narrative the negative view of his kingdom begins (cf. Bodner, *Royal Drama*, 32–34). In 1 Kings 5:4, Solomon, speaking to (the servants of) Hiram of his plan to build a temple for Yahweh, says, "Yahweh God has given me rest on every side. There is neither adversary (שָׂטָן) nor misfortune." The mention of "adversaries" here in chapter 11 is clear evidence that the situation has changed.
14. Some English translations (e.g., ESV, NASB) put "also" in this verse, but it is not in the Hebrew. Those English translations blur the difference between Hadad and Rezon and Jeroboam.

saying "By establishing a pattern of description and then breaking the pattern, the author signals that a new phase of his history is beginning."[15]

The two key words in this introduction, "servant" (עֶבֶד) and "hand" (יָד), are significant for the narrator's purpose, and immediately remind a careful reader of Yahweh's judgment speech to Solomon in 1 Kings 11:11–13:

> Therefore Yahweh said to Solomon, "Since this has been your practice and you have not kept my covenant and my statutes that I have commanded you, I will surely tear the kingdom from you and will give it to your servant (עֶבֶד). Yet for the sake of David your father I will not do it in your days, but I will tear it out of the hand (יָד) of your son. However, I will not tear away the entire kingdom, but I will give one tribe to your son, for the sake of David my servant and for the sake of Jerusalem that I have chosen."

Therefore, these two key words signal that "the fulfillment of Yahweh's threat is at hand."[16] Jeroboam is not one of the "adversaries," but is the "servant" of Solomon who Yahweh said would be the recipient of the tribes of the torn kingdom. And this "servant" will raise his hand against the king.

The narrator clarifies at the outset that the following account (11:27b–40) is allotted to showing "the reason (הַדָּבָר) he [Jeroboam] raised [his] hand against the king" (v. 27a). The word הַדָּבָר is worth noting here. Walsh translates the clause this way: "This is the word (הַדָּבָר) that raised a hand against the king." He argues, "The *dābār* in question is, literally, a divine 'word,' the prophetic oracle Ahijah delivers in verses 31–39."[17] Given that it is Ahijah's oracle that initiates Jeroboam's "rebellion" in the following account, and that the word of Yahweh is described as the driving force behind the human events, this wordplay seems to point to the narrator's emphasis on the power of the word of Yahweh. It may also betray the narrator's view of the prophetic word as the first cause for the human events in the history of Israel. Therefore, despite the expression "Jeroboam . . . raised his hand against the king," the narrator finds the fundamental cause of the rebellion in the word of Yahweh.

The last background verse (v. 28) tells of Jeroboam's ability and his promotion by Solomon. Jeroboam has a humble familial background ("the son of a widow," v 26). Bodner argues, "The purpose of this parental notice is to

15. Cohn, "Literary Technique," 26.
16. Walsh, *1 Kings*, 143.
17. Walsh, *1 Kings*, 143.

highlight Jeroboam's roots: the description of his parents does not imply a powerful or well-connected family, not part of the Jerusalem elite, nor the typical recipients of Solomonic favor."[18] On the other hand, the adjectives that describe him ("very able," גִּבּוֹר חַיִל, and "industrious," עֹשֵׂה מְלָאכָה) are very positive. Having seen Jeroboam's ability and diligence, Solomon "gave him charge over all the forced labor of the house of Joseph" (v. 28). The reader senses that he might be the "servant" whom Yahweh mentioned before in 1 Kings 11:11–13. Also, his northern origin is clear from the statement that Solomon put him in charge of all the forced labor of the house of Joseph, which may serve as foreshadowing that he will be a new king of the seceded northern tribes.[19]

Ahijah's Prophecy and Solomon's Reaction (11:29–40)

The phrase "at that time" (בָּעֵת הַהִיא) signals the beginning of a new account. The lengthy scene that follows this phrase (vv. 29–40) describes the historic encounter between the prophet Ahijah and Jeroboam, which fits well the category of the report of prophetic symbolic actions.

Key words found in the first part of the scene are significant for their symbolic connotations and also their connections with the story in 1 Kings 13. Ahijah met him "when Jeroboam was leaving Jerusalem," which seems to be "an apt emblem for what Ahijah is about to announce,"[20] that is, Jeroboam's (northern tribes') departure from the house of David. Then Ahijah "found" (מצא) Jeroboam "on the way" (בַּדֶּרֶךְ) (v. 29; cf. 13:24), and "took hold of" (וַיִּתְפֹּשׂ) the new robe[21] and "tore it" (וַיִּקְרָעֶהָ) into twelve pieces (v. 30).[22] He delivered the message: "Thus says Yahweh, the God of Israel, 'Behold, I am about to tear (קרע) the kingdom from the hand (יָד) of

---

18. Bodner, *Royal Drama*, 43.

19. Also, the term "Ephratite" contributes to clarify his origin from the North. See Walsh, *1 Kings*, 143, and Bodner, *Royal Drama*, 42–43.

20. Walsh, *1 Kings*, 143.

21. Some scholars maintain Jeroboam not Ahijah is the one clothed in the new robe (e.g., Cogan, *I Kings*, 339; Chun, "A Note on 1 Kings xi 29–30," 268–74; Bodner, *Royal Drama*, 51–52). In contrast to these scholars' views, however, the symbolic meaning of the narrative is hardly changed, and thus who was wearing the robe does not make much difference to the interpretation of the meaning of the symbolic action. For Stacey's discussion on this matter, see Stacey, *Prophetic Drama*, 79.

22. It is also noticeable that the words "took hold of" (תָּפַשׂ) and "tore" (קָרַע) appear in chapter 13 (v. 4 and vv. 3, 5 respectively).

THE FATE OF THE MAN OF GOD FROM JUDAH

Solomon and will give you ten tribes'" (v. 31). The key words "found" (מצא) and "on the way" (בַּדֶּרֶךְ) here are conspicuous, since they play a significant role in the story of the man of God, where the man of God sets out on a journey, and the old prophet of Bethel and the lion both "found" the man of God "on the way" (13:14, 24, 28). Already here we see parallels forming between Jeroboam and the man of God. Bodner argues, "Use of the exact same terms certainly is not random but meant to illustrate that the journey of Jeroboam parallels that of the man of God."[23] He continues,

> Both figures, after all, are the recipients of a word from God that, for modulated reasons, they abandon in pursuit of a different way. In spatial terms, both depart from the road and venture to Bethel—the man of God returns to Bethel, the city of Jeroboam has consecrated (for political security). Both are raised up to counter illicit cultic activity, and both survive attempts at arrest by formidable monarchs. Yet both Jeroboam and the man of God detour from their mandates, and are penalized with a violent, premature demise.[24]

If this observation is correct, the narrator's use of these words is very intentional.

The tearing of the robe symbolizes God's tearing the kingdom from the hand of Solomon. There may be a wordplay between the term for robe (שלמה) and the name Solomon (שלמה), as these two words in the Hebrew manuscripts were indistinguishable from each other.[25] This wordplay may be "to signal a reversal of fortune, and the torn coat certainly points to an extraordinary reversal of Solomonic fortune."[26] Just as שלמה is torn in pieces, so will the kingdom of שלמה be torn apart, and ten tribes will be given over to his "servant." Ironically, however, this reversal of fortune will happen one more time later in chapter 13, where Jeroboam attempts to "seize" (תִּפְשֵׂהוּ) the man of God from Judah (13:4; cf. 11:30). Then the altar is "torn down" (נִקְרָע), which signals another reversal of fortune, but, at this time, that of Jeroboam. Just as the "torn" robe symbolized the decline of the Solomon's kingdom, so the "torn" altar symbolizes the fall of the house of Jeroboam. Furthermore, in chapter 11, which depicts the rise of Jeroboam, it is announced that Yahweh will tear out the kingdom from the "hand"

---

23. Bodner, *Royal Drama*, 113.
24. Bodner, *Royal Drama*, 113.
25. For this, see Watson, *Classical Hebrew Poetry*, 246, and Walsh, *1 Kings*, 143–4.
26. Bodner, *Royal Drama*, 52.

(יָד) of Solomon and give ten tribes to Jeroboam, but in chapter 13, which depicts the fall of Jeroboam, we see that Jeroboam's "hand" is withered. The reversal of Jeroboam's fortune comes into sharp relief when we read these two accounts together.

The reason for these measures from Yahweh is that Solomon forsook God and worshipped Ashtoreth, Chemosh, and Milcom, and "they[27] have not walked in my ways, doing what is right in my sight and keeping my statutes and my rules, as David his father did" (v. 33). Solomon's violation of God's commands is blamed for the "rebellion" of Jeroboam and the northern tribes. What is notable is that Jeroboam's "rebellion," in contrast to other rebellions (those of Absalom and Sheba, for example), "is orchestrated by God through the hand of Ahijah the prophet."[28] In other words, Jeroboam is "divinely sponsored to raise his hand against Solomon's corruption."[29]

Ahijah's oracle, meanwhile, concerns not only the birth of the Northern Kingdom but also the future of the Southern Kingdom. While God promises that he will give Jeroboam ten tribes, he announces his plan for the house of David: "To his son I will give one tribe, so that there may be a lamp for my servant David forever before me in Jerusalem—the city where I have chosen to establish my name" (v. 36, also v. 32). As Walsh puts it, "perhaps the 'lamp' refers to a 'glimmer of hope' for the future of the dynasty, still burning in the midst of the dark doom Yahweh is bringing upon Solomon."[30] This statement may betray the point of view of the Judean historian. The Judean historian, while describing the northern tribes' rebellion as the will of God, ensures that it does not mean God's revocation of his earlier promise to David (2 Sam 7:16). The promise has been qualified but has not been completely revoked (v. 39).

Ahijah's oracle ends with both a promise and a warning for Jeroboam (vv. 37–38). The promise is that "I will be with you, and I will build for you a sure house as I did for David" (v. 38b). The promise of "a sure house" that is now being given to Jeroboam is certainly reminiscent of God's promise to David. Thus, the privilege and favor promised to Jeroboam are elevated to the same level as God's promise to David. The promise is genuine, and

---

27. The subject of the actions is plural, "they"; thus, the blame is not limited to Solomon, but is directed also to all Israel. It implies that the people have followed and joined Solomon in his idolatry.

28. Bodner, *Royal Drama*, 47.

29. Bodner, *Royal Drama*, 48.

30. Walsh, *1 Kings*, 145. The reference to "lamp" is made also in 1 Kgs 15:4 and 2 Kgs 8:19 in the Book of Kings (cf. 2 Chr 21:7).

THE FATE OF THE MAN OF GOD FROM JUDAH

we do not sense God's deception. Knoppers states, "In this narration Jeroboam is not only one of the deity's instruments to effect retribution upon Solomon, but also a key figure called out by the deity, signaling new hope for (northern) Israel."[31] On the other hand, however, a warning is clearly discernible in the conditionality of the promise: "If you heed all that I command you, and walk in my laws and commandments as my servant David did . . ." (v. 38a). Walsh comments on this:

> It ends, in words that have no parallel in the first part of the oracle, by promising Jeroboam the same sort of blessings David enjoyed if his obedience is modeled on David's. In this context such a promise is problematic. What can it mean to promise 'to build for you an enduring house, as I built for David' in the middle of an oracle announcing Yahweh's devastating punishment on that very house of David? David's kingdom is about to disintegrate because of Solomon's disobedience and will endure only in severely reduced circumstances. Is this a presage of a tragic destiny for Jeroboam as well?[32]

Thus, the conditionality of the promise here functions as foreshadowing in the sense that it hints at what will occur later in the story. Cohn remarks, "The prophet's final words, 'And I will afflict the seed of David for this, but not forever' (v. 39), look darkly upon the ultimate success of Jeroboam's kingdom."[33]

Ahijah's prophetic symbolic actions and his oracle are followed by the narrator's rather unexpected statement about Solomon's response: "Solomon sought to put Jeroboam to death, but Jeroboam promptly fled to King Shishak of Egypt and remained in Egypt till the death of Solomon" (v. 40). Given Solomon's earlier favor for Jeroboam, this reversal in Solomon's attitude is unexpected. It is not clear what caused the change in his attitude toward Jeroboam, because it is not likely that Solomon knew of this prophecy (the text says, "two of them [Ahijah and Jeroboam] were alone in the open country," v. 29), but the narrator, by arranging the two events together, clearly associates Ahijah's oracle with Solomon's attempt to kill Jeroboam. In other words, the text, as it stands, leads the reader to believe that Ahijah's prophecy (vv. 29-39) was the reason why Solomon "sought to kill

---

31. Knoppers, *Two Nations under God*, 2:186.
32. Walsh, *1 Kings*, 146.
33. Cohn, "Literary Technique," 27.

Jeroboam" (v. 40).[34] Cohn argues, "He [the author] implies that Solomon acts because of the prophecy and compounds his sin by attempting to defy the divine will. It is no wonder that the formulaic report of Solomon's death follows immediately!"[35]

Regnal Resume (11:41–43)

A regular regnal formula describes the end of the days of Solomon. The length of Solomon's reign is recorded here, and, more importantly, his death is mentioned. The significance of the report of Solomon's death is to be found in God's promise that he would not take the kingdom out of Solomon's hand as long as he lived (v. 34). Now Solomon is dead, and his son Rehoboam succeeds him as king; hence the oracle that Ahijah delivered to Jeroboam is ready to be fulfilled.

Conclusion

In sum, the first section of the Jeroboam narrative describes how Jeroboam's raising his hand against Solomon has begun. This section is best understood in the context of Yahweh's judgment on the house of Solomon. Ahijah's prophecy is the beginning of the fulfillment of Yahweh's oracle against Solomon that Yahweh would "tear" the kingdom and give it to one of Solomon's servants (1 Kgs 11:11–13). Thus the northern tribes' rebellion is blamed on Solomon's apostasy, which justifies Yahweh's qualification of his previous promise to David of "a sure house."[36] In fact, the first section of the Jeroboam narrative functions as the hinge between the Solomonic narrative and the Jeroboam narrative, as is seen in the fact that the regnal formula of King Solomon appears in 11:41–43. "The last element of the symmetrical organization of Solomon's story is the first element of Jeroboam's."[37]

The division of the kingdom is described to be from God, but at the same time, God's continuing mercy for the house of David will not cease. The overall tone of the narration is not pessimistic, nor critical of Jeroboam,

---

34. Cohn, "Literary Technique," 27–28.

35. Cohn, "Literary Technique," 27–28. For a discussion on the correlations between the story of Jeroboam, Solomon, and Ahijah and the story of David, Saul, and Samuel, see Walsh, *1 Kings*, 148.

36. Sweeney, *I & II Kings*, 159.

37. Walsh, *1 Kings*, 204.

THE FATE OF THE MAN OF GOD FROM JUDAH

at this point of the narrative, but the intended reader of the Book of Kings may already be aware of what has become of the house of Jeroboam, which only makes the reader curious to learn how "a turn of affairs" will be brought about (12:15). In terms of the characterization of Jeroboam, as Walsh puts it, "Jeroboam remains something of an enigma. What is he really like, and how well will he live up to the destiny to which Yahweh calls him?"[38] The conditions presented for "a sure house" may function as a foreshadowing of what will unfold in the rest of the Jeroboam narrative. Overall, the literary function of Ahijah's prophecy is to emphasize the word of Yahweh as the driving force of the history of Israel.

The Rise of Jeroboam and the Secession of the Northern Tribes (12:1–25)

This pericope describes how Ahijah's prophecy regarding Jeroboam has been fulfilled. After the death of Solomon, Rehoboam succeeded him as king (11:43). How Jeroboam raised his hand against the king, which the narrator promised to show earlier in 11:27, is related here. Ahijah's prophecy finds its fulfillment through complicated human events and relationships. Rehoboam, whose regnal account is found in 1 Kings 14, appears as a main character in this account. Sweeney states, "By focusing initially on Rehoboam ben Solomon, who has his own discrete regnal account in 1 Kgs 14:21–31, the narrative recounts the failure of Rehoboam to obtain the Israelite throne as a prelude to the return and accession of Jeroboam."[39] Three observations can be made as to the narrator's intention and emphasis in this account: (1) the narrator blames Rehoboam for Israel's revolt, (2) Jeroboam's involvement in the revolt is minimized, and (3) the secession of the northern tribes is attributed to Yahweh. Our discussion of this section will proceed in the order of these three topics.

THE FLAWED CHARACTER OF REHOBOAM BLAMED FOR ISRAEL'S REVOLT

The secession of the northern tribes is conceived in their grievance over Solomon's excessive imperialistic internal policies and his unfair treatment

---

38. Walsh, *1 Kings*, 149.
39. Sweeney, *I & II Kings*, 161.

A Literary Analysis of the Jeroboam Narrative

of them. In effect, "all Israel"[40] came to Shechem, "an early political center of Israel,"[41] to acclaim Rehoboam as king. They notify Rehoboam of the heavy forced labor that Solomon imposed on the northern tribes and make a request that Rehoboam lighten "the harsh labor and the heavy yoke" (v. 4). The absence of any objection on the part of Rehoboam at the time of their request implies Rehoboam's "admission of Solomon's discriminatory internal policies and fiscal parochialism."[42] Sweeney writes, "A fundamental issue is the unfair treatment of the northern tribes, insofar as Solomon imposed upon them far greater responsibility for the support of the royal court and military establishment (1 Kgs 4:7–19), the labor corvée that built the temple and royal palace complex (1 Kgs 5:26–32), and the ceding of territory to Hiram of Tyre (1 Kgs 9:10–14)."[43] The representatives of the northern tribes make the request with all respect for Rehoboam, whom they are now about to acclaim as king. "In return for a lessening of the service (*'bdh*) expected of them, the Israelites pledge to serve (*'bd*) the new king."[44] How Rehoboam would respond to the request becomes the center of attention. Rehoboam asks for three days to give them his answer.

The process of Rehoboam's decision-making (vv. 6–11), which is bracketed by Rehoboam's three-day notice (v. 5) and the people's coming back in three days (v. 12), moves slowly through a series of direct speeches. The direct speeches "slow the development and create considerable tension."[45] King Rehoboam takes counsel from two different groups of advisers, "the elders (הַזְּקֵנִים) who had stood before his father Solomon" (v. 6) and "the boys (הַיְלָדִים) who had grown up with him and were standing before him" (v. 8). In this scene, the elders are contrasted with the boys, and the servant-leadership[46] with the oppressive leadership.

---

40. Walsh points out that "all Israel" refers to "Israel," the northern tribes, which is the case with 12:1. See Walsh, *1 Kings*, 160.

41. Sweeney, *I & II Kings*, 168.

42. Bodner, *Royal Drama*, 65. From the historical point of view, it may be debatable whether or not the people of Israel, not only the Canaanites, were also drafted for forced labor (compare 1 Kgs 5:13–18 with 1 Kgs 9:15–22). The unfair treatment of the northern tribes, however, is presumed in the text and forms the basis of their request.

43. Sweeney, *I & II Kings*, 169.

44. Walsh, *1 Kings*, 161.

45. Walsh, *1 Kings*, 167.

46. Fretheim points out that this kind of leadership for the kingship is unparalleled in the Hebrew Bible (see Fretheim, *First and Second Kings*, 72). One of the closest concepts of kingship may be found in Deuteronomy 17:14–20. John Bright states, "the feeling was

THE FATE OF THE MAN OF GOD FROM JUDAH

The narrator calls the second group of advisers "boys" (הַיְלָדִים), which is a term used more commonly for children than for adults. Thus "the narrator's sympathy is clearly for the old men; his emphasis here is on the youth and inexperience of the 'boys' who belong to Rehoboam's own generation."[47] As Sweeney notes, "this label is striking for the comrades of a forty-one-year-old man!" (1 Kgs 14:21).[48] It seems that the term reflects the narrator's derogatory perspective. Bodner makes insightful comments about the "boys": "Undeniably there is something unique about Rehoboam's gang: they are the first generation of Israelites to enjoy wealth on an unprecedented scale, the urban courtiers whose standard of living comes at the expense of the ordinary taxpayer."[49] It is unfortunate that Rehoboam was closer to the "boys" than to the elders, which is shown in his words to the elders and to the boys respectively; He keeps some distance between the elders and himself when he says, "how would *you* advise [*me*] to return to this people regarding the matter?"; while he identifies himself with the "boys," saying, "What would you advise me that *we* reply to this people . . . ?"

The kind of leadership that the elders propose that the king should adopt is servant-leadership, accompanied by "kind words" (דברים טובים): "If you will be a *servant* to this people today and *serve* them and speak good words to them when you answer them, they will be your servants forever" (v. 7). Rehoboam is advised to replace his father's oppressive leadership style with one based on serving. That the assembly of Israel is now asking for a different policy from Rehoboam is notable in the contrast between "your father" (אָבִיךָ) and "you" (אַתָּה) (vv. 4, 10). Rehoboam, however, takes the advice of the "boys" and "answered the people harshly" (v. 13),[50] as is seen in the repeated pronoun (v. 14): ". . . אָבִי . . . וַאֲנִי . . . אָבִי . . . וַאֲנִי . . . אָבִי." The advice of the "boys" (vv. 10–11) and Rehoboam's answer based on it

---

deep-seated in northern circles, a feeling reflected in the law of Deuteronomy (17:14–17), that a king ought to be as little like Solomon as possible" (*Kingdom of God*, 49).

47. Walsh, *1 Kings*, 162. Walsh further argues, "The meaning of 'my little one' . . . is uncertain. If, as some scholars suspect, it is gutter language for the male organ, Rehoboam's young advisers are coarse as well as crude" (164).

48. Sweeney, *I & II Kings*, 170. 3 Rgns 12:24a says that Rehoboam was sixteen years old when he began to reign, though 3 Rgns 14:21 says differently that he was forty-one years old.

49. Bodner, *Royal Drama*, 67.

50. The word "harshly" (קָשָׁה) contains the denotation of "stubborn" (cf. Judg 2:19). This word is applied to Israel when Aaron made the golden calf, where the word is usually translated "stiff-necked" (Exod 32:9; 33:3, 5).

only highlight their immaturity: "My little finger [קָטָנִּי literally translated 'my littleness,' which is most likely a reference to his penis] is thicker than my father's loins" (v. 10). The narrator in his description of this incident emphasizes Rehoboam's folly and stupidity in rejecting "the advice that the elders had given him" but following "the advice of the boys" (vv. 13–14). "The reader is reminded," Bodner states, "that the kingdom is about to be passed on to a servant who is poised for a substantial inheritance."[51] The narrator's intention is clear: he blames Rehoboam's folly and recalcitrance for the secession of the northern tribes. Rehoboam is held responsible for the choice he has made.

Jeroboam Plays a Minor Role in the Revolt

While Rehoboam's folly is highlighted, Jeroboam's role in the secession is described as surprisingly limited or passive. Jeroboam is "still" (עוֹד) in Egypt, when all Israel went to Shechem to acclaim Rehoboam as king (12:2). Jeroboam "hears of it" (v. 2) but he does not take the initiative in taking any action. In the Hebrew Bible, as opposed to the Septuagint rendition, Jeroboam did not come back to Shechem until they [all Israel] sent for him from Egypt.[52] Sweeney says, "The narrative emphasizes that

---

51. Bodner, *Royal Drama*, 65.

52. In Septuagint and Vulgate, along with 2 Chr 10:2, Jeroboam returns from Egypt when he hears of Solomon's death. The Septuagint includes a long alternative version of Jeroboam's career after 3 Reigns 12:24 (1 Kgs 12:24 of the Hebrew Bible). This insertion (3 Rgns 12:24) brings in some information that is not known in the Hebrew Bible, but, overall, does not provide a reliable chronological development of the events. One thing that is noteworthy is that Jeroboam, according to the Septuagint rendition, is characterized as a man of aspiration to become king: he went back to the land of Israel from Egypt as soon as he heard of the death of Solomon (3 Rgns 11:43). He was very determined to return to Israel when he heard of Solomon's death (3 Reigns 12:24d–f), because "he was aspiring to the kingdom" (3 Rgns 12:24b). J. Montgomery states that the Septuagint rendition shows "none of the cool objectivity" of the Hebrew Bible (*The Book of Kings*, 254). The brief comparison of the Septuagint and the Hebrew Bible provides some clues to the Hebrew narrator's narrative strategy in portraying Jeroboam. Jeroboam did not actively initiate the rebellion against the house of David. Scholars have various hypotheses regarding the Septuagint version. For example, J. Gray sees this version as an independent northern tradition worked over by a Judean editor (*I & II Kings*, 287). R. Cohn says, "[I]t demonstrates the existence of a variety of tales about Jeroboam from which our author chose in creating his narrative" ("Literary Technique," 24). On a different note, the discrepancy between 1 Kings 12:2 and 2 Chr 10:2 seems to be due to a scribal error; 2 Chr 10:2b reads וַיֵּשֶׁב יָרָבְעָם מִמִּצְרָיִם, whereas 1 Kgs 12:2b reads וַיֵּשֶׁב יָרָבְעָם בְּמִצְרָיִם. NRSV emends the vocalization of "he lived" (וַיֵּשֶׁב) to "he returned" (וַיָּשָׁב), but, as Bodner

THE FATE OF THE MAN OF GOD FROM JUDAH

Jeroboam played no direct role in fomenting revolt against the house of David."[53] The reason all Israel called for Jeroboam is not provided. It is probably because Jeroboam was a leader when Solomon "gave him charge over all the forced labor of the house of Joseph" (11:28), and they now need someone to represent them as they are prepared to make a request to the new king. It is inferred from the text, as Walsh also argues, "the Israelites have kept contact with Jeroboam even in his exile," which implies a high respect for Jeroboam.[54] Some intertextual connections may be noticeable here. Fretheim says, "Moses-like, he was called upon to lead a delegation to Rehoboam to request relief from the crown's forced labor policies, language reminiscent of Israel's life in Egypt."[55] All this seems to contribute to a positive characterization of Jeroboam.

On the other hand, the northern tribes' expectation of Jeroboam seems to have been greater than simply needing him to represent them in their request to Rehoboam.[56] "It is," Bodner states, "as though a great deal of northern hope now rests on Jeroboam's shoulders."[57] This hope or expectation is manifested when Rehoboam refused to comply with their request. The representatives of the northern tribes who came to Rehoboam twice were presumably led by Jeroboam (vv. 3, 12). Nevertheless, the role of Jeroboam in all this matter is enigmatic. Jeroboam "plays a minor role in the revolt."[58] It is notable that Rehoboam's answer is directed to *the people* (v. 13), and the reaction to the king's answer and their rebellion are ascribed completely to *the people* while Jeroboam remains silent until all Israel summons him to the assembly (v. 20). Bodner states, "Yet Jeroboam's own perspective on the matter is cloaked in silence, and this silence is what directs attention to the enigmatic role of Jeroboam throughout the proceedings."[59] It seems that the narrator has intentionally omitted Jeroboam from this matter. Jeroboam's ascension to kingship is requested by "all Israel," and

---

argues, such emendation is unnecessary because 1 Kings 12:2 is making a point that the northern tribes have taken the initiative in sending for Jeroboam and bringing him back to Israel (*Royal Drama*, 61–62).

53. Sweeney, *I & II Kings*, 167.
54. Walsh, *1 Kings*, 161.
55. Fretheim, *First and Second Kings*, 72.
56. Walsh, *1 Kings*, 161.
57. Bodner, *Royal Drama*, 62.
58. Sweeney, *I & II Kings*, 168.
59. Bodner, *Royal Drama*, 63.

Jeroboam's role in all this is only passive (v. 20). As Sweeney points out, "the MT places him at the assembly but gives him no evident speaking or leadership roles."[60]

Some scholars see a discrepancy between vv. 3 and 12 and v. 20.[61] In contrast to Jeroboam's involvement in the people's request to Rehoboam in the earlier parts (vv. 3, 12), v. 20 seems to suggest that Jeroboam did not enter into this matter. The Chronicler attempts to harmonize the tension in the text by dropping the verse (2 Chr 10). Robert Cohn says of this seemingly discrepancy, "Although the inclusion of Jeroboam in the Hebrew v. 3. 12 may well be secondary, the final author of Kings, by offering two views of when Jeroboam returned, nicely underscores the basic tension between human and divine plans which informs the story."[62]

On this matter, however, Walsh's explanation may be more plausible. He notes that "the 'assembly' of v. 3 and that of v. 20 are different words in Hebrew" and "this suggests that two different gatherings, for two different purposes, may be in view."[63] The summons of Jeroboam described in v. 20 is a different "convocation, where they made him king over all Israel."[64] At any rate, in the present form of the Hebrew Bible, Jeroboam does not take any action until v. 25, and it is only in vv. 26–31 that we hear him speak for the first time. Cohn argues correctly, "The story of his accession to power seems designed to create sympathy for him. Against the apostasy of Solomon and the stupidity of his son Rehoboam, Jeroboam is depicted as the right man in the right place."[65] The narrator characterizes Jeroboam as someone who patiently waits for his turn to hold power rather than as one who aspires to acquire power.

---

60. Sweeney, *I & II Kings*, 170.

61. Fretheim understands "v. 20 functions as a summary statement in the present text, not as a report of his return" (*First and Second Kings*, 72), but, as Walsh notes, the "assembly" in v. 3 and the "assembly" in v. 20 are different in Hebrew, so v. 20 does not have to be a summary statement (*1 Kings*, 166–67).

62. Cohn, "Literary Technique," 30.

63. Walsh, *1 Kings*, 166–67.

64. Walsh, *1 Kings*, 167.

65. Cohn, "Literary Technique," 25.

THE FATE OF THE MAN OF GOD FROM JUDAH

The Secession Is Attributed to Yahweh

Although the blame of the secession is ascribed to Rehoboam's folly, the secession of the Northern Kingdom is attributed to Yahweh. King Rehoboam did not listen to the people "because it was a turn of affairs brought about by Yahweh in order to fulfill the promise that Yahweh had made through Ahijah the Shilonite to Jeroboam son of Nebat" (v. 15). Also, Rehoboam sends Adoram, only to have him stoned to death by an angry Israel (v. 18). Then he prepares for a war against "the house of Israel" (v. 21), but the word of God comes to Shemaiah, the man of God, saying, "Say to King Rehoboam son of Solomon of Judah, and to all the House of Judah and Benjamin and the rest of the people: Thus says Yahweh, 'You shall not set out to make war on your brothers, the Israelites. Let every man return to his home, *for this thing has been brought about by me*'" (vv. 23–24).

Surprisingly enough, Rehoboam and all the house of Judah and Benjamin listen to the oracle with no obvious objection: "They obeyed the word of Yahweh and turned back to walk according to the word of Yahweh" (v. 24b).[66] Judah's surprising obedience will be contrasted with Jeroboam's disobedience, which will be described in the following chapter. This rather surprising obedience of Rehoboam to the word of Yahweh serves to make "Rehoboam and the southern kingdom actually appear in a positive light," and more importantly, "it furthers the theme of prophetic power introduced earlier, and will continue to hover over the Jeroboam story."[67] This theme certainly appears multiple times throughout the Jeroboam narrative and especially so in the frame of the overarching theme of the prophecy and fulfillment in the Jeroboam narrative. The narrator's attribution of the secession to Yahweh's will causes some confusion for the reader as to the interrelationship between the prophecy (Yahweh's will) and humans' choice. The will of Yahweh does not acquit Rehoboam, and Rehoboam is held responsible for his choice, but Yahweh's plan encompasses even Rehoboam's folly (this topic will be discussed in more detail in chapter 4). The narrator emphasizes that God's will delivered in the form of prophecy is certainly fulfilled through human choices, though the consequences of the choices will be borne out by humans.

---

66. Amos Frisch discusses 1 Kings 12:21–24 from the perspective of the two opposed interpretations of the schism, that is, Rehoboam's political interpretation and Shemaiah's religious view ("Shemaiah the Prophet," 466–8).

67. Bodner, *Royal Drama*, 77.

A Literary Analysis of the Jeroboam Narrative

Through this account, the narrator depicts God letting the nation be divided into two and be two nations under one God. These two nations are "brothers" (v. 24).[68] Knoppers says, "By orchestrating the division according to his standard typology of sin, punishment, and divine deliverance, the Deuteronomist endorses the creation of two nations under one God. A common heritage and a common cultic obligation to the Jerusalem temple characterize nascent Israel and Judah, but their separate polities are divinely ordained."[69]

Conclusion

In this section, Ahijah's oracle is fulfilled, and as a fulfillment of the prophecy, the rise of Jeroboam and the "rebellion" (12:19) of the northern tribes are described. Rehoboam's oppressive policy toward the northern tribes and insensitive folly become the cause of the secession of the northern tribes. Jeroboam, a servant of Solomon's, becomes the king of the northern tribes. His role in the secession, however, is surprisingly minimal, and thus the characterization of Jeroboam remains positive throughout the course of "rebellion." Some scholars notice the tension in the text between the view that sees the secession as something brought about by Yahweh (1 Kgs 12:15, 24) and another view that considers it as the northern tribes' rebellion against the house of David (1 Kgs 12:19).[70] The narrator, however, clarifies that the secession is from Yahweh, and this reveals the narrator's theological view that Yahweh's providence is played out in human history. Now, "the prospects of two separate kingdoms allied by a common faith-tradition emerge in this phase of the story, and there is every hope for a successful coexistence."[71] The certainty of the fulfillment of the prophet's prophecy is emphasized, and Yahweh's providence works with human decisions in a mysterious way. The narrator makes it clear that the political separation of Judah and Israel is made according to the will of Yahweh,

---

68. Frisch notes that the word "brethren" "expresses kinship and also equality of status," which "contrasts sharply with the views of Rehoboam and his advisers throughout the narrative of xii 1–20." See Frisch, "Shemaiah the Prophet," 466.

69. Knoppers, *Two Nations under God*, 2:5.

70. Sweeney says this verse ("so Israel has been in rebellion against the house of David to this day") indicates that the narrative "dates to the reign of Hezekiah, since northern Israel did not exist following its destruction by the Assyrians in 722/721 BCE" (*I & II Kings*, 171).

71. Bodner, *Royal Drama*, 142.

but as we will see in the next part, "the religious unity of Yahweh's people" should not be affected.⁷²

The Sin of Jeroboam (12:26–31)

This part of the Jeroboam narrative depicts a turning point in the fate of Jeroboam. Up until this point, the narrator depicted the rise of Jeroboam, showing how Ahijah's prophecy regarding Jeroboam was fulfilled. Jeroboam's role in bringing about the "rebellion" was minimal, which contributes to the overall positive characterization of Jeroboam. The sudden change in Jeroboam's attitude described in this part may surprise the reader. The narrator focuses on the motivation behind the change, which made Jeroboam turn away from walking after God's commands.

This account begins with Jeroboam's inner soliloquy. Though it is a soliloquy in his heart, this is the first time Jeroboam utters a word in the form of a direct speech. The reader is perplexed, as soon as Jeroboam reveals what is in his heart, because the face of Jeroboam, which has been hidden until this point, has now appeared: "Jeroboam said in his heart (בְּלִבּוֹ), 'Now the kingdom will return to the house of David. If this people goes up to offer sacrifices in the house of Yahweh in Jerusalem, the heart of this people will return to their master Rehoboam, king of Judah, and they will kill me and go back to Rehoboam, king of Judah'" (vv. 26–7). The word לֵב, occurring twice here, grabs the reader's attention. It shows that the narrator finds the problem of Jeroboam's apostasy in his "heart." Cohn notes that the narrator mentions heart "at the outset ('he said in his heart,' v. 26) and at the conclusion ('he devised in his heart,' v. 33)."⁷³ The anxiety in his heart was that "the *heart* of this people might turn back" to Rehoboam and kill him (v. 28). Bodner states, "The most litigious moment in the story—Jeroboam's disclosure of his fear of mutiny—is presented as an interior monologue so the reader can further understand the kind of inner fear that eventually

---

72. Walsh, *1 Kings*, 203. In addition, the political separation seems, in the narrator's view, rather temporary (cf. 12:19). The narrator's editorial comment betrays that the separation is extending even to his own time, but at the same time, as Fretheim remarks, "this suggests that the break is not seen to be finally permanent" (*First and Second Kings*, 73). This reveals the narrator's view on the secession. F. M. Cross opines, "Ahijah added the qualification that while the seed of David would be chastised for a season, God would not afflict Judah forever. In this statement we must understand that the oracle presumes an ultimate reunion of the two kingdoms under a Davidid" (*Myth and Hebrew Epic*, 279).

73. Cohn, "Literary Technique," 31.

results in the alternative liturgy."[74] The Deuteronomist often finds the origin of apostasy of kings in their not walking before God with all their *heart* (לְבָב/לֵב) (cf. 1 Kgs 2:4; 3:6; 8:23; 9:4; 11:4; 14:8; 15:3, 14; 2 Kgs 20:3; 23:3, 25).[75] In the Jeroboam narrative, Jeroboam is pointed out as not having been like "my servant David who kept my commandments and followed me with all his *heart*..." (14:8).

Jeroboam's soliloquy makes a sharp contrast with the positive characterization of him before this point of the narrative. Thus, it "marks a transition in the audience's understanding of the protagonist [Jeroboam]."[76] Jeroboam's fear seems ungrounded, especially when we consider the kind of relationship that the northern tribes have had with Jeroboam. Walsh states,

> His next words, "they will kill me," hardly ring true either. The narrator has shown us no grounds to suppose such a danger. Indeed, everything points to the high regard Israel has for Jeroboam: they kept in contact with him in his exile, recalled him as soon as possible, made him part of the team that negotiated with Rehoboam, and finally chose him as their king. Jeroboam's fears strike us as unrealistic and reinforce our impression that he does not trust in Yahweh's continuing favor.[77]

Instead of heeding God's command to "walk in my ways" given as a condition for God's promise of "a sure house" (11:38), Jeroboam now explores a different way to secure his house on his own. This anxiety compels him to "make" golden calves. The narrator adds a brief comment that "the king took counsel," just as Rehoboam did (v. 28; cf. 12:6, 8).[78] The counsel did not stop him from moving away from God, but he moved forward with his plan—"So the king took counsel and made two golden calves"—which may suggest that the king and the counsellors were not very different from each other in terms of their allegiance to Yahweh.

We notice that the word "to make" (עָשָׂה) is repeated many times in this short block of text (vv. 27, 28, 31[x2], 32[x4], 33[x2]), which signifies the narrator's emphasis on Jeroboam's new cultic inventions. Cohn says, "Hammering out the verb *'āśâ* ('he made') nine times (v. 28–33), the

---

74. Bodner, *Royal Drama*, 144–5.
75. Von Rad, *Studies in Deuteronomy*, 87–88.
76. Bodner, *Royal Drama*, 84.
77. Walsh, *1 Kings*, 172.
78. It is not stated in the text who Jeroboam took counsel with. Sweeney assumes that Jeroboam took counsel with his subjects (*I & II Kings*, 176).

narrator depicts Jeroboam's acts as self-willed and self-serving."[79] The inventions are "two golden calves" (v. 28), "shrines on high places" (v. 31), non-Levite "priests" (v. 31), and a feast (v. 32). Among these new cultic inventions, the golden calves receive the primary attention. Many scholars argue that the golden bulls, like the cherubim in the Jerusalem temple, might have been pedestals for the throne of the invisible Yahweh,[80] but John Bright points out that "the bull motif was apparently too closely associated with the symbolism of the Baal cult for the taste of purists."[81] Whatever Jeroboam's original motivation for the making of the golden calves may have been, he is clearly presented as an idolater in the text.

Jeroboam's pronouncement of this new cultic center is familiar to the reader: "Behold, your gods, O Israel, who brought you up from the land of Egypt!" (v. 28). This statement is almost a verbatim repetition of what the Israelites said when they created the golden calf in the wilderness (Exod 32:4).[82] Though which text is prior to the other remains controversial among scholars, there is no doubt that Jeroboam's sin of idolatry is depicted in an extremely heretical way. He sets up one calf in Bethel and the other in Dan. The narrator adds, "This matter (הַדָּבָר הַזֶּה) became a sin, and the people went to the one as far as Dan" (v. 30). Jeroboam's idolatry is portrayed as influential. Fretheim says, "From the narrator's perspective, they were deeply problematic from the beginning; they 'became' a sin and led Israel into sin (12:30; 13:34; 14:15–16). Jeroboam becomes, in effect, a new Aaron."[83]

Graeme Auld observes an interesting connection between the Exodus account and this event in Kings: "In both Exodus and Kings the making of the 'true' shrine is reported first and in greatest detail (Exod 25–31 and 1 Kgs 5–8), then the 'distortion' more briefly (Exod 32 and 1 Kgs 12). Both texts are designed to legitimate the shrine in Jerusalem, and its furniture, and its priesthood (cf. v. 31)."[84] The literary effect may be twofold: the legitimization of the temple in Jerusalem and the maximization of the condemnation of the sin of Jeroboam. The list of his sins is expanded in v. 31: "He made shrines on the high places, and he made [appointed] priests out of anyone

---

79. Cohn, "Literary Technique," 31.
80. E.g., F. M. Cross, John Bright, and M. Sweeney (*I & II Kings*, 177).
81. Bright, *Kingdom of God*, 50–51. See also Cross, *Myth and Hebrew Epic*, 73.
82. Hosea also condemns "the calf of Samaria" (Hos 8:4b–6).
83. Fretheim, *First and Second Kings*, 76.
84. Auld, *Kings*, 88.

A Literary Analysis of the Jeroboam Narrative

of the people who were not Levites." There is no doubt that Jeroboam's inventions listed here violate prohibitions in Deuteronomy, which is "presupposed throughout the DtrH," hence the concerns of the Deuteronomist:[85] the centralization of cultus (Deut 12:5–7, 11, 13–14), the removal of the high places (Deut 12:2), and the sacrifice only by the Levites (Deut 18:1–8), the first of which is condemned this time (12:30), and the second and third later in chapter 13 (13:34). With this regard, the condemnation of the altar at Bethel and Dan betrays Judean polemical interests.

Conclusion

This section divides the Jeroboam narrative into two symmetrical halves, because everything about Jeroboam before this section is positive and everything about Jeroboam after this section is negative. Walsh states, "The center of the story of Jeroboam and its literary pivot is therefore the account of his cultic innovations, particularly the establishment of calf-idols at Bethel and Dan. This is the heart of Jeroboam's sin and the cause of his downfall."[86] Jeroboam's soliloquy, the first utterance made by Jeroboam, reveals the dark side of his *heart*, which betrays his lack of trust in Yahweh's word. As a result, he makes golden calves and proclaims them as the God who brought Israel up from the land of Egypt, which is reminiscent of a similar incident in the wilderness. "This thing became a sin" (12:30a). John Bright states,

> No doubt ignorant people did come to worship them. Jeroboam was to live in the hearts of posterity as the man who "made Israel to sin" (I Kings 15:34). His cult was probably the entering wedge for all sorts of paganism. In any case pagan practices did enter (as the reader of Hosea well knows). What was worse, Yahweh—God of Israel—became, in the minds of many, all too very much like Baal.[87]

This new cultic invention of Jeroboam signals the fall of Jeroboam from the height of his career to an idolater. The repetition of the words "to make" in this section indicates Jeroboam's cultic inventiveness. The emphasis in this section falls on the important theological term "sin," which will be

---

85. Sweeney, *I & II Kings*, 178.
86. Walsh, *1 Kings*, 203.
87. Bright, *Kingdom of God*, 51.

THE FATE OF THE MAN OF GOD FROM JUDAH

repeatedly mentioned in the rest of the Book of Kings. Jeroboam's sin of idolatry causes the decline not only in the fate of his own "house" (dynasty), but also in the fate of the Northern Kingdom.

Ahijah's Prophecy Regarding the Fall of Jeroboam (14:1–20)

While chapter 13 provides the reader with illustrative events that show the irrevocable destruction of the house of Jeroboam, this part describes the beginning of the actual fall of the house of Jeroboam. The narrator does it by reversing the promise that the prophet Ahijah had delivered at the time of his first encounter with Jeroboam (11:29–39). The prophet Ahijah appears on both scenes, located at the beginning and end of the Jeroboam narrative respectively. These two parts correspond to each other and signify together the purpose of the narrative, which is to depict how the rise and fall of Jeroboam was brought about.

After 1 Kings 13, the reader now expects to see how God's judgment on the house of Jeroboam will take place. Thus, as Fretheim notes, the reader knows far more than Jeroboam does about the fate he is now facing.[88] In this part of the narrative, the sickness of Abijah,[89] one of Jeroboam's sons, becomes an occasion through which Yahweh's will of judgment is delivered to the house of Jeroboam. This section is mainly comprised of two parts: Jeroboam's wife's visit to the prophet Ahijah (vv. 1–6), and Ahijah's "harsh" words for the house of Jeroboam (vv. 7–18); vv. 19–20 are the conclusion to the entire Jeroboam narrative. The second part (vv. 7–18) can be further divided into four subunits: accusations (vv. 7–9), the disaster to fall upon the house of Jeroboam (vv. 10–14), Israel to be uprooted (vv. 15–16), and a partial fulfillment of the prophet Ahijah's pronouncement (vv. 17–18).

The account begins with the phrase בָּעֵת הַהִיא "at that time" (v.1), which ties the following events to the previous events (1 Kgs 12:32—13:34) thematically as well as temporarily. More importantly, this adverbial phrase links the following account with the account of Ahijah's earlier prophecy (1 Kgs 11:29–39), which began with the same phrase (1 Kgs 11:29). This

---

88. Fretheim, *First and Second Kings*, 84.

89. It has been noted by scholars that the sons of Jeroboam and those of Aaron share the similar names: Jeroboam's sons—אֲבִיָּה ("Yah is father") and נָדָב ("generous, noble")—and two of Aaron's sons—נָדָב and אֲבִיהוּא ("He is father"). The significance of the same names is heightened by the fact that both Aaron and Jeroboam "made" golden calves. Whether the narrator intended this connection and what significance this connection might have is not obvious, however.

connection seems intentional in that the prophecy that follows reverses the promise that the prophet Ahijah had delivered in his earlier prophecy.[90] Unlike in his first encounter with Ahijah, Jeroboam now avoids direct contact with Ahijah and sends to him his wife, instead of himself, and that, in disguise.[91] This may betray the psychological distance between him and Ahijah and also "a pang of guilt" in him.[92]

The reversal of the fate of Jeroboam is further suggested in the common words used in both accounts: Jeroboam raised his יָד, "hand," against the king (11:26, 27), and the prophet Ahijah in his first encounter with Jeroboam told him to קַח־לְךָ, "take for yourself," עֲשָׂרָה, "ten," pieces of the garment (11:31). God said that he would "take" the kingdom out of Rehoboam's "hand" and give "ten" tribes to him (11:34–35). Jeroboam's "hand," however, was once withered, which symbolizes the withering of his power (13:4). Now in this counter-prophecy, Jeroboam tells his queen to "take ten" loaves in her "hand" (14:3), only to hear the harsh words spoken by the prophet Ahijah (14:18). These connections seem to intentionally signify the reversal of the fate of Jeroboam. What had been handed into the hand (or power) of Jeroboam through the prophet is now taken back from Jeroboam.

Sending his wife to Ahijah, Jeroboam has a vague hope of receiving a good message regarding the sickness of his son, Abijah, because he remembers that Ahijah had said good things of him before (v. 2). This time, however, the aged Ahijah is "sent to you with a harsh (קָשָׁה) message" (v. 6). Ahijah's "harsh" message begins with accusations (vv. 7–9). The oracular formula "Thus says Yahweh, the God of Israel" is found only once more in the Jeroboam narrative, in 11:31, which is another indicator of the parallels between the two oracles. The accusations are based on the promise and warning that had been given in 11:29–39, as some of the key words are repeated here: "tear" (v. 8; cf. 11:30, 31; 13:3, 5), "keep my commandments"

---

90. Walsh, *1 Kings*, 193.

91. For the motif of disguise either by or in the presence of a king (e.g., 1 Sam 28; 1 Kgs 22; 2 Chr 35; 1 Kgs 14), see Coggins, "On Kings and Disguises," 55–62, and Bodner, *Royal Drama*, 126–7. Bodner also notices the commonality between 1 Kings 11 and 14 in the shared motif of clothes. He argues, "Here, the wife's change of appearance is an attempt to stave off judgment against his house by deceiving that same prophet. It is entirely plausible that the biblical writer deploys these two completely different uses of clothing as a sign to illustrate the regression of Jeroboam's fortunes from riches to rags" (*Royal Drama*, 128).

92. Bodner, *Royal Drama*, 130. See also Knoppers, *Two Nations under God*, 2:82.

(v. 8; cf. 11:34, 38; 13:21), "walk" (vv. 8, 9; cf. 11:33, 38; 13:9, 10, 12, 16–17). Walsh states, "These and other allusions to the earlier oracle emphasize the contrast between Yahweh's approval of Jeroboam there and the condemnation here."[93] Also, the main accusation is directed against making "other gods and molten images" (v. 9), which refers back to Jeroboam's golden calves (12:26–31).

The judgment is directed to "the house of Jeroboam": every male will be "cut off from Jeroboam," and the house of Jeroboam will be burnt up until it is all gone (v. 10). This prophecy is fulfilled later through Baasha (15:29). The pronouncement of the child's death (Abijah) is clearly set in the context of judgment pronouncement (vv. 12–13). There is no doubt that the death of this child has a symbolic significance that shows the beginning of the "cutting off" of the house of Jeroboam. Thus Knoppers argues, "The demise of Jeroboam's son prefigures, even secures, the demise of Jeroboam's dynasty and kingdom."[94] Seow suspects that, from the fact that all Israel lamented over the death of Abijah, he might have been the heir to the throne of Jeroboam,[95] hence his death was "understood as symptomatic of an epidemic that is spreading in Jeroboam's kingdom."[96]

The oracle about Jeroboam's son Abijah demands some attention. Verse 13 says, "And all Israel shall mourn for him and bury him, for he alone of Jeroboam's family shall come to the grave, because in him something good was found toward the Lord God of Israel in the house of Jeroboam." Though, as Bodner states, "the narrator does not state whether the illness is a sign of divine judgment or the dark inevitability of human mortality,"[97] it is certain that this child's death is not the punishment for his own sin, but rather his death is depicted only in relation to God's judgment on the house of Jeroboam. Thus, this child who dies rather innocently becomes a symbol of the destruction of the house of Jeroboam. As Fretheim remarks, the mourning of all Israel over the death of the child "mirrors God's own response to all that has happened."[98] In this sense, this child shares some similarities with the man of God from Judah in chapter 13, and

---

93. Walsh, *1 Kings*, 196.

94. Knoppers, *Two Nations under God*, 2:10. For Knoppers's comparison between 2 Samuel 7:5–16 and 1 Kings 14:7–16, see Knoppers, *Two Nations under God*, 2:9–10.

95. Seow, "I & II Kings," III.

96. Bodner, *Royal Drama*, 120.

97. Bodner, *Royal Drama*, 123.

98. Fretheim, *First and Second Kings*, 86.

the connection may be suggested by the two common words "mourn" and "bury" (cf. 13:29–30). Just as the man of God was mourned for and buried and put in the grave, this son of Jeroboam will be mourned for and buried and come to the grave.

This link between the two deaths may be more significant than it looks. The narrator may have implied some resemblance in the symbolism of both deaths. Most scholars would say that these two scenes come from two different traditions. The deaths of the man of God from Judah and Abijah do appear entirely unrelated to each other. The positioning of these two deaths one after another, however, may be considered strategic within the overall narrative architecture. Arranging the deaths of these two figures might reveal intentionality in the structural design of the narrative. The man of God from Judah bore the disgrace, fulfilling his role as a symbol of Jeroboam, and likewise, the child, though being pronounced to have "something pleasing to Yahweh, the God of Israel," dies to symbolize the end of the house of Jeroboam.[99] These parallels may clarify the significance of the man of God's death in 1 Kings 13.

On the other hand, while vv. 10–14 pronounce the destruction of the house of Jeroboam, vv. 15–16 go one step further and pronounce the fall of the Northern Kingdom (cf. 2 Kgs 17:1–23). The judgment that is looming over the house of Jeroboam even extends to the entire Northern Kingdom. As Fretheim notices, it is "the first clear reference since Deuteronomy" to the fall of the Northern Kingdom.[100] The Deuteronomist's attribution of the destruction of the Northern Kingdom to the sin of Jeroboam is found in one of the key Deuteronomistic passages (2 Kgs 17:21–23):

> When he had torn Israel from the house of David, they made Jeroboam the son of Nebat king. Then Jeroboam drove Israel away from following Yahweh and made them commit a great sin. And the sons of Israel walked in all the sins of Jeroboam which he did; they did not depart from them, until Yahweh removed Israel from his sight, as he spoke through all his servants the prophets. So Israel was carried away into exile from their own land to Assyria until this day.

---

99. Walsh, *1 Kings*, 199. Further potential parallels between 1 Kings 13 and 14 are to be found in that the judgment will be executed through a king to be born (13:2 and 14:14). This king, unlike the son to be born prophesied in 13:2, is referring to a relatively imminent king, King Baasha.

100. Fretheim, *First and Second Kings*, 85.

THE FATE OF THE MAN OF GOD FROM JUDAH

The Deuteronomistic characteristics of this part of the Jeroboam narrative then are noticeable. Knoppers finds parallels between this part of the Jeroboam narrative and 2 Samuel 7:5–16:

> Drawing upon traditions dealing with Jeroboam's sick son, the Deuteronomist creates a mixed genre to address the fate of the kingdom entrusted to Jeroboam. In this regard, the heavily edited judgment oracles of 1 Kgs 14:7–11, 12–16 play a critical role in northern history analogous to the role of 2 Sam 7:5–16 in southern history. As the Deuteronomist links the fate of David, his seed, dynasty, temple, and people in 2 Sam 7:5–16, so he links the fate of Jeroboam, his son, dynasty, cultus, and people in 1 Kgs 14:7–16.[101]

These Deuteronomistic elements indicate that the Jeroboam narrative forms an integral part of the Deuteronomistic History.

In the rest of the text, Jeroboam's wife goes back to Tirzah, and the child dies as was predicted by Ahijah, and they (all Israel) bury him and laments over him "according to the word that Yahweh had spoken through his servant the prophet Ahijah" (v. 18; cf. vv. 12–13). And vv. 19–20 conclude the whole Jeroboam narrative with a standard "regnal formula."

Conclusion

Ahijah's second prophecy described in this account reverses his first prophecy where God promised Jeroboam a sure house. The employment of some key words that were used in the first prophecy links this prophecy with the earlier prophecy and contributes to the literary purpose of this part, which is to describe the reversal of the fate of Jeroboam. Ahijah's oracle does not concern the fate of Jeroboam only, but it goes further and announces judgment on Israel (vv. 15–16). The death of Jeroboam's son, Abijah, signals the fall of the house of Jeroboam.

The Theme of the Jeroboam Narrative

So far, I have discussed individual units that constitute the Jeroboam narrative and showed how the narrator artfully arranged them. We now turn to the discussion of the theme of the Jeroboam narrative. For Marvin A. Sweeney, 1 Kings 11:41—14:20 "presents an account of the establishment

---

101. Knoppers, *Two Nations under God*, 2:9–10.

of the northern kingdom of Israel as a consequence of Solomon's apostasy following his death."[102] Thus the Jeroboam narrative depicts "the revolt of the northern tribes and the establishment of the northern kingdom of Israel under the rule of Jeroboam ben Nebat in 1 Kgs 12:1—14:20."[103] Sweeney's view reflects an important element of the Jeroboam narrative, that is, the division of the kingdom, but it does not explain the purpose of the Jeroboam narrative, especially in relation to the main character Jeroboam.

As we saw earlier in the outline (in the section titled "Overall Structure of the Jeroboam Narrative"), Ahijah's prophecies paralleled at the beginning and end of the Jeroboam narrative show that this extended coverage of the first king of the Northern Kingdom is depicting the rise and fall of the house of Jeroboam. At the center of the Jeroboam narrative is placed Jeroboam's cultic inventions, which describes the turning point of Jeroboam's career. What is notable is that Jeroboam's personal rise is closely tied with the beginning of the Northern Kingdom, and that, in the same way, with the announcement of Jeroboam's fall, the end of the Northern Kingdom is also pronounced (1 Kgs 14:15–16). Thus in the mind of the narrator, Jeroboam is not just the first king of the Northern Kingdom, but he is the archetypal evil ruler, *Unheilsherrscher*, through whom the sin of apostasy was brought into the Northern Kingdom, and then all the subsequent kings of the kingdom repeated the sin. Thus, Cohn's statement is suitable here:

> It is not surprising that Jeroboam, infamous as the arch-apostate to whom every subsequent king of Israel is compared, should be the subject of an extended literary treatment. For he presents a difficult theological problem for the Judahite historian who included his "biography" in Kings. Although Jeroboam had successfully supplanted the reign of the Davidic dynasty over the northern tribes, his kingdom ultimately failed. The author, therefore, must explain both why God allowed Jeroboam to inherit the greatest part of the kingdom promised to the descendants of David, but also why Jeroboam's dynasty and his kingdom, having been so favored, came to ruin. The historian accomplishes these two aims by pausing long enough over the career of Jeroboam to depict his transformation from God's chosen instrument to his despised enemy.[104]

---

102. Sweeney, *I & II Kings*, 161.
103. Sweeney, *I & II Kings*, 161.
104. Cohn, "Literary Technique," 25.

THE FATE OF THE MAN OF GOD FROM JUDAH

Therefore, understanding the Jeroboam narrative merely as a report of the division of the Davidic kingdom does not suffice as the theme of this literary unit. The narrator carefully constructed the narrative so as to depict the rise and fall of Jeroboam. By depicting Jeroboam's transformation from someone who received Yahweh's promise of "a sure house" (1 Kgs 11:38) to the culprit who introduced the destructive sin of idolatry into the Northern Kingdom, the narrator warns the reader of the consequence of apostasy and also justifies the fall of the Kingdom.

1 KINGS 12:32—13:34 IN THE JEROBOAM NARRATIVE

In this chapter I demonstrated that the Jeroboam narrative is a tightly formulated literary unit and that identifying the literary connections among the texts helps the interpretation of the individual parts of the Jeroboam narrative. In the previous discussion I excluded 1 Kings 12:32—13:34 and here will briefly summarize the conversation between 1 Kings 12:32—13:34 and the rest of the Jeroboam narrative. The purpose of this discussion is to clarify that 1 Kings 13 can be properly interpreted only in relation to the rest of the Jeroboam narrative and also to support my earlier conclusion that 1 Kings 13 has been placed in its current location to serve its function in the Jeroboam narrative.

The Literary Connections of the Story of the Man of God (1 Kings 12:32—13:34) with Other Parts of the Jeroboam Narrative

The literary connections between 1 Kings 12:32—13:34 and the rest of the Jeroboam narrative are as follows. Some of them have already been noted before, but they are included here and discussed in relation to 1 Kings 12:32—13:34.

First, the phrase בית דוד "the house of David" (1 Kgs 13:2): This phrase appears in the earlier parts of the Jeroboam narrative (1 Kgs 12:19, 20, 26), mostly in the contexts of the northern tribes' rebellion against the Davidic dynasty. Thus, the man of God's prophecy that "a son will be born to the house of David" implies that God's mercy will not leave the house of David and also betrays a Judean polemic against the Northern Kingdom. The phrase occurs once more in the second prophecy of Ahijah to refer to Yahweh's giving the ten tribes to Jeroboam: ". . . and tore the kingdom away from the house of David and gave it to you" (1 Kgs 14:8). Thus "the house of David" is portrayed as being in tension with "the house of Jeroboam" (13:34; 14:10 (x2), 13, 14). It is not surprising to see the phrase in the story where God's judgment on the house of Jeroboam is depicted.

Second, דבר יהוה/האלהים "the word of Yahweh (or God)": These phrases appear not only in 1 Kings 13 but throughout the Jeroboam narrative (1 Kgs 12:15, 22, 24; 13:1, 2, 3, 5, 9, 17, 18, 20, 26, 32; 14:11, 18). The repetitive use of the phrase reveals the narrator's theology that Yahweh *speaks* and accomplishes his words through all human events in history. The word of Yahweh is emphasized the most in 1 Kings 13 to visualize the importance of keeping God's command and hence to maximize the seriousness of Jeroboam's deserting the command of God.

Third, the rise and fall of Jeroboam is depicted by the use of the key words such as יָד "hand" (11:26, 27, 31, 34, 35; 13:4, 6; 14:3) and תָּפַשׂ "to grasp" (11:30) or "to seize" (13:4). As I previously discussed it (in the section titled "Ahijah's Prophecy and Solomon's Reaction"), the narrator, using these words, describes the reversal of the fate of Jeroboam. The withering of Jeroboam's hand in 1 Kings 13 is a very symbolic event that shows the turn of the fate of Jeroboam.

Fourth, some Deuteronomistic key words link 1 Kings 13 with earlier parts of the Jeroboam narrative as well as other key passages of the Deuteronomistic History: צוה "to command" or "commandment(s)" (11:38; 13:9, 21; cf. 11:10–11), שָׁמַר "to keep (commandments)" (11:34, 38; 13:21; 14:8), and הלך בדרך "to walk in the way" (11:33, 38; 13:10, 12, 17, etc.). These key words are an indicator of the Deuteronomist's hand in 1 Kings 13 and show that 1 Kings 13 contributes to the overall theological schema of the Deuteronomistic History.

Fifth, the vocabulary related to God's judgments appears mostly in chapter 13 and chapter 14: מות "to die" or "to kill" (13:24, 26, 31; 14:11, 12, 17), קבר "to bury" or "grave" (11:43; 13:22, 29, 30, 31; 14:14, 18), and ספד "to mourn" (13:29, 30; 14:13, 18). These words are used to show God's judgment on the man of God and on the house of Jeroboam in 1 Kings 13 and 14. The fate of Jeroboam has made its turn downhill.

These literary connections bind the different parts of the Jeroboam narrative together and contribute to the overall depiction of the rise and fall of the house of Jeroboam. They display the narrator's literary skills and artistry. Bodner correctly evaluates that the Jeroboam narrative displays "a literary achievement of great subtlety and a highly complex characterization."[105]

---

105. Bodner, *Royal Drama*, 1.

THE FATE OF THE MAN OF GOD FROM JUDAH

The identification of the literary connections assist in the proper interpretation of 1 Kings 13.

The Location and Function of the Story of the Man of God (1 Kings 12:32—13:34) in the Jeroboam Narrative

The location and function of this narrative in the Jeroboam narrative is significant. While 1 Kings 12:26-31 provides a turning point of Jeroboam's career and identifies "the sin of Jeroboam" as making golden calves (vv. 26-30) and making high places and non-Levitical priests (v. 31), 1 Kings 12:32—13:34 continues the theme of the sin of Jeroboam, but by focusing on the events at Bethel, the narrator illustrates the fall of Jeroboam.[106] Cohn notes the location of this narrative in the Jeroboam narrative and says, "At the height of Jeroboam's career and at the center of the chiasmus, the oracle of the man of God from Judah ominously prophesies the end of his cult at the hands of Josiah."[107] The function of the narrative is not, however, limited to the condemnation of his cult but is more about depicting Jeroboam's disobedience and recalcitrance; Jeroboam not only left the way of Yahweh, but did not turn away from his evil way. Without the story of the man of God, the narrator could not have presented persuasively why Jeroboam had to be condemned so much. Jeroboam refused to turn away from his evil way despite the two signs: the sign of the torn altar, and the sign of the death of the man of God.

Therefore, Jeroboam is portrayed as the arch-apostate and the sin of Jeroboam the archetype of the sins of every subsequent king of Israel; thus the cause of the destruction of the Northern Kingdom is to be found in the epidemical influence of the sin of Jeroboam (1 Kgs 14:15-16; cf. 1 Kgs 12:30). Von Rad remarks, "The doom of the northern kingdom is really

---

106. Sweeney understands the narrative (1 Kgs 12:32—13:34) to be a polemic against Jeroboam's appointment of non-Levitical priests. He notes that the narrative "depicts Jeroboam's attempt to offer incense at the Beth El altar a prerogative reserved only for the high priest (Exod 30:1-10; see also Num 16; 17:5; 2 Chr 26:16-21; Lev 10:1-3)" (*I & II Kings*, 176). This observation is insightful in part because the narrative depicts Jeroboam who offers incense, not being a high priest (12:33b—13:1), and 1 Kgs 13:33-34 mentions specifically Jeroboam's appointment of non-Levitical priests as a cause for the fall of the house of Jeroboam. Jeroboam's appointing non-Levitical priests, however, is also depicted in 1 Kgs 12:31, and it does not provide the lens through which to read the whole narrative. It is hard to consider the whole narrative as a polemic against appointing non-Levitical priests.

107. Cohn, "Literary Technique," 25.

A Literary Analysis of the Jeroboam Narrative

sealed with the first sin, the apostasy of Jeroboam I. The stereotyped observation about the real guilt of all the other kings is that they walked in the sin of Jeroboam."[108] Sweeney also states that Jeroboam's "apostasy earns him the hardest condemnation in the DtrH as the monarch who set in motion the pattern of evil behavior on the part of all northern kings such apostasy ultimately caused the destruction of northern Israel according to the DtrH theological schema (see esp. 2 Kgs 17)."[109]

CONCLUSION

In this chapter I have broadened the range of my study to the entire Jeroboam narrative. This study used a holistic and synchronic approach to the Jeroboam narrative, giving special attention to the narrator's literary artistry. I argued that 1 Kings 11:26—14:20 should be considered a literary unit that has been arranged in a concentric structure and that the Jeroboam narrative as a whole describes the rise and fall of Jeroboam. The constituent subunits of the Jeroboam narrative are in frequent communication with one another by means of repeated motifs and key words. A proper interpretation of 1 Kings 13, therefore, demands the reader understand the text of 1 Kings 13 in relation to the entire Jeroboam narrative, which supports my earlier conclusion that the theme of the 1 Kings 13 should be delineated in its literary context and in relation to the fate of Jeroboam.[110]

In his depiction of the rise and fall of Jeroboam, the narrator describes the transformation of the first king of the Northern Kingdom from a chosen servant of Yahweh to the main culprit, which in turn foreshadows the tragic fate of the kingdom itself and justifies God's judgment of the kingdom. In line with this framework, 1 Kings 13, which is a dramatization of the sin and fall of Jeroboam, plays an essential role in shaping the overall theme of the Jeroboam narrative. This point lays a foundation for the discussion in chapter 4,[111] where I shall argue that the Jeroboam narrative as a literary unit constitutes an integral part of the Deuteronomistic History in contributing to the formation of the Deuteronomist's theology.

---

108. Von Rad, *Studies in Deuteronomy*, 83.

109. Sweeney, *I & II Kings*, 159.

110. For my discussion on the theme of the story, go to the section titled "The Certainty of God's Judgment on the House of Jeroboam" in chapter 2.

111. For this, see the sections titled "The Deuteronomist's View on the Role of the Prophets" and "The Story's Literary Effects on the Reader" in chapter 4.

4

A Theological Approach to the Jeroboam Narrative

INTRODUCTION

THE PURPOSE OF THIS chapter is to address the theological concepts that the Jeroboam narrative (especially 1 Kings 13) expresses. The moral or theological implications of 1 Kings 13 have discomforted many readers; it seems great injustice was done to the innocent man of God from Judah, and the characterization of God in the chapter is harsh and even violent toward the man of God. Hence J. Gray judged the chapter to be containing a "mechanical and a-moral conception of the operation of the word of God."[1] My discussion in this chapter shows that such a view does not do justice to the theology of the text.

In this chapter I will delineate the theological concepts found in the Jeroboam narrative and how they fit into the larger theological framework of the Deuteronomist. I use the term "the Deuteronomist" to refer to the one who is responsible for the final form of the text. To this end, I will, first, review briefly several theological problems that biblical scholars have raised regarding 1 Kings 13 and then review theological frameworks that some of the main biblical scholars have suggested for the Book of Kings

---

1. Gray, *I & II Kings*, 294.

A Theological Approach to the Jeroboam Narrative

and the Deuteronomistic History.[2] I will show how the Jeroboam narrative—and 1 Kings 13 specifically—fits into these theological frameworks and argue that the Jeroboam narrative is to be understood as an integral part of the Deuteronomistic History.

This discussion will highlight the important role that prophets played in the history of Israel. Especially, I will revisit and expand on the theme of prophets' suffering that they had to bear in the course of fulfilling their prophetic duties (ch. 2). This will revise the view that the chapter presents "a mechanical and a-moral conception of the operation of the word of God."[3] Second, I will expand on the concept of prophecy and fulfillment, as presented by the Deuteronomist(s), and investigate further the Deuteronomist's perspective on the interrelationship between God's will and human's decisions. Lastly, I will discuss the literary effects that the Deuteronomist might have designed for the intended reader. I would argue that the story, as has been configured and presented by the narrator, demands a particular response from the reader, that is, repentance.

THEOLOGICAL THEMES OF THE JEROBOAM NARRATIVE

Theological Problems Raised Regarding 1 Kings 13

The evaluations by the past scholarship regarding the theology of 1 Kings 13 have been generally negative and somewhat harsh. Gressmann, for example, states conclusively about 1 Kings 13: "Yahweh is reduced to a magician, the word of God to a magic formula which demands unconditional submission. The smallest deviation, no matter how understandable, brings death ... This legend is, viewed religiously and morally, of little value."[4] A similarly degrading evaluation was made by Mauchline, who says, "The mechanical, unethical relationship of the prophet to his message, as exemplified in the second part of the story, is indicative of an immature outlook."[5] Robinson also says, "The story ... shows him [Yahweh] as applying retributive justice in a narrowly mechanical and impersonal way; the actions of a harsh tyrant ... the view of God's nature underlying this

---

2. Noth, von Rad, Cross, Provan, and Brueggemann. Marvin A. Sweeney includes 1 Kings 13 in his discussion on the Josianic edition of the DtrH (*I & II Kings*, 15–20).

3. Gray, *I & II Kings*, 294.

4. Gressmann, *Die älteste Geschichtsschreibung*, 248–49.

5. Mauchline, "I and II Kings," 344.

THE FATE OF THE MAN OF GOD FROM JUDAH

chapter is crude and insensitive."[6] Along similar lines, John Gray judges that the chapter betrays the Deuteronomist's "mechanical view of prophecy and its authentication familiar from Deuteronomy."[7]

It is admitted that the story in 1 Kings 13, when read from an ethical/moral point of view, can raise many questions and that God's treatment of the innocent man of God looks unfair. I would argue, however, that these views result from a failure to recognize the nature of the story as prophetic symbolic actions, as already discussed in a previous chapter (ch. 2), and also the Deuteronomist's theological emphases on the special role of prophets as agents of the word of Yahweh.

Theological Approaches to the Book of Kings and the Deuteronomistic History

Most scholars would agree that the Book of Kings is a theological writing rather than "exact writing of history."[8] Thus the book reflects the author's particular theological perspective. At the beginning of his commentary on the "The Division of the Kingdom," Fretheim writes, "while a coherent history of the divided kingdoms is sketched, the narrator is interested fundamentally in religious and theological matters. Prophets will play a particularly prominent role in what follows."[9] As Fretheim correctly states, the narrator describes the history of both kingdoms with his distinct theological perspective, and the prophets' role stands out in the historical narrative as the reader reads it carefully. In this part of our study, therefore, we will focus on the theological ideas that are highlighted in the text.

Most scholars ascribe 1 Kings 13 and the entire Jeroboam narrative to the Josianic (Deuteronomistic) editor of the Deuteronomistic History (e.g., F. M. Cross, John Gray, Gary Knoppers, T. Fretheim, and M. Sweeney). Even though this view is a generally accepted one, it would not mean that the whole Jeroboam narrative *in its present form* was finished by the

---

6. Robinson, *The First Book of Kings*, 162.

7. Gray, *I & II Kings*, 294. I. Benzinger argues that this story reflects a rather mechanistic concept of prophetism in later Judaism (*Die Bücher der Könige*, 90–93).

8. Von Rad attends to a distinctive nature of the Deuteronomistic history in that the author exercises the practice of a historian in making a constant reference to his sources, and at the same time, it has a "unique theological stamp on it" (*Studies in Deuteronomy*, 74).

9. Fretheim, *First and Second Kings*, 70.

A Theological Approach to the Jeroboam Narrative

hand of the Josianic editor. Rather, it has been noted by multiple scholars that the view of the exilic editor is clearly discernible in the text.[10] In any case, we will not be able to clearly tell which editor is responsible for what portion of the Jeroboam narrative, though such attempts should not be abandoned completely. It is not my concern, therefore, in this discussion to reconstruct the intention of any particular Deuteronomistic editor of the Jeroboam narrative, but rather to identify theological themes contained in the present form of the narrative, which also reflects the concerns of the exilic community.

Many scholars tried to delineate theological themes that run through the Deuteronomistic History, and the Book of Kings has been always important in these discussions. Martin Noth, for example, argued that the Deuteronomistic author had addressed his work to the exiles and explained and justified that the exile was God's judgment on his people for their sins.[11] Gerhard von Rad, while accepting the exilic composition of the Deuteronomistic History, added a new dimension to Noth's understanding. He noted the motif of judgment that came as a result of breaking covenant law but also argued that the theme of grace was also to be found in the Deuteronomistic History, especially in the Book of Kings. According to von Rad, the theme of grace is found in God's eternal promise to David, and hence the ground of hope was present, which is presented clearly in the Nathan's oracle to David in 2 Samuel 7.[12]

H. W. Wolff agrees with von Rad in broad lines but takes a step further and argues that the theme of a call for repentance is to be repeatedly found in important Deuteronomistic passages that promise that, when Israel cries out to God and turns away from her apostate ways, God will restore them to his covenant.[13] Walter Brueggemann puts these ideas together (those of Noth, von Rad, and Wolff) and adds one more element, the motif of "good" (טוֹב)."[14] He shows that the motif of "good" is found throughout the Deuteronomistic History and argues that God's good word to David provides a basis for the summons to repentance. Thus God's "goodness" becomes

---

10. Lemke, "The Way of Obedience," 310–26.
11. Noth, *Deuteronomistic History*, 145.
12. Von Rad, *Studies in Deuteronomy*, 85.
13. Wolff, "Kerygma," 62–78.
14. Brueggemann, "Kerygma," 387–402.

THE FATE OF THE MAN OF GOD FROM JUDAH

a motivation of repentance. Here the two motifs, "good" (טוֹב) and "turn" (שׁוּב), are closely linked with each other in the Deuteronomistic History.[15]

On the other hand, F. M. Cross, in his discussion on the structure of the Deuteronomistic History, synthesized the results of previous studies on the subject and argued for two editions of the Deuteronomistic history, Dtr[1] (the Josianic edition of the Deuteronomistic History) and Dtr[2] (the Exilic edition). Then he argued that an editor wrote "in the era of Josiah as a programmatic document of his reform and of his revival of the Davidic state,"[16] and another editor, about 550 BC, "not only updated the history by adding a chronicle of events subsequent to Josiah's reign," but "also attempted to transform the work into a sermon on history addressed to Judaean exiles."[17] For the Josianic edition, which covers most of the Book of Kings up to King Josiah, Cross argues that two themes are operative: the theme of the sin of Jeroboam and the theme of "the faithfulness of David and Josiah."[18] The exilic editor, on the other hand, blames the fall of Jerusalem on the wickedness of Manasseh (2 Kgs 21:7–14) but emphasizes that Yahweh will not forget the covenant of their fathers and the promise of return from their captivity if they would repent (Deut 4:27–31; 30:1–10).[19]

More recently, McConville, in his discussion on the theology of Deuteronomy and its influence on Joshua through 2 Kings, traced scholarly discussions on the tension that may exist between the themes of promise/grace and law/judgment in the Deuteronomistic History.[20] He does not attribute these two conflicting themes to different layers or different Deuteronomists but to one author, who showed through "the subtle ironies of the literature" that, although God brought judgment on Israel for her failure in

15. Brueggemann, "Kerygma," 401–2.

16. Cross, *Myth and Hebrew Bible*, 287.

17. Cross, *Myth and Hebrew Bible*, 287.

18. The optimistic tone regarding the house of David occurs more than once in the Jeroboam narrative (1 Kgs 11:13; 13:2–3). J. Gordon McConville argues "a qualification of the condemnation of Solomon" ("for the sake of Jerusalem, which I have chosen" [1 Kgs 11:13]) leaves "a door open for the later fulfillment of the Davidic promise in Judah" and that the prophecy of the reform by Josiah in 1 Kings 13:2–3 looks forward to the future with hope (*Grace in the End*, 79). On the other hand, McConville adds his criticism of Cross's theory. For this, see McConville, *Grace in the End*, 80–82, and "Narrative and Meaning," 31–49.

19. For more views on the composition of the Deuteronomistic History, see Provan, *Hezekiah and the Books of Kings* (1988); Smend, "Das Gesetz und die Völker," 494–509; Hoffmann, *Reform und Reformen* (1980).

20. McConville, *Grace in the End*, 65–122.

A Theological Approach to the Jeroboam Narrative

keeping God's covenant, God's overpowering grace made them survive as a nation. He concludes that the two books of Kings are best understood "in a context in which temple and monarchy have disappeared" and that they thus "have (in common with some Psalms, especially Ps 89) the particular characteristic that they reflect on the meaning of the promises concerning David and Zion in the light of their apparent dereliction."[21] According to McConville, however, Noth's pessimistic view is wrong because "the prayer of Solomon at the dedication holds out hope that the covenantal relationship between God and Israel may survive even this cataclysm (1 Ki 8:46–53)."[22] Therefore, for McConville, the two books of Kings "issue a call to repent and leave open the question how God might then respond in grace."[23]

THE DEUTERONOMIST'S THEOLOGY OF THE WORD OF YAHWEH

The above review is significant for the current study of the theology of the Jeroboam narrative. In this part of our discussion, we will, first, focus on von Rad's emphasis on the word of Yahweh in his coverage on "the Deuteronomistic theology of history in the Books of Kings."[24] Von Rad focused on the interrelationship between the word of Yahweh and the history of both kingdoms. He showed that the catastrophes of 721 BC and 587 BC are simply the fulfillment of the word of Yahweh when Israel and Judah had refused or failed to keep "the ordinances, commandments, and statutes of the Yahweh."[25] Here the element of obedience is an important "fundamental element in the Deuteronomistic presentation of the history."[26] The kings failed to "trust" (בָּטַח, 2 Kgs 18:5) Yahweh and to be "perfect with Yahweh" (שָׁלֵם עִם יְהוָה, 1 Kgs 11:4; 15:3, 14) in keeping his commandments; while the element of obedience constitutes the "subjective" aspect of the Deuteronomist's history, a more "objective" element is the manner of the divine

---

21. McConville, *Grace in the End*, 89.
22. McConville, *Grace in the End*, 89.
23. McConville, *Grace in the End*, 90.
24. Von Rad, *Studies in Deuteronomy*, 74–91.
25. These three words in various combinations frequently occur throughout the Book of Kings (cf. 1 Kgs 2:3; 6:12; 8:58; 9:4; 11:33, 38; 14:8; 18:8; 2 Kgs 17:13, 34, 37; 18:6; 23:3).
26. Von Rad, *Studies in Deuteronomy*, 78.

THE FATE OF THE MAN OF GOD FROM JUDAH

intervention in history,[27] that is, Yahweh intervenes actively in the history of Israel by speaking to his people.

Von Rad's point is well summarized in the following statement: "There exists an inter-relationship between the word of Jahweh and history in the sense that Jahweh's word, once uttered, reaches its goal under all circumstances in history by virtue of the power inherent in it."[28] This interrelationship is clearly visible in the prophecy and fulfillment structure in the Book of Kings, which von Rad calls "a theological schema."[29] The repeated mentions of prophecies and their fulfillment throughout the Book of Kings are hardly ignorable and demand the attention of the reader. Von Rad then provides a list of them from the Book of Kings:[30]

1. 2 Sam 7:13—1 Kgs 8:20
2. 1 Kgs 11:29ff.—1 Kgs 12:15b
3. 1 Kgs 13—2 Kgs 23:16-18
4. 1 Kgs 14:6ff.—1 Kgs 15:29
5. 1 Kgs 16:1ff.—1 Kgs 16:12
6. Josh 6:26—1 Kgs 16:34
7. 1 Kgs 22:17—1 Kgs 22:35f.
8. 1 Kgs 21:21f.—1 Kgs 21:27-29
9. 2 Kgs 1:6—2 Kgs 1:17
10. 2 Kgs 21:10ff.—2 Kgs 24:2 and 2 Kgs 23:26
11. 2 Kgs 22:15ff.—2 Kgs 23:30

Therefore, there seems to be no doubt that this theological schema provides the Book of Kings with a theological structure and that the Deuteronomist had it in mind when he was shaping the Book of Kings. Von Rad says, "In actual fact, in this connection the Deuteronomist demands the keenest attentiveness on the part of his readers: they are to discern this all-prevailing correspondence between the divine word spoken by prophets and the historical events even in those cases where notice is not expressly drawn to it."[31]

27. Von Rad, *Studies in Deuteronomy*, 78.
28. Von Rad, *Studies in Deuteronomy*, 78.
29. Von Rad, *Studies in Deuteronomy*, 78–80.
30. Von Rad, *Studies in Deuteronomy*, 78–81.
31. Von Rad, *Studies in Deuteronomy*, 81.

A Theological Approach to the Jeroboam Narrative

Then, it seems natural to ask why this theological schema was so important to the Deuteronomist; why did he, as he was shaping this historical writing, want to emphasize the power of the word of Yahweh to such an extent? Von Rad gives an answer to this question; it was to speak of "Jahweh immanent in history, acting in judgment or mercy."[32] That is to say, Yahweh was immanent in the history of Israel through his spoken words. This theological emphasis highlights the creative power of the words of Yahweh which are fulfilled without fail in history.[33] The Deuteronomist's theological stance is that "the history of the two kingdoms is simply the will of Jahweh and the word of Jahweh actualized in history."[34] Then, the purpose of this theological work was to show Yahweh's active intervention in the history of Israel and Judah. The way in which Yahweh intervenes the history of Israel is through his words, which, I believe, comes to its partial expression in 2 Kings 17:13:

> Yahweh warned Israel and Judah by every prophet (and) every seer, saying, "Turn back from your wicked way, and observe my commandments and my laws, according to all the teaching that I commanded your fathers and that I transmitted to you *through my servants the prophets.*"[35] (Italics added.)

That Yahweh's will spoken out in the form of the word of Yahweh is actualized without fail in history becomes a clear message to the readers that their current situation is the consequence of their and their fatahers' disobedience to the word of Yahweh. Conversely, since Israel and Judah are suffering the punishment of their disobedience to the word of Yahweh, they could find a hope of a future in another word of Yahweh, that is, Yahweh's promise to David through Nathan in 2 Samuel 7. This prophetic tradition, which von Rad judges "wholly undeuteronomistic," forms another theological dimension in the Deuteronomistic History. He sees the "judging and destroying" function (that is, as law) of the word of Yahweh fused with the "saving and forgiving" function (that is, as gospel) of the word of Yahweh

---

32. Von Rad, *Studies in Deuteronomy*, 83.
33. Von Rad, *Studies in Deuteronomy*, 83.
34. Von Rad, *Studies in Deuteronomy*, 83.
35. The expression "my servants the prophets" in slight variation appears across the prophetical books of the Hebrew Bible, mostly in 2 Kings and Jeremiah (2 Kgs 9:7; 17:13, 23; 21:10; 24:2; Ezra 9:11; Jer 7:25; 25:4; 26:5; 29:19; 35:15; 44:4; Ezek 38:17; Dan 9:6, 10; Amos 3:7; Zech 1:6).

THE FATE OF THE MAN OF GOD FROM JUDAH

in the Deuteronomistic presentation of the history of Judah.[36] The Nathan promise for David runs through the history of Judah and remains a hope of future, as is shown in the brief mention of Jehoiachin's exaltation at the end of the Book of Kings (2 Kgs 25:27–30).

The Deuteronomist's View on the Role of the Prophets

Von Rad delineated the theology of the word of Yahweh in the Book of Kings clearly by showing how the history of Israel was shaped by the theological notion of the interrelationship between the word of Yahweh and its fulfillment in the history.[37] That said, however, one thing that was not fully articulated in his treatment is the role of the prophets of Yahweh. Considering that the narrator sees history as developing from the word of Yahweh, I cannot emphasize enough the importance of the agents through whom the word of Yahweh was spoken and the role that they played in the history of Israel, which I now turn to in the following discussion.

Our review of von Rad's treatment of the theology of the Book of Kings is relevant to our discussion. 1 Kings 13 and, more broadly, the Jeroboam narrative fit into the Deuteronomist's theological framework better than they seem to at first glance. It is notable that prophetic activity begins to multiply in the Jeroboam narrative in contrast to the Solomonic narrative and that most events in the Jeroboam narrative are directed by and correspond to the prophets' words. Walsh comments on this phenomenon,

> In 1 Kings 1:1—11:25, Yahweh speaks four times to Solomon. The divine word does not dominate or direct the story but acts more as a commentary on preceding events and a warning about the future. With the appearance of Jeroboam in 11:26, however, the word of Yahweh takes on a much greater role. It is central to five of the seven major sections of the Jeroboam story, and its power directs the plot at each step. In contrast to Solomon, though, Yahweh never addresses Jeroboam directly. The word comes to him through prophetic figures. This points forward to the major role that prophets and men of God will play in the subsequent stories of the kings.[38]

---

36. Von Rad, *Studies in Deuteronomy*, 89.

37. Regarding the theme of promise and fulfillment, see von Rad, "Deuteronomic Theology," 208–14; Würthwein, "Prophetische Wort und Geschichte, 399–411; Weippert, "'Histories' and 'History,'" 46–61.

38. Walsh, *1 Kings*, 204. Yahweh's interactions with Solomon are direct and is done

A Theological Approach to the Jeroboam Narrative

The phenomenon is indeed notable in the Jeroboam narrative: (1) Jeroboam's rise along with the secession of the northern tribes is proclaimed through Ahijah (11:29–39); (2) the secession of the northern tribes is approved of and supported by Yahweh through Shemaiah (12:22–24); (3) the destruction of the Bethel altar is predicted by the man of God from Judah and is confirmed by the old prophet of Bethel (13:2, 30); and (4) last of all, the fall of Jeroboam's house is proclaimed by Ahijah (14:1–16). The sudden increase of the prophetic words in the Jeroboam narrative, along with the heavy emphasis on the word of Yahweh in 1 Kings 13, reflects the Deuteronomist's theology of the word of Yahweh, which becomes more obvious in the rest of the books of Kings. The word of Yahweh in all this *decisively* shapes the human events throughout the Jeroboam narrative.[39] In addition, the prophets' words do not speak only about the times of Jeroboam but go further and predict the events of the distant future: The man of God's condemnation of the Bethel altar goes on to predict Josiah's reformation work in the northern territories some three hundred and fifty years later (2 Kgs 23), thus forming a prophecy and fulfillment correspondence between the time of Jeroboam I and the time of Josiah. Also, in 1 Kings 14, we see that Ahijah's condemnation of Jeroboam's house goes on to predict the fall of Samaria (1 Kgs 14:15–16).[40]

Thus, the Deuteronomist's theology is clearly discernible in the Jeroboam narrative. Von Rad argues that Ahijah's prophecy (11:29–39) "stands entirely within the context of the specifically Deuteronomistic question as to Jahweh's plans with the heirs to the throne and kingdom of David."[41] Especially, 1 Kings 11:36 contains the combined form of the Deuteronomistic theology of the cult-place, Yahweh's "name," and the Nathan

---

not through prophets throughout Solomon's life (1 Kgs 3:5–14; 6:11–13; 9:2–9;11:11–13); a prophet's proclaiming the word of Yahweh in the Book of Kings does not occur until Ahijah's encounter with Jeroboam (11:29–39). Nathan plays a role in making Solomon king in chapter 1, but his role as a prophet does not appear there. The prophet's role as the messenger of Yahweh is absent. The absence of prophetic activity during Solomon's reign hints at Solomon's negative aspects for some scholars. Bodner comments, "After 1 Kings 1 Nathan is not heard from again, and once Solomon secures the throne, prophets are conspicuously absent, leading one to speculate that such voices are not particularly welcome in his kingdom. Indeed, as Solomon's empire expands prophetic involvement shrinks to nothing, causing one to think that the king is more interested in profits than prophets" (*Royal Drama*, 27).

39. Fretheim, *First and Second Kings*, 70.
40. Blenkinsopp, *History of Prophecy*, 164.
41. Von Rad, *Studies in Deuteronomy*, 81–82, footnote 1.

prophecy in 2 Samuel 7.⁴² The matter of obedience of the king whom Yahweh appointed over Israel is also emphasized in the repeated key words such as "to command" or "commandment" (vv. 9 and 21). It all shows that the Deuteronomist's theology is deeply embedded in this story and that the Jeroboam narrative as a whole is an integral component of the Deuteronomistic History rather than a discrete or foreign composition that was inserted into the overall Deuteronomistic History. If the Deuteronomist was showing "a process of history which is formed by the word of Jahweh continually intervening in judgment and salvation and directed towards a fulfillment,"⁴³ we see the same emphasis operating in the Jeroboam narrative. The history-shaping power of the word of Yahweh is predominant in the Jeroboam narrative.

The Prophet as a Sign (מוֹפֵת)

This phenomenal role assigned to prophets, I would argue, finds one of its most extreme forms in 1 Kings 13. The man of God's commission as the messenger of the word of Yahweh deserves special attention. The man of God from Judah delivers and proclaims the word of Yahweh, and he even dies in the course of fulfilling his prophetic commission, which in turn becomes a warning to Jeroboam in the story. Thus, not only his message but the man of God himself becomes a *sign* (מוֹפֵת) for Jeroboam, and the whole story illustrates the importance of obeying the word of Yahweh. The man of God's fate as a messenger of Yahweh thus includes suffering, which is in this case his death and not being buried in his father's grave.

Many instances of a prophet becoming a sign (מוֹפֵת) for others (kings and the people) are to be found in other parts of the Hebrew Bible (Isa 8:18; 20:3; Ezek 12:6, 11; 24:24, 27; Zech 3:8). Isaiah says he and his children "are the signs (אֹתוֹת) and portents (מֹפְתִים) in Israel from Yahweh of hosts" (Isa 8:18). Ezekiel is another, and a better, example of becoming a sign for his people; he is commanded by Yahweh to perform a series of symbolic actions, and he not only performs those actions but is himself called a sign (מוֹפֵת, Ezek 12:6, 11; 24:24, 27). In these symbolic actions, the prophet functions as "a living image of God's judgment and the people's fate,"⁴⁴ and

---

42. Von Rad, *Studies in Deuteronomy*, 85.
43. Von Rad, *Studies in Deuteronomy*, 91.
44. Davis, *Swallowing the Scroll*, 83.

in that sense, "The medium has become the message."⁴⁵ The prophet's tragedy or suffering (Ezek 24:15–27) becomes a means by which God's message is heard more clearly by the ears of the recipients of the message.

The suffering of prophets as messengers of Yahweh is not an unfamiliar theme to the reader of the Hebrew Bible, as we see it in the cases of Moses, Jeremiah, the servant of Yahweh in Isaiah, and Micaiah in 1 Kings 22. What is conspicuous in the story of the man of God from Judah is that his suffering itself has become a sign for Jeroboam; Hosea may be a close example. Though it is possible that "the pain that Hosea experienced caused him to understand his marital relationship in terms of Yahweh's relationship with Israel," and thus that "the crucial activity of the prophet lies in the 'seeing' and in the interpretation, rather than in the conditions themselves," the text as it stands in the present form depicts Hosea's marriage as a prophetic symbolic action commanded by God to be performed to illustrate the relationship between God and Israel (Hos 1:2–3; 3:1).⁴⁶ In performing these symbolic actions, Hosea experiences and bears the suffering in himself, which reveals the degree of God's pain caused by his own people. More examples of prophets' suffering, though in different degrees, are to be found in prophetic literature of the Hebrew Bible.

This theme of prophets' suffering as the messengers of Yahweh, I argue, is found in 1 Kings 13 in a very extreme form; the man of God from Judah suffered the loss of his life in the course of fulfilling his prophetic duties, and his death itself became a message/sign for Jeroboam. Here again we see the Deuteronomist assigning to prophets a special role for their prophetic commission. According to the Deuteronomist, the prophets were not only speakers of the word, but they themselves often became the word, a *sign*. This uncommon command or request by God to his prophets indicates the extreme spiritual condition of Israel of the day. The injustice done to the man of God from Judah only serves to emphasize the seriousness of the sin of Jeroboam. Therefore, Stacey's observation that the prophetic symbolic actions "emerge only in the most critical circumstances, when words have proved inadequate" holds true of 1 Kings 13 as well as Hosea 1 and 3.⁴⁷ Thus we conclude that John Gray's judgment that 1 Kings 13 contains

---

45. Block, *The Book of Ezekiel*, 371.
46. Stacey, *Prophetic Drama*, 219.
47. Stacey, *Prophetic Drama*, 217.

THE FATE OF THE MAN OF GOD FROM JUDAH

"the mechanical and a-moral conception of the operation of the word of Yahweh" does not do justice to the story.[48]

Given the seriousness of the sin of Jeroboam from the Deuteronomistic historian's perspective, it may be understandable that this extreme form of prophetic symbolic action had to be employed at this point of the history. The death of the man of God from Judah betrays the Deuteronomist's strongest condemnation of the sin of Jeroboam. It shows that the Northern Kingdom contained too great a sin from the outset of its existence, which would continue and only grow until the end of the kingdom. Therefore, the graveness of the sin of Jeroboam, in some sense, demanded this extreme form of prophetic symbolic action. If our reading of 1 Kings 13 is legitimate, we learn that the Deuteronomist held prophets in high esteem as the messengers of Yahweh and also deeply sympathized with the burden that they had to bear in order to fulfill their prophetic calling, which could extend even to their lives.

GOD'S WILL AND HUMANS' DECISION

Our discussion on the Deuteronomist's theological view on the word of Yahweh and his understanding regarding the role of prophets as the agent of the word of Yahweh leads to another theological topic, that is, the correlation between God's will and humans' decisions.

In the Jeroboam narrative, with the sudden increase of prophetic words and their corresponding fulfillment, the problem of potential conflicts between the will of God and the humans' decisions arises. Though this topic is not limited to the Jeroboam narrative, it becomes an important element in the plot of the narrative. The interrelationship between the will of Yahweh spoken through prophets and the decisions made by human characters as delineated in the narrative is mysterious. Yahweh's words to Solomon about the "tearing" of the kingdom (11:11–13) proclaim the division of the kingdom, and Ahijah's oracle (11:29–39) predicts Jeroboam's future. These prophecies find their fulfillment in a series of complex human events (1 Kgs 12:16–25). In between the prophecies and their fulfillment, Rehoboam's hardening his heart against the northern tribes is commented on by the narrator (12:15):

---

48. Gray, *I & II Kings*, 294.

> So the king [Rehoboam] did not listen to the people, for it was *a turn of affairs brought about by Yahweh* that he might fulfill his word, which Yahweh spoke by Ahijah the Shilonite to Jeroboam the son of Nebat. (Italics added)

According to the narrator, Rehoboam's decision was in some sense *predestined* by the word of Yahweh that Ahijah spoke to Jeroboam. It is clear, however, that Rehoboam was not aware of the prophecy and acted on his own initiative. "The mysterious stupidity of his free decision comes about as Yhwh's way of bringing about the fulfillment of Ahijah's word."[49] Sweeney ponders the implication of the narrator's comment in 12:15:

> Verse 15 explains the reason for Rehoboam's ill-considered response as divine intervention—that is, YHWH had caused a *sibbâ*, literally "a turning (of events)" so that Rehoboam would follow the advice of his comrades and confirm Ahijah's prophetic word concerning Jeroboam's kingship (1 Kgs 11:26–40). Such a statement is particularly controversial because it indicates divine intervention to ensure the downfall of an otherwise innocent man. Some might understand it as a reference to absolute divine power and freedom, but it points to YHWH as a trickster who works to undermine the human protagonists (cf. 1 Kgs 22) . . . YHWH's action might be justified in relation to Solomon on account of his apostasy (1 Kgs 11:1–13), but this is a case of the sins of the father visited on the son (cf. Deut 5:9–10; Exod 20:5–6; contra Ezek 18; Jer 31:29–30). Rehoboam has done nothing to justify divine punishment (contra Walsh, *1 Kings*, 165).[50]

It is not likely the narrator is dealing with the issue of the sins of the father being visited on the son here, though it is a legitimate question to ask.[51] Rather, the emphasis is that Yahweh was behind Rehoboam's foolish

---

49. Goldingay, *Old Testament Theology*, 649. Goldingay discusses the topic of "how Yhwh works" in his treatment of the monarchic period of the Israelite history and articulates five ways (not necessarily excluding one another) Yahweh works: (1) "Using natural and human processes," (2) "Taking initiatives behind the scenes," (3) "Sending prophets with bewildering commissions," (4) "Using the chance and the inexplicable," and (5) "Acting through supernatural and natural force and violence." He includes the narrator's comment in 1 Kgs 12:15 in the first category (648–56).

50. Sweeney, *I & II Kings*, 171.

51. Moreover, 2 Kings 14:6 records that Amaziah did not put to death the children of the murderers "according to what is written in the Book of the Law of Moses, 'Fathers shall not be put to death because of their children, nor shall children be put to death because of their fathers. But each one shall die for his own sin.'"

THE FATE OF THE MAN OF GOD FROM JUDAH

decision. Subsequent to this event, Rehoboam attempts to take a military action against the northern tribes for their rebellion, but it is frustrated by Shemaiah the man of God, who delivers the same idea as that of the narrator (12:24):

> Thus says Yahweh, "You shall not go up or fight against your relatives the people of Israel. Every man, return to his home, *for this thing is from me.*" So they listened to the word of Yahweh and went home again, according to the word of Yahweh. (Italics added.)

The emphasis seems to be on Yahweh's approval of the secession of the northern tribes. In the narrator's view, the secession was Yahweh's alternative plan to a "whole" kingdom of David, because of the sin of Solomon. In the course of the fulfillment of the will of Yahweh, Rehoboam unconsciously made a choice that contributed to the fulfillment of the will of Yahweh. Rehoboam's foolish choice should not be understood just as a necessary literary device here. The narrator believed that Yahweh's will is fulfilled mysteriously through human decisions and events. This view of the narrator is discernible throughout the Jeroboam narrative.

The man of God's prophecy of Josiah's reformation is another example (1 Kgs 13:2). In 2 Kings 23:15–20, Josiah fulfills the prophecy without being aware of it, and only after he has already fulfilled the prophecy does he hear of it (vv. 16–18). Also, the prophecy that the body of the man of God shall not enter the grave of his fathers is fulfilled through the passers-by, who tell of the death of the man of God in the city where the old prophet lived, and also through the old prophet himself, who brings the body back and buries him in his own grave out of a different motive than fulfilling the prophecy (vv. 25–30). Jeroboam's wife in chapter 14 heard an ominous oracle from Ahijah that "when your feet enter the city, the child shall die" (14:12). Then Jeroboam's wife "arose and departed and came to Tirzah. And as she came to the threshold of the house, the child died" (v. 17). Here again we see that Yahweh's will expressed in the form of prophecy is fulfilled apart from the intention of Jeroboam's wife. It seems that any accounts of prophecy and fulfillment in the Hebrew Bible necessarily entail this kind of interrelationship between the spoken will of Yahweh and humans' involvement in the process. Walsh states of prophetism in the Jeroboam narrative,

> The correlation of prophecy and fulfillment is not simply a narrative technique; behind it lies a profound theological understanding of Israel's history and Yahweh's role in it. The narrator believes that events are caused by human behavior: for instance, Rehoboam's

A Theological Approach to the Jeroboam Narrative

diplomatic heavy-handedness precipitated the secession of the northern tribes. But they are also, and more primally, Yahweh's doing (see 12:15). Prophecy and fulfillment do not merely reveal the interconnectedness of history. The word of Yahweh itself, with or without human cooperation, drives history and brings it into being. Israel's history—which is that of the narrator and of his intended readers as well—is *co-created* by Yahweh and Yahweh's people.[52]

Therefore, it is clear that the Deuteronomist believed that the spoken word of Yahweh has the power to accomplish itself in human history, and the decisions that humans make, regardless of their intention, contribute to the fulfillment of the divine will.

Dual Causality Principle

According to the theological framework of the Deuteronomist, the course of events happens according to the will of God, but at the same time, the things unfold in the web of complex human relationships and interactions, without one conflicting with another. Thus, in a mysterious way, human events interact with the divine will. Fretheim notices such an interaction in 1 Kings 11:27:

> The reference to Jeroboam's rebellion (v. 27) is not inconsequential; causation in this situation is not ascribed only to God and God's word. Though this part of the story is delayed until chapter 12 and God's powerful word through the prophet fills this scene, the word "rebellion" stands at the beginning of this narrative and has important content (as will be evident in chap. 12) . . . For one thing, God works in and through what people do and say. This has just been made clear regarding Solomon's external adversaries (see at 11:14–25). What Jeroboam has done and will now do counts in charting a future course, not simply what God does or what God's prophet says. Both Jeroboam and God's word are effective agents.[53]

In the Book of Kings as well as other books of the Deuteronomistic History the reader notices the concept of God at work behind the scenes of human history. Especially, in the Jeroboam narrative, God is not directly involved

---

52. Walsh, *1 Kings*, 205.
53. Fretheim, *First and Second Kings*, 68–69.

in the events as in the time of Solomon, but he, in a more indirect way, supervises everything to accomplish his plan and will. It is difficult to draw a distinguishing line between humans' actions and God's will. God does not step up in the forefront of the story, but things eventually happen according to his will, which has been revealed by the means of dreams, prophecies, or the narrator's or a character's words.

Yairah Amit discusses this theological concept in her article titled "Dual Causality."[54] She traces this theological concept back to von Rad, who called this literary phenomenon "a new technique in narrative."[55] Von Rad argues that it is a "secularized" rendition of Yahweh's activity in human history which was begun in the early monarchial period (or during the period of the united monarchy).[56] Around that time, according to von Rad, God's activity began to be explained in a new way, and there came into being a new way of narration, which indicates a transition from miraculous episodes to the writing of a comprehensive historical composition. This signaled for von Rad a change in the way of writing history from "a sacral narrative-form" to a "completely new way of picturing Jahweh's action in history" in which the story-tellers "have no need of wonders or the appearance of charismatic leaders—events develop apparently in complete accord with their own inherent nature."[57] Although he is still believed to be acting in history and is the cause of all things, and the link between the course of events and divine providence and will is noted, Yahweh's action is more hidden and does not need to be as apparent as before.

Von Rad does not say this new "literary technique" means "any abandonment of belief in Jahweh, nor was it a veering to an attenuated rationalized piety,"[58] but it rather signaled Israel's ability "to make herself the object of consideration and large-scale interrogation" and to "deal with extensive complexes of connected history."[59] Among the examples provided by von Rad are Yahweh's causing a deep sleep to come over Saul and his men in 1 Samuel 26, "Rehoboam's insensate rejection of the counsel of the older men" being "due to a 'turn of affair' (1) (סבה Kgs 12:15), Yahweh's causing the evil spirit to come upon Saul (1 Sam 16:14), and the story of Ruth (Ruth

---

54. Amit, "Dual Causality," 385–400.
55. Von Rad, *Old Testament Theology* 1, 52–53.
56. Von Rad, *Old Testament Theology* 1, 52–53.
57. Von Rad, *Old Testament Theology* 1, 53.
58. Von Rad, *Old Testament Theology* 1, 53.
59. Von Rad, *Old Testament Theology* 1, 49–50.

1:8f.; 2:12, 20).⁶⁰ In this discussion, von Rad was concerned in pointing out a change in the mode of history writing begun in the period of the united monarchy.

Amit borrows the term "dual causality" from Kaufmann for this literary phenomenon, that is, "the indirect governing of history by God and the granting of a wider scope to human initiative."⁶¹ Through the principle of dual causality, Amit explains events that occur through "both natural causes and divine guidance which determines a purpose for the events."⁶² She develops von Rad's view, which links

> dual causality with the form of narration, and consider[s] its implementation as a process of "secularization" of history, which was achieved by granting a central place on the stage of events to human action while distancing God to a place behind the scenes and depicting him as a vigilant and supervising eye, this being in fact the central though covert reason for the course of events.⁶³

The aim of employing the principle of dual causality is, according to Amit, to "refrain from describing God as directly guiding history and as playing an all-pervading and active role in the course of events."⁶⁴ She qualifies, however, the above statement by saying, "Despite this, the place of God as a supervising and magisterial being with events occurring as a result of his command and will is preserved in these stories."⁶⁵ As Amit observes, in the stories where this principle has been employed, "man is assigned the greater time of narration," but "man, albeit subconsciously, is subjugated to the divine plan."⁶⁶ As a result, "the reader of these stories may explain oc-

---

60. Exodus 6 to 15, in my judgment, may be included in the list, where Pharaoh is blamed for not listening to Moses, but at the same time Yahweh's hardening of the heart of Pharaoh is described as a determining cause of Pharaoh's obduracy.

61. Amit, "Dual Causality," 388. Y. Kaufmann presents the story of the downfall of Ai and the victory over it (Josh 7–8) as a good example where dual causality operates, and his emphasis is on the historicity of the story (*The Book of Joshua*, 128). For more discussion on this phenomenon, see von Rad, *Old Testament Theology*, 36–68, and Seeligmann, "Menschliches Heldentum," 385–411. Walter Brueggemann uses the term "the double agency" in a similar sense ("Why the Old Testament Must Not Go Away," 262–75, esp. 265–6).

62. Amit, "Dual Causality," 388.
63. Amit, "Dual Causality," 390.
64. Amit, "Dual Causality," 390–1.
65. Amit, "Dual Causality," 391.
66. Amit, "Dual Causality," 391.

currences by two systems of interpretation—the divine system and the human system—without one system contradicting or invalidating the other."[67]

Amit includes 1 Kings 13:2–3 in the stories where dual causality principle is operative; the prophecy uttered by the man of God from Judah reveals the will of God, but events will occur through dual causality, that is, through both natural causes and divine guidance. In my judgment, along with 1 Kings 13:2–3, Jeroboam's ascension to the kingship of the Northern Kingdom (1 Kgs 11–12) and Rehoboam's folly as a means by which Jeroboam's ascension is accomplished fall well under this category. God's will is proclaimed in the form of prophecy, and human events fulfill the prophecies. Notably, "God's supervision is conspicuous in a prophecy which is going to be fulfilled in the sequence of events."[68] This observation opens up our perspective to the narrator's understanding of God's role in history. The Deuteronomist strongly believes that everything is done according to the providential will of God and that whatever is revealed as the will of God through the mediums of dreams or prophecies will eventually come true through the humans' decisions.

Amit's observation is insightful and helpful; the principle of dual causality is operative throughout the Jeroboam narrative. In in my judgment, however, one important aspect has not been explored enough, which is *how* humans' decisions become part of the divine plan, especially when the decisions are *bad/evil* ones. The narrator does not attribute bad decisions of biblical characters (e.g., Rehoboam's folly, Jeroboam's stubbornness, etc.) to God, but at the same time they still become the means by which God's will is fulfilled. We will discuss this topic in the following section.

God Is not Held Responsible for Humans' Sins or Errors

Robert L. Cohn states of the correlation between divine will and humans' decision in the Book of Kings,

> The formulaic language and the omniscient Deuteronomistic hand of judgment in the accounts of the kings produce a tediousness and repetitiveness relieved mainly by the interposed prophetic stories. Yet even here there is clear evidence of conscious artistry in the very splicing of the annalistic and prophetic, *a splicing which*

---

67. Amit, "Dual Causality," 391.
68. Amit, "Dual Causality," 400.

sets human's behavior against divine purpose in the complex unfolding of history.[69] (Italics added)

The kings in the Book of Kings repeatedly disobey the commands of Yahweh, but their apostasy cannot exclude God's will from the history of Israel. God reveals his will through prophecy and wondrously works behind humans' decisions and events. In this sense, God is the author of history. Who then is responsible for humans' sins and errors when God's supervision is operative behind humans' decisions and events?

The Hebrew Bible does not support fatalism, but the biblical characters still have the freedom of choice, and the God of the Hebrew Bible does not manipulate the mind of the characters.[70] In other words, the emphasis on the fulfillment of the word of Yahweh in the Book of Kings is not to usurp from humans the freedom to make their own choices, but only to claim Yahweh's immanency in and direction of the history of Israel.

In the case of the secession of the northern tribes, the fulfillment of Ahijah's prophecy depends not on Jeroboam, but on Yahweh's faithfulness to his words. Since it is a promise for Jeroboam, the fulfillment depends on Yahweh who keeps the promise. The narrator clarifies that Rehoboam's listening not to the elders but to younger counselors comes from Yahweh (1 Kgs 12:15). Rehoboam's folly, however, is ascribed to himself, not to Yahweh. Fretheim says,

> Again, Rehoboam is the subject of the verb 'listen'; that he did not listen is something that he himself did. It is not clear what the "turning" means or even who the subject is (this word occurs only here in the Hebrew Bible), but it does not imply that God micromanaged his mind . . . At the same time, the claim is clear that Rehoboam did not act alone. God was at work in this situation on behalf of the future outlined by Ahijah, even through the bumbling efforts of Rehoboam's listening and not listening, and that the work of God was effective in this instance toward that end.[71]

Also, we note that the narrator does not make God a liar or a deceiver in the case of Jeroboam. The conditionality of Yahweh's promise to Jeroboam has been noted by scholars. From the literary perspective, it may serve as foreshadowing of Jeroboam's apostasy at a later stage of his life, but from the theological standpoint, it may raise a theological question: "Is God being

---

69. Cohn, "Literary Technique," 23–24.
70. Fretheim, *First and Second Kings*, 74.
71. Fretheim, *First and Second Kings*, 74.

deceptive here to Jeroboam and giving him this promise with the condition, knowing that Jeroboam will not able to meet the conditions?" This question is legitimate, given that the God in the Book of Kings speaks out his will regarding the future through his prophets. The God in our story, however, is not deceptive toward the human characters, and his promise has a genuine possibility. With regards to this, Fretheim makes an interesting point:

> What Jeroboam has done and will now do counts in charting a future course, not simply what God does or what God's prophet says. Both Jeroboam and God's word are effective agents. And Jeroboam's faithfulness (v. 38) is seen to be crucial for the course which that future takes. Moreover, the future possibility that God's word gives to Jeroboam in verse 38 is real; it has not been "closed off by prophetic foreknowledge" (contra Nelson, 73). The text gives us no reason to believe that God is being deceptive here, as if God knows for sure that this future will not come to pass but lays it out anyway. (See at 9:1–9 for God's knowledge of the future not being absolute; see also at 22:1–53 for divine deception.) This word to Jeroboam is *a genuine possibility* for the future, for *both* Jeroboam and God. God here treats Jeroboam *with integrity* in the outline of possible futures.[72]

The narrator's knowledge of Jeroboam's failure in the future may be betrayed in the narrator's wording, but he does not allude to the possibility that there may be deception on the part of Yahweh. Jeroboam's future depends on his own decisions, and it remains unpredictable until he has become a king of the Northern Kingdom.

In sum, the interrelationship between God's word (or God's will expressed in his word) and its unfolding in the history of Israel through humans' decision/events is an interesting theological topic worth our special attention and discussion. It reveals the Deuteronomist's view on God's intervention into the history of Israel, and this theological understanding is manifested in the stories in the Jeroboam narrative.

THE STORY'S LITERARY EFFECTS ON THE READER

In chapter 2, I argued that 1 Kings 13 is about showing that God's judgment on the house of Jeroboam was irrevocable and certain. I also argued

---

72. Fretheim, *First and Second Kings*, 69.

A Theological Approach to the Jeroboam Narrative

that the prophecy and fulfillment structure of the chapter contributes to the theme of the story. In chapter 3, I expanded the scope of this study to the Jeroboam narrative and argued that the narrator was not concerned with the fate of the house of Jeroboam only but also had in view the end of the Northern Kingdom. The house of Jeroboam and the northern kingdom share the same fate, and what binds the two together is the "sin of Jeroboam."[73] The removal of the sin of Jeroboam is prophesied and will be fulfilled by Josiah.

In the current chapter, I argue that 1 Kings 13 and the rest of the Jeroboam narrative in its present form reflect the theology of the Deuteronomist. This confirms Lemke's argument that 1 Kings 13 "forms an integral part of the structure and theology of the Deuteronomistic History."[74] Lemke contends as follows:

> Affinities with such other key Deuteronomistic passages as I Samuel 12 and II Kings 17 and 23 suggest that our story in its present context is to be viewed as another pivotal passage in the Deuteronomistic History, which is illustrative of the Historian's theology and over-all proclamation. For one, it fits admirably into the larger scheme of prophecy and fulfillment observable throughout the Deuteronomistic History. It provides one of the more impressive examples of the realization of the divine word as mediated through the prophets, which brackets virtually the entire history of the divided monarchy.[75]

This shows that 1 Kings 13 is significant "for an assessment of the structure and theology of the Deuteronomistic History."[76]

With all this in mind, I now situate 1 Kings 13 in the context of the Deuteronomistic History. This discussion will address how the narrator shaped the text to create a particular intended effect on the reader. The tone of judgment employed by the narrator warns the intended reader to respond to the warning in a proper way.[77]

---

73. 1 Kgs 12:30; 13:34; 14:16; 15:26, 30, 34; 16:2, 19, 20; 22:52; 2 Kgs 3:3; 10:29, 31; 13:2, 6, 11; 14:24; 15:9, 18, 24, 28; 17:21; 23:15.

74. Lemke, "The Way of Obedience," 303–4. Lemke does not specify what he means by "the Deuteronomistic editor," though it seems that he accepts M. Noth's view of an exilic editor. He argues that a Deuteronomistic editor is responsible for both the insertion of the story (vv. 1–32) and the immediate literary framework (12:26–33 and 13:33–34).

75. Lemke, "The Way of Obedience," 317.

76. Lemke, "The Way of Obedience," 303–4.

77. On the intended reader and repentance, in texts typically called

THE FATE OF THE MAN OF GOD FROM JUDAH

H. W. Wolff in his essay titled "The Kerygma of the Deuteronomistic Historical Work" argued that the theme of repentance provides an important theological frame for the Deuteronomistic History.[78] In the essay he accepts Noth's view that the Deuteronomy was written in the exile, but he raises a question about Noth's view that "the actual *purpose* of his [the Deuteronomist's] entire historical presentation" was to show that the exile must "be understood as divine judgment"[79] (italics added). While this view of Noth's leaves no room for a future of hope, Wolff asks a legitimate question: "one can only ask why an Israelite of the sixth century B.C. would even reach for his pen if he only wanted to explain the final end of Israel's history as the righteous judgment of God."[80] He concludes that Noth's view does not explain satisfactorily the purpose of the Deuteronomistic History and suspects that the Deuteronomist might have "a rather complex intention in mind."[81] He finds the answer to the question in the theme of repentance. He says, "The Deuteronomist wanted Israel to read his whole work from its beginning as a summons to return in the midst of judgment"[82] (cf. Judg 2:11–23; 1 Sam 12:19), thereby providing "a limited ray of hope on the basis on which Israel's continued, or renewed, existence as the people of God might be assured."[83] The catchword שוב repeatedly occurs throughout the Deuteronomistic History in the passages that are crucial for the frame of history (1 Sam 7:3; 1 Kgs 8:33, 35, 46–53; 2 Kgs 17:13; 23:25; Deut 4:29–31; 30:1–10). Then the Deuteronomist shows through this historical writing that Israel's cry to Yahweh (repentance) and their turning back from their evil ways might bring about Yahweh's compassion on them, and this is the

---

"Deuteronomistic," see Seitz, "The Place of the Reader," 67–75. The approach taken in this study is similar to the one Seitz articulates in his essay. Seitz is concerned to "comprehend the final shaping of the book of Jeremiah without ignoring the fact of its complex prehistory, with the hope that by understanding this shaping, clues might be given about how readers might appropriate the message of the book" (70). He argues that the final shaping of Jeremiah allowed "the reader to participate in the refusal of an earlier generation to heed God's calls to repentance and to experience the judgment they eventually experienced, though now with a clear confession of wrongdoing and an acknowledgment that Jeremiah was a true prophet sent by God—something for which he was persecuted rather than honored and heeded" (71–72).

78. Wolff, "Kerygma," 62–78.
79. Noth, *Uberlieferungsgeschichtlich Studien I*, 109.
80. Wolff, "Kerygma," 64.
81. Wolff, "Kerygma," 66.
82. Wolff, "Kerygma," 72.
83. Lemke, "The Way of Obedience," 311–12.

A Theological Approach to the Jeroboam Narrative

"sermon" or the basic kerygmatic thrust that the Deuteronomist intended to give to "his sixth-century contemporaries."[84]

Wolff did not include 1 Kings 13 or the Jeroboam narrative in his discussion, but I would argue that the theme of repentance is clearly discernible in this chapter. First, it is found in the first part of our story (vv. 1–10), where Jeroboam attempts to have the man of God from Judah arrested.[85] He stretched out his hand from the altar, saying "Seize him," only to find his hand withered. Simultaneously, the altar was torn down and the ashes were poured out from the altar. Then Jeroboam in a surprising reversal asked the man of God from Judah for his prayer (1 Kgs 13:6):

> And the king said to the man of God, "Entreat now the favor of Yahweh your God, and pray for me (וְהִתְפַּלֵּל בַּעֲדִי), that my hand may be restored to me." And the man of God entreated Yahweh, and the king's hand was restored (וַתָּשָׁב) to him and became as it was before.

The abrupt change in the king's attitude toward the man of God and his request to him for his prayer is surprising, and though there are many speculations as to the motive of the king's appeal, the phrase used here seems to hint at the change in Jeroboam's heart. This interpretation is supported by the occurrence of the same phrase in 1 Sam 12:19:

> And all the people said to Samuel, "Pray for your servants (הִתְפַּלֵּל בְּעַד־עֲבָדֶיךָ) to Yahweh your God, that we may not die, for we have added to all our sins this evil, to ask for ourselves a king."

The basic tone of both requests is similar, and the construct of the verb "to pray" and the preposition "on behalf of" is significant. This construct is one of the phrases that has been frequently employed by the Deuteronomist in the situations where a prophet prays for the people who sinned or for someone who needed God's mercy.[86]

---

84. Brueggemann agrees with Wolff on the presence of the theme of repentance in the Deuteronomistic History and builds upon Wolff's work in suggesting the Deuteronomist summons the exilic readers to repentance by reminding them of God's goodness that was promised to David.

85. See my discussion on v. 6 in the section titled "The First Set of 'Word' and Fulfillment" in chapter 2.

86. The combination of "to pray" and "on behalf of" occurs thirteen times in the Hebrew Bible (Gen 20:7; Num 21:7; Deut 9:20; 1 Sam 12:19; 12:23; 1 Kgs 13:6; Job 42:10; Ps 72:15; Jer 7:16; 14:11; 29:7; 37:3; 42:20), eight times of which are found in the Book of Samuel (two times), the Book of Kings (once), and the Book of Jeremiah (five times).

THE FATE OF THE MAN OF GOD FROM JUDAH

Wolff considers 1 Samuel 12:19 as one of the key verses that form the theological frames of the Deuteronomistic History. Jeroboam's request, when read against the background of 1 Samuel 12:19 and alongside the key word of 1 Kings 13 "to return," could well be perceived as a hint of Jeroboam's repentance, or at least, a change in his attitude toward the messenger of the word of Yahweh. Moreover, the fact that Yahweh heard the prayer of the man of God from Jeroboam and healed the withered hand of Jeroboam supports such an interpretation. The slight hope of Jeroboam's repentance at the beginning of the story remains somewhat unclear until the end of the story, and the story moves on to the next scene, which describes the incidents between the man of God from Judah and the old prophet of Bethel. The hope of Jeroboam's repentance, however, turns out to be a groundless one when the reader reads through the tragic story of the man of God and the narrator's comment at the end of the story (13:33–34):

> After this thing Jeroboam did not turn (לֹא־שָׁב) from his evil way, but he turned (וַיָּשָׁב) and made priests for the high places again from among all the people. Any who would, he ordained to be priests of the high places. And this thing became sin to the house of Jeroboam, so as to cut it off and to destroy it from the face of the earth.

The Deuteronomist's hand is obvious in these two verses, as one of the Deuteronomistic expressions, "turn from his evil way," shows.[87] One of the key words that is crucial for the theme of repentance, שׁוב, appears here with rich theological significance. It is noteworthy that the catchword—to borrow Wolff's term—שׁוב occurs in this story sixteen times, which is "more than in any other chapter in the entire Old Testament, except for Jeremiah 3 where the root occurs an equal number of times."[88] Jeroboam did not "turn" (שׁוב), but he "turned" (שׁוב)—meaning "continued"—and stayed in his evil way. Thus, because of the sin that Jeroboam committed by refusing to turn away from his evil way, his house (or dynasty) will be "cut off" and "destroyed" from the face of the earth. The expression "turn from his evil way" occurs once more in 2 Kings 17:13 which is generally agreed to be another key Deuteronomistic passage. The combination of the verb שׁוב with

---

87. Lemke, "The Way of Obedience," 305. Lemke suggests that this idiom "turn from the way" "was characteristic of the late pre-exilic or exilic prose tradition which found its literary deposit in the book of Jeremiah and Ezekiel" (310).

88. Lemke, "The Way of Obedience," 310.

the noun דֶּרֶךְ might well be considered as the hand of the Deuteronomist.[89] Thus the chapter ends with the profound disappointment that Jeroboam did not *repent*. Jeroboam did not turn from his evil way, and thus the destruction of his house is irreversible, and the influence of this sin on the Northern Kingdom only grows until the kingdom is completely destroyed.

This story's thematic structure leads us to the particular literary effects that the Deuteronomist intended to make on the intended reader.[90] The editorial comment that begins with the statement "After this Jeroboam did not turn away from his evil way" suggests to some commentators that Jeroboam might have heard about the tragic events that had happened to the man of God from Judah, which then must have provided him with a chance to "turn from his evil way." It is not clear, however, in the text whether or not Jeroboam heard about this. Rather, what is more important may be that the comment seems to be targeted to the *reader*. In other words, the Deuteronomist is giving the reader a clear message here: "Jeroboam did not turn from his evil way even after this thing, and as a result, his house could not avoid being cut off and being destroyed, so the reader should take a lesson from this story of Jeroboam." Lemke says, "Our story thus could be seen as a negative illustration of this theme [the theme of repentance], pointing to the dire consequences which ensued when a man on the one hand turned from his divinely ordained way, and on the other failed to turn from his evil ways and persisted in them in spite of all warnings."[91] Admittedly, Lemke did not read the story (vv. 11–32) as an incident that illustrates or symbolizes Jeroboam's disobedience or attempt to read the story in the context of the Jeroboam narrative. Yet he finds the theme of repentance operating in the story. At any rate, the literary effects on the reader seem to be clear.

F. M. Cross also noticed the theme of repentance in the story of 1 Kings 13. He states,

> In particular, the document speaks to the North, calling Israel to return to Judah and to Yahweh's sole legitimate shrine in Jerusalem, asserting the claims of the ancient Davidic monarchy upon all Israel. Even the destruction of Bethel and the cults of the high

---

89. Lemke, "The Way of Obedience," 310–13. Lemke argues that when these two words are combined by means of the preposition *min* in 1 Kings 13, the expression has "a transferred or metaphorical meaning" as in 1 Kgs 13:33 (310).

90. Cohn, "Literary Technique," 23.

91. Lemke, "The Way of Obedience," 311–12.

> places were predicted by the prophets, pointing to the centrality of Josiah's role for northern Israel. It speaks equally or more emphatically to Judah. Its restoration to ancient grandeur depends on the return of the nation to the covenant of Yahweh and on the wholehearted return of her king to the ways of David, the servant of Yahweh. In Josiah is centered the hope of a new Israel and the renewing of the "sure mercies" shown to David.[92]

Cross, dating the composition of the Jeroboam narrative to the days of Josiah, argues that the message of the Josianic editor is directed to the North about their coming back to Judah and to Jerusalem. This element is discernible in the narrative, for example, in the repeated designation of the man of God as the man of God from Judah. The meaning of the Judean prophet's coming to the first king of the northern kingdom and speaking against the counter-cultus in Bethel becomes clear. As Cross himself mentions, however, this story should have meant much for the exilic people as well. That is, the exilic readers must have read this story as a summons to turn from their evil ways to go back to the covenant of Yahweh in the hope that Yahweh might restore them to himself by delivering them from the exile.

As briefly mentioned previously, McConville understands 1 and 2 Kings as a call for the exilic community to repent. He concludes that the Book of Kings promotes "the ideas of Deuteronomy, first, in their concern for right worship, reflected in the belief that Yahweh is the proper object and the temple at Jerusalem the proper location. Second, they share Deuteronomy's concern for right leadership, addressing the issue in connection with the kings of Israel and Judah."[93] What did these themes of the Book of Kings mean to the exilic Judah? McConville continues,

> The consideration of these themes, however, is in a context in which temple and monarchy have disappeared. The two books of Kings, therefore, have (in common with some Psalms, especially Ps 89) the particular characteristic that they reflect on the meaning of the promises concerning David and Zion in the light of their apparent dereliction. Being under Deuteronomic influence, 1, 2 Kings know full well the possibility of the covenantal curse. Noth is wrong, however, to think that it proclaims only this, for the prayer of Solomon at the dedication of the temple holds out hope that the covenantal relationship between God and Israel may

---

92. Cross, *Myth and Hebrew Epic*, 284.
93. McConville, *Grace in the End*, 89.

survive even this cataclysm (1 Ki 8:46–53). The implicit call to repent is ubiquitous and also implies the possibility of a future. As we have seen, however, there is no strand of 1, 2 Kings that imagines that the future lies along the path of a restored monarchy. It is significant that the prayer of Solomon, the most articulate expression of hope for the future in the books, anticipates no such thing, not even a return to the land. The two books of Kings issue a call to repent and leave open the question how God might then respond in grace.[94]

The problem of "the sin of Jeroboam" is a heavy issue that the Deuteronomist is dealing with in and throughout the Jeroboam narrative. Walsh observed the growth of "sin" in the Jeroboam narrative:

> Where Jeroboam made golden calf-idols, the people of Israel make *ăšērîm* (NRSV, "sacred poles"), or cult objects representing the goddess Asherah. Like Jeroboam's, Israel's idolatry "provokes Yahweh to anger" (v. 15; cf. v. 9). These parallels point to a deeper connection between Jeroboam's sin and Israel's that the last words of Ahijah's speech bring out. Jeroboam's sin also *caused* Israel to sin. The "sin" of Jeroboam (a thematic phrase that will recur frequently in 1–2 Kings) has come to term. It was first simply "sin" (12:30), then "the sin of the house of Jeroboam" (13:34), and finally "the sin which he sinned and which he caused Israel to sin" (14:16).[95]

This sin did not stay in the house of Jeroboam, but it "became" a sin and "caused Israel to sin" (14:16). This is why Ahijah's condemnation (1 Kgs 14) is not limited to the house of Jeroboam only but extends to the entire northern kingdom. The Deuteronomist finds the fundamental cause of the fall of the northern kingdom in the deadly and transmittable sin of Jeroboam.

Thus, the Deuteronomist's intention for the reader is clear; that is, he both explains the irrevocability of the fall of Jeroboam (and of the Northern Kingdom) and urges the reader not to walk in the same way as Jeroboam did. Wolff observes, "It is not so much the total apostasy which makes judgment final as the contemptuous disregard of the call to repentance."[96] This seems to be the message for the reader, and the story has been shaped for the reader rather than for Jeroboam. In his treatment of this serious issue of sin, the Deuteronomist maximizes the theme of repentance through the

---

94. McConville, *Grace in the End*, 89–90.
95. Walsh, *1 Kings*, 198.
96. Wolff, "Kerygma," 70.

use of the key term "turn/return." As Nelson argues, "The use of "turn/return" (*shub*) in this chapter resonates with the call for the exilic audience to repent (*shub*; 8:48)."[97]

CONCLUSION

In this chapter, I have approached the Jeroboam narrative from a theological point of view. I have endeavored to demonstrate that there are two theological emphases that come to the fore in the Jeroboam narrative and that reflect the Deuteronomist's theological views.

First, I argued that the Deuteronomist's strong belief in the word of God as the driving force behind the history of Israel is surfacing in the Jeroboam narrative for the first time and is highlighted with much emphasis in 1 Kings 13. An important theological schema, that is, the pattern of prophecy and fulfillment, which reflects the Deuteronomist's view of history, multiplies in the Jeroboam narrative (1 Kgs 11:29–39—1 Kgs 12:15b; 1 Kgs 13—2 Kgs 23:16–18; 1 Kgs 14:6–14—1 Kgs 15:29). Thus, it becomes clear that Yahweh's intervention into the history of Israel is made through the word spoken by his prophets. Necessarily, prophets, the agents of the word of Yahweh, play important roles in the Deuteronomist's articulation of history. Especially in the Jeroboam narrative, when compared with the Solomonic narrative, these agents of the word of Yahweh (prophets and the man of God) begin to increase with surprising frequency.

With such an emphasis on the role of the prophets in the Jeroboam narrative, the Deuteronomist's presentation of the man of God in 1 Kings 13 is particularly eye-catching. The man of God himself becomes a *sign* to Jeroboam and thus visualizes the consequence of Jeroboam's disobedience to Yahweh's command. In the course of fulfilling his prophetic duty, the man of God gets killed. In this sense, the man of God joins other prophets in the suffering that they bore as the messengers of the word of Yahweh. This theological theme of Yahweh's prophets' suffering for their prophetic commission is to be found throughout the prophetical books of the Hebrew Bible, but one of the most extreme cases is found in 1 Kings 13.

---

97. Nelson, *First and Second Kings*, 89. Again, it is not my primary concern to argue for a particular position about the date of composition, that is, whether it is pre-exilic or exilic. Though most of the text may be attributed to the pre-exilic editor, the present form most likely reflects the theology of the exilic editor as well.

Second, the Deuteronomist's special emphasis on Yahweh's intervention into the history of Israel through his word leads to another theological topic that is also emphasized in the Jeroboam narrative, that is, the interrelationship between God's will and human's decision. God's will is spoken through his prophets, and the spoken will of God always finds its fulfillment through a complicated web of human events and decisions. These two elements, the will of God and the freedom of human decisions, could conflict with each other, but the Deuteronomist depicts the process of the fulfillment of God's words with not much difficulty. The unfolding of human history is attributed to the complete will of Yahweh. Humans' sins—in this case, Solomon's sin and failure to meet Yahweh's requirements—qualifies Yahweh's earlier promises (Yahweh's promise to David), but they cannot nullify them completely, and the promise is still alive. The revised plan of Yahweh (the secession of the northern tribes) is proclaimed through his prophet (Ahijah), and the word of Yahweh is fulfilled in a mysterious way through Rehoboam's stupidity and recalcitrance, while Rehoboam's decision remains his own. The Deuteronomist's historical writing thus reveals the principle of dual causality at work. God is described as behind the history and is portrayed as the one who supervises the development of human events rather than as the one who is acting in the forefront of the events. The human events still unfold in accordance with the will of God. They happen in the principle of natural causality but still succumb to the will of Yahweh. While human events are depicted to be happening in accordance with the will of God, humans' sins are not attributed to God. Also, God does not micromanage humans' mind, and humans make their moral decisions on their own.

Lastly, I drew attention to the literary effects of 1 Kings 13 on the intended reader. The Deuteronomist seems to have shaped the story of the man of God for the purpose of justifying God's judgment on the house of Jeroboam. The death of the man of God was supposed to serve as a warning to Jeroboam and thereby provides Jeroboam with a chance to repent from his evil way. This sin of Jeroboam, however, did not end with him, but continued until the end of the Northern Kingdom. Therefore, Jeroboam is condemned as someone through whom the sin of idolatry came and thus affected the fate of the whole kingdom. Therefore, it is not surprising that the Deuteronomist spared much space to describing the rise and fall of Jeroboam and the cause of his fall. The Deuteronomist uses the series of events to urge his exilic reader to be warned by the story. The story as it

THE FATE OF THE MAN OF GOD FROM JUDAH

stands in its final form functions as a summons to repent and "turn" back to Yahweh. This is the message for the people who have now lost temple and monarchy. They need to repent of their past sins and cry out to God in the hope that God will turn his favor toward them again.

Conclusion & Future Study

THE PURPOSE OF THIS study was to address the scholarly issues such as the theme, function, and ethical/theological problems that past scholarship has raised regarding this bizarre story of 1 Kings 13. A plethora of themes have been proposed for 1 Kings 13; a multitude of interpreters attempted to solve the difficult aspects of the story; nevertheless, in my judgment, a new approach was necessary to provide a coherent reading of the narrative. This dissertation was an attempt to take on the task by means of a literary and theological reading of the narrative.

THEME AND GENRE

A literary analysis of 1 Kings 13 showed that it had been shaped around the framework of prophecy and fulfillment (vv. 3–6 and 20–26; v. 2 and 32), which in turn contributed to the theme of the story, the certainty of God's judgment on the house of Jeroboam. The narrator (or the Deuteronomist) presents Jeroboam as the archetypal *Unheilsherrscher* ("evil ruler") who brought into the Northern Kingdom apostasy, which is repeated in all the subsequent kings. The sin of Jeroboam is condemned to the same degree as the grievous sin of Israel in the wilderness (Exod 32:4; cf. 1 Kgs 12:28). Thus, in the eyes of the Deuteronomist, the sin of Jeroboam foreshadows the tragic end of the Northern Kingdom.

Against this backdrop 1 Kings 13 was placed in the midst of the Jeroboam narrative. Placed right after the beginning of Jeroboam's downfall (12:26–31), 1 Kings 13 justifies the inevitability of Jeroboam's fall. Jeroboam's disobedience to the command of Yahweh, which was given to him at the outset of his career (1 Kgs 11:38), and his refusal to turn away from his evil way (1 Kgs 13:33), are dramatized in the story of the man of

THE FATE OF THE MAN OF GOD FROM JUDAH

God from Judah. The reason for the narrator's inclusion of the story in the Jeroboam narrative thus becomes clear. The man of God becomes a *sign* (מוֹפֵת) for Jeroboam in his obedience, his disobedience, and God's punishment of it. An important argument of this dissertation was, therefore, that the narrator shaped the story around the centrality of prophetic symbolic actions, where the man of God is *portrayed* as performing a series of actions that symbolize Jeroboam's rise, disobedience, and fall.

One of the implications of this interpretation is that the text does not intend to give the reader a full and connected circumstantial picture regarding the motives of the characters, or at least it is not the emphasis of the story. Within the framework of the symbolic actions, "the desire for completeness and full clarification of the circumstances is restricted solely to the preaching aspect of the action,"[1] which explains the text's silence about the motive of the old prophet's lie, often regarded as the key to the interpretation of the story.

LOCATION AND FUNCTION

The theme and function of 1 Kings 13 is in line with the overall structure of the Jeroboam narrative. This study argued that the Jeroboam narrative (11:26—14:20) displays artistic unity and thus should be considered a literary unit. The Jeroboam narrative as a whole describes the rise and fall of Jeroboam. With the sin of Jeroboam placed at the center (12:26–31), the first half of the Jeroboam narrative describes the rise of Jeroboam (11:26–43; 12:1-25), whereas the second describes the fall of Jeroboam (12:32—13:34; 14:1–20). Jeroboam's minimal role in his ascension contributes to the positive characterization of Jeroboam, but a sudden change is made to the portrayal of Jeroboam as soon as his "heart" is revealed through his soliloquy (12:26). The new cultic invention of Jeroboam signals the turning point in relation with his fate; Jeroboam falls from the peak of his career to the status of the main culprit who is responsible for the destruction of the kingdom. The reversed fate of Jeroboam is highlighted in the prophetic words through Ahijah (1 Kgs 14), which is paralleled with and reverses his earlier prophecy (1 Kgs 11).

---

1. Zimmerli, *Ezekiel I*, 157.

THEOLOGY

The sudden increase of prophetic words in the Jeroboam narrative signals the full-scale development of the Deuteronomist's theology that operates throughout the rest of the Book of Kings, that is, the prophecy and fulfillment schema. It reveals the Deuteronomist's conviction regarding God's intervention in human history. The role of Yahweh's prophets as the messengers of God's words stands out, one of the most extreme examples of which is found in 1 Kings 13: the man of God *gave his life* in order that the word of Yahweh might be proclaimed by becoming a sign for Jeroboam; in this sense, the man of God joins other prophets of Yahweh in his suffering for the prophetic commission from Yahweh. We find the instances of prophets themselves becoming a sign (מוֹפֵת) for Israel in many places in the Hebrew Bible.

The Deuteronomist's emphasis on the word of Yahweh leads to another theological investigation into the interaction between the divine will and humans' decisions. The principle of dual causality is operative in the theology of the Deuteronomist. In this theological framework, God's will is delivered in the form of prophecy, but God remains a supervisor behind the scene; humans make decisions on their own initiative and human events unfold in the web of natural causality but in a mysterious way co-operate with God's sovereign plan. Lastly, 1 Kings 13 in its present form functions as a summons for the intended reader, that is the exilic community, to repentance. The recalcitrance of Jeroboam and his consequential downfall become a powerful summons for the exiles to act differently and to call upon God's grace, which was promised to David (2 Sam 7).

IMPLICATIONS AND FURTHER STUDY

This study showed that understanding the story in 1 Kings 13 as prophetic symbolic actions resolves many of the ethical/theological questions often raised by the past scholarship, and if our reading of this story is in the right direction, this study may lead to a further investigation into the Deuteronomist's peculiar view of Yahweh's prophets as the bearer of Yahweh's words and also how the Hebrew Bible understands the suffering of Yahweh's prophets. Interestingly, we find a similar perspective operating in the words of Jesus in the New Testament. Jesus compares the life and ministry of John the Baptist and his own to children's "singing a dirge" and "playing flute" to their playmates in the marketplaces (Matt 11:16–19, NRSV):

> But to what will I compare this generation? It is like children sitting in the marketplaces and calling to one another, "We played the flute for you, and you did not dance; we wailed, and you did not mourn." For John came neither eating nor drinking, and they say, "He has a demon"; the Son of Man came eating and drinking, and they say, "Look, a glutton and a drunkard, a friend of tax collectors and sinners!" Yet wisdom is vindicated by her deeds.

In this parable, Jesus presents their lives and ministry as a kind of prophetic drama played before Israel to which the people of Israel refused to pay attention, and thus the word of Yahweh spoken through them has been rejected by the people. Jesus, however, ends his parable with a statement that God's wisdom is vindicated (or justified) by her deeds, that is, the lifestyles of both John and Jesus.[2] Thus the word of Yahweh is vindicated by the lived vocations of his prophets.

---

2. Carson, *Matthew*, 270–71.

Bibliography

Aberbach, Moses, and Leivy Smolar. "Aaron, Jeroboam, and the Golden Calves." *JBL* 86 (1967) 129–40.
Alter, Robert. *The Art of Biblical Narrative*. New York: Basic Books, 1981.
Amit, Yairah. *Reading Biblical Narratives: Literary Criticism and the Hebrew Bible*. Minneapolis: Fortress, 2001.
Angel, Hayyim. "When God's Will Can and Cannot Be Altered: The Relationship between the Balaam Narrative and 1 Kings 13." *JBQ* 33 no 1 (2005) 32–39.
Ash, Paul S. "Jeroboam I and the Deuteronomistic Historian's Ideology of the Founder." *CBQ* 60 (1998) 16–24.
Auld, A. Graeme. *Kings*. Daily Study Bible. Louisville: Westminster John Knox, 1986.
Avioz, Michael. "The Book of Kings in Recent Research (Part II)." *CBR* 5/1 (2006) 11–57.
Balthasar, Hans Urs von. *The Theology of Karl Barth*. Translated by John Drury. San Francisco: Ignatius, 1992.
Barstad, Hans M. "The Understanding of the Prophets in Deuteronomy." *SJOT* 8 (1994) 236–51.
Barth, Karl. *Church Dogmatics*, Vol. II/2, Sections 34–35: *The Doctrine of God*, Study Edition. Edited by G. W. Bromiley and T. F. Torrance; Translated by G. W. Bromiley et al. London: T. & T. Clark, 2010.
Bartlett, J. R. "An Adversary against Solomon, Hadad the Edomite." *ZAW* 88 (1976) 205–26.
Barton, John. *Oracles of God: Perceptions of Prophecy in Israel after the Exile*. New York: Oxford University Press, 1986.
Beal, Lissa M. Wray. *The Deuteronomist's Prophet: Narrative Control of Approval and Disapproval in the Story of Jehu (2 Kings 9 and 10)*. LHBOTS 478. London: T. & T. Clark, 2007.
Blenkinsopp, Joseph. *A History of Prophecy in Israel*. Louisville: Westminster John Knox, 1996.
Blum, Erhard. "Die Lüge des Propheten: Ein Lesevorschlag zu einer befremdlichen Geschichte (I Reg 13)." In *Mincha: Festgabe für Rolf Rendtorff zum 75. Geburtstag*, edited by Erhard Blum, 27–46. Neukirchen: Neukirchener, 2000.
Bodner, Keith. *Jeroboam's Royal Drama*. Biblical Refigurations. Oxford: Oxford University Press, 2012.
Boer, Roland. "National Allegory in the Hebrew Bible." *JSOT* 74 (1997) 95–116.
Bosworth, David. "Revisiting Karl Barth's Exegesis of 1 Kings 13." *BI* 10 (2002) 360–83.

Bibliography

———. *The Story within a Story in Biblical Hebrew Narrative*. CBQMS 45. Washington, DC: Catholic Biblical Association of America, 2008.

Branch, Robin Gallaher. *Jeroboam's Wife: The Enduring Contributions of the Old Testament's Least-Known Women*. Peabody, MA: Hendrickson, 2009.

Briend, Jacques. "Du message au messager: remarques sur 1 Rois XIII." In *Congress Volume: Paris, 1992*, 13–24. VTSup 61. Leiden: Brill, 1995.

Brueggemann, Walter. *1 & 2 Kings*. Smyth and Helwys Bible Commentary. Macon, GA: Smyth & Helwys, 2000.

Calvin, John. *Institutes of the Christian Religion*. Edited by John T. McNeill. Translated by Ford Lewis Battles. 2 vols. Library of Christian Classics 20–21. Philadelphia: Westminster, 1960.

Campbell, Antony F. "Martin Noth and Deuteronomistic History." In *The History of Israel's Traditions: The Heritage of Martin Noth*, edited by Steven L. McKenzie and M. Patrick Graham, 31–62. JSOTSup 182. Sheffield: Sheffield Academic, 1994.

Campbell, Edward F., Jr. "A Land Divided: Judah and Israel from the Death of Solomon to the Fall of Samaria." In *The Oxford History of the Biblical World*, edited by Michael D. Coogan, 206–41. New York: Oxford University Press, 1998.

Carroll, Robert P. *When Prophecy Failed: Redactions and Responses to Failure in the Old Testament Prophetic Traditions*. London: SCM, 1979.

Childs, Brevard S. *Biblical Theology of the Old and New Testaments*. Minneapolis: Fortress, 1993.

———. *Old Testament Theology in a Canonical Context*. Philadelphia: Fortress, 1985.

Chun, S. Min. "Whose Cloak Did Ahijah Seize and Tear? A Note on I Kings xi 29–30." *VT* 56 (2006) 268–74.

Chung, Youn Ho. *The Sin of the Calf: The Rise of the Bible's Negative Attitude toward the Golden Calf*. LHBOTS 523. London: T. & T. Clark, 2010.

Cochell, Trevor. "The Religious Establishments of Jeroboam I." *SCJ* 8 (2005) 85–97.

Cogan, Mordechai, and Hayim Tadmor. *II Kings: A New Translation with Introduction and Commentary*. AB 11. New York: Doubleday, 1998.

Cogan, Mordechai. *I Kings: A New Translation with Introduction and Commentary*. AB 10. New York: Doubleday, 2001.

Coggins, Richard. "On Kings and Disguises." *JSOT* 50 (1991) 55–62.

Cohn, Robert L. "Convention and Creativity in the Book of Kings: The Case of the Dying Monarch." *CBQ* 47 (1985) 603–16.

———. "Literary Techniques in the Jeroboam Narrative." *ZAW* 97 (1985) 23–35.

Conti, Marco, ed. *1–2 Kings, 1–2 Chronicles, Ezra, Nehemiah, Esther*. Ancient Christian Commentary on Scripture: Old Testament 5. Downers Grove, IL: IVP, 2008.

Crenshaw, James L. *Prophetic Conflict: Its Effect upon Israelite Religion*. Atlanta: Society of Biblical Literature, 2007.

Cross, Frank Moore. *Canaanite Myth and Hebrew Epic: Essays in the History of the Religion of Israel*. Cambridge: Harvard University Press, 1973.

Culler, Jonathan. *The Pursuit of Signs: Semiotics, Literature, Deconstruction*. Ithaca, NY: Cornell University Press, 1981.

Davis, Ellen F. *Swallowing the Scroll: Textuality and the Dynamics of Discourse in Ezekiel's Prophecy*. BLS 21. Sheffield: Almond, 1989.

De Moor, Johannes C., and Harry F. Van Rooy, eds. *Past, Present and Future: The Deuteronomistic History and the Prophets*. Oudtestamentische Studiën 44. Leiden: Brill, 2000.

Bibliography

Deboys, David G. "1 Kings 13–A 'New Criterion' Reconsidered." *VT* 41 (1991) 210–12.
DeVries, Simon J. *Prophet against Prophet: The Role of the Micaiah Narrative (I Kings 22) in the Development of Early Prophetic Tradition*. Grand Rapids: Eerdmans, 1978.
———. *1 Kings*. WBC 12. Waco, TX: Word, 1985.
Dietrich, Walter. *The Early Monarchy in Israel: The Tenth Century BCE*. Translated by Joachim Vette. BE 3. Atlanta: Society of Biblical Literature, 2007.
Dietrich, Walter, and Dwight R. Daniels. "Martin Noth and the Future of Deuteronomistic History." In *The History of Israel's Traditions: The Heritage of Martin Noth*, edited by Steven L. McKenzie and M. Patrick Graham, 153–75. JSOTSup 182. Sheffield: Sheffield Academic, 1994.
Dozeman, Thomas B. "The Way of the Man of God from Judah: True and False Prophecy in the Pre-Deuteronomistic Legend of 1 Kings 13." *CBQ* 44 (1982) 379–93.
Edelman, Diana V. "Solomon's Adversaries Hadad, Rezon and Jeroboam: A Trio of 'Bad Guy' Characters Illustrating the Theology of Immediate Retribution." In *The Pitcher is Broken: Memorial Essays for Gösta W. Ahlström*, edited by Steven W. Holloway and Lowell K. Handy, 166–91. Sheffield: Sheffield Academic, 1995.
Eynikel, Erik. "Prophecy and Fulfillment in the Deuteronomistic History (1 Kgs. 13; 2 Kgs. 23:16–18)." In *Pentateuchal and Deuteronomistic Studies*, edited by C. Brekelmans and J. Lust, 227–37. Bibliotheca Ephemeridum theologicarum Lovaniensium 94. Louvain: Leuven University Press, 1990.
Floyd, Michael H. "Basic Trends in the Form-Critical Study of Prophetic Texts." In *The Changing Face of Form Criticism for the Twenty-First Century*, edited by Marvin A. Sweeney and Ehud Ben Zvi, 298–311. Grand Rapids: Eerdmans, 2003.
Fohrer, Georg. "Die Gattung der Berichte über symbolische Handlungen der Propheten." *ZAW* 64 (1952) 101–20.
———. *Die symbolischen Handlungen der Propheten*. 2nd ed. Zürich: Zwingli, 1968.
Frei, Hans W. *The Eclipse of Biblical Narrative: A Study in Eighteenth and Nineteenth Century Hermeneutics*. New Haven: Yale University Press, 1974.
Fretheim, Terence E. *Deuteronomic History*. Interpreting Biblical Texts. Nashville: Abingdon, 1983.
———. *First and Second Kings*. Westminster Bible Companion. Louisville: Westminster John Knox, 1999.
Friebel, Kelvin. "A Hermeneutical Paradigm for Interpreting Prophetic Sign-Actions." *Didaskalia (Otterburne, Man.)* 12.2 (2001) 25–45.
Frisch, Amos. "Jeroboam and the Division of the Kingdom: Mapping Contrasting Biblical Accounts." *JANES* 27 (2000) 15–29.
———. "Shemaiah the Prophet versus King Rehoboam: Two Opposed Interpretations of the Schism (I Kings XII 21–4)." *VT* 38 (1988) 466–68.
Fritz, Volkmar. *1 & 2 Kings*. Translated by Anselm Hagedorn. Continental Commentary. Minneapolis: Fortress, 2003.
Gibson, David. *Reading the Decree: Exegesis, Election and Christology in Calvin and Barth*. T. & T. Clark Studies in Systematic Theology. London: T. & T. Clark, 2009.
Gomes, Jules Francis. *The Sanctuary of Bethel and the Configuration of Israelite Identity*. BZAW 368. Berlin: de Gruyter, 2006.
Gravett, Sandra L., Karla G. Bohmbach, F. V. Greifenhagen, and Donald C. Polaski. *An Introduction to the Hebrew Bible: A Thematic Approach*. Louisville: Westminster John Knox, 2008.
Gray, John. *I & II Kings: A Commentary*. OTL. Philadelphia: Westminster, 1970.

Bibliography

Gressmann, Hugo. *Die älteste Geschichtsschreibung und Prophetie Israels (von Samuel bis Amos und Hosea) übersetzt, erklärt und mit Einleitungen versehen*. 2nd ed. Die Schriften des Alten Testaments 2/1. Göttingen: Vandenhoeck & Ruprecht, 1921

Gross, Walter. "Lying Prophet and Disobedient Man of God in 1 Kings 13: Role Analysis as an Instrument of Theological Interpretation of an OT Narrative Text." *Semeia* 15 (1979) 97–135.

Gunneweg, Antonius H J. "Die Prophetenlegende I Reg 13—Missdeutung, Umdeutung, Bedeutung. " In *Prophet und Prophetenbuch: Festschrift für Otto Kaiser zum 65. Geburtstag*, edited by Volkmar Fritz et al., 73–81. BZAW 185. Berlin: de Gruyter, 1989.

Hagan, G. Michael. "First and Second Kings." In *Complete Literary Guide to the Bible*, edited by Leland Ryken and Tremper Longman III, 182–92. Grand Rapids: Zondervan, 1993.

Hens-Piazza, Gina. *1–2 Kings*. Abingdon Old Testament Commentaries. Nashville: Abingdon, 2006.

Herr, Bertram. "Der wahre Prophet bezeugt seine Botschaft mit dem Tod: Ein Versuch zu 1 Kön 13. " *BZ* 41 (1997) 69–78.

Holder, John. "The Presuppositions, Accusations, and Threats of 1 Kings 14:1–18." *JBL* 107 (1988) 27–38.

Hossfeld, Frank L., and Ivo Meyer. *Prophet gegen Prophet: Eine Analyse der alttestamentlichen Texte zum Thema: Wahre und falsche Propheten*. Biblische Beiträge 9. Fribourg: Schweizerisches Katholisches Bibelwerk, 1973.

House, Paul R. *1, 2 Kings*. New American Commentary 8. Nashville: Broadman & Holman, 1995.

Hunsinger, George. *How to Read Karl Barth: The Shape of His Theology*. New York: Oxford University Press, 1991.

Jepsen, Alfred. "Gottesmann und Prophet (Anmerkungen zum Kapitel 1. Könige 13)." In *Probleme biblischer Theologie: Gerhard von Rad zum 70. Geburtstag*, edited by Hans Walter Wolff, 171–82. Munich: Kaiser, 1971.

Jones, Gwilym H. *1 and 2 Kings, Volume I*. New Century Bible Commentary. Grand Rapids: Eerdmans, 1984.

Klopfenstein, M. A. "1 Könige 13." In *Parresia: Karl Barth zum achtzigsten Geburtstag*, edited by Eberhard Busch et al., 639–72. Zurich: EVZ, 1966.

Knoppers, Gary N. "Aaron's Calf and Jeroboam's Calves." In *Fortunate the Eyes That See: Essays in Honor of David Noel Freedman in Celebration of His Seventieth Birthday*, edited by Astrid B. Beck et al., 92–104. Grand Rapids: Eerdmans, 1995.

———. *Two Nations under God: The Deuteronomistic History of Solomon and the Dual Monarchies*. Vol. 1, *The Reign of Solomon and the Rise of Jeroboam: The Deuteronomistic History of Solomon and the Dual Monarchies*. HSM 52. Atlanta: Scholars, 1993.

———. *Two Nations under God: The Deuteronomistic History of Solomon and the Dual Monarchies*. Vol. 2, *The Reign of Jeroboam, the Fall of Israel, and the Reign of Josiah*. HSM 53. Atlanta: Scholars, 1994.

Koch, Klaus. "The Language of Prophecy: Thoughts on the Macrosyntax of the *dĕbar YHWH* and Its Semantic Implications in the Deuteronomistic History." In *Problems in Biblical Theology: Essays in Honor of Rolf Knierim*, edited by Henry T. C. Sun and Keith L. Eades, 210–21. 1997. Reprint, Eugene, OR: Wipf & Stock, 2011.

Kruger, Paul A. "מוֹפֵת." In *NIDOTTE* 2:879–81.

Bibliography

Laderman, Shulamit. "Biblical Controversy: A Clash between Two Divinely Inspired Messages?" In *Iconoclasm and Iconoclash: Struggle for Religious Identity*, edited by Willem van Asselt et al., 143–56. Jewish and Christian Perspectives Series 14. Leiden: Brill, 2007.

Lasine, Stuart. "Reading Jeroboam's Intentions: Intertextuality, Rhetoric, and History in 1 Kings 12." In *Reading between Texts: Intertextuality and the Hebrew Bible*, edited by Danna Nolan Fewell, 133–52. Louisville: Westminster John Knox, 1992.

Leithart, Peter J. *1 & 2 Kings*. Brazos Theological Commentary on the Bible. Grand Rapids: Brazos, 2006.

Lemke, Werner. "The Way of Obedience: 1 Kings 13 and the Structure of Deuteronomistic History." In *Magnalia Dei, The Mighty Acts of God: Essays on the Bible and Archaeology in Memory of G. Ernest Wright*, edited by Frank Moore Cross et al., 301–26. Garden City: Doubleday, 1976.

Leuchter, Mark. "Jeroboam the Ephratite." *JBL* 125 (2006) 51–72.

———. *Josiah's Reform and Jeremiah's Scroll: Historical Calamity and Prophetic Response*. Hebrew Bible Monographs 6. Sheffield: Sheffield Phoenix, 2006.

Levin, Christoph. "Amos und Jerobeam I." *VT* 45 (1995) 307–17.

Long, Burke O. *1 Kings, with an Introduction to Historical Literature*. FOTL 9. Grand Rapids: Eerdmans, 1984.

———. *2 Kings*. FOTL 10. Grand Rapids: Eerdmans, 1991.

Long, Jesse C. *1 & 2 Kings*. College Press NIV Commentary. Joplin, MO: College Press, 2002.

March, W. Eugene. "Prophecy." In *Old Testament Form Criticism*, edited by John H. Hayes, 141–77. San Antonio: Trinity University Press, 1977.

Marcus, David. "Elements of Ridicule and Parody in the Story of the Lying Prophet from Bethel." In *Proceedings of the Eleventh World Congress of Judaism: Jerusalem, June 22–29, 1993*, edited by David Assaf, 67–74. Jerusalem: World Union of Jewish Studies, 1994.

McConville, J. G. *God and Earthly Power. An Old Testament Political Theology: Genesis—Kings*. LHBOTS 454. London: T. & T. Clark, 2006.

McKenzie, Steven L. *The Trouble with Kings: The Composition of the Book of Kings in the Deuteronomistic History*. VTSup 42. Leiden: Brill, 1991.

McKenzie, Steven L., and M. Patrick Graham, eds. *The History of Israel's Traditions: The Heritage of Martin Noth*. JSOTSup 182. Sheffield: Sheffield Academic, 1994.

Mead, James K. "Kings and Prophets, Donkeys and Lions: Dramatic Shape and Deuteronomistic Rhetoric in 1 Kings XIII." *VT* 49 (1999) 192–205.

Meier, Samuel A. *Themes and Transformations in the Old Testament*. Downers Grove, IL: IVP Academic, 2009.

Miscall, Peter D. "Introduction to Narrative Literature." In *The New Interpreter's Bible*, edited by Leander E. Keck, 2:539–52. Nashville: Abingdon, 1998.

Mitchell, Margaret M. "Rhetorical and New Literary Criticism." In *The Oxford Handbook of Biblical Studies*, edited by John W. Rogerson and Judith M. Lieu, 615–33. Oxford: Oxford University Press, 2006.

Montgomery, James A. *A Critical and Exegetical Commentary on the Books of Kings*. International Critical Commentary. Edinburgh: T. & T. Clark, 1951.

Morgenstern, Julian. *Amos Studies* I. Cincinnati: Hebrew Union College Press, 1941.

———. "Amos Studies. II, The Sin of Uzziah, the Festival of Jeroboam and the Date of Amos." *HUCA* 12 (1938) 1–53.

Bibliography

Mulder, Martin J. *1 Kings*. Historical Commentary on the Old Testament. Leuven: Peeters, 1998.

Mullen, E. Theodore, Jr. "The Sins of Jeroboam: A Redactional Assessment." *CBQ* 49 (1987) 212–32.

Münderlein, Gerhard. *Kriterien wahrer und falscher Prophetie: Entstehung und Bedeutung im Alten Testament*. Europäische Hochschulschriften 23: Theologie 33. Bern: Lang, 1974.

Nelson, Richard D. *The Double Redaction of the Deuteronomistic History*. JSOTSup 18. Sheffield: JSOT Press, 1981.

———. *First and Second Kings*. Interpretation. Atlanta: John Knox, 1987.

Noll, K. L. "Deuteronomistic History or Deuteronomic Debate? (A Thought Experiment)." *JSOT* 31 (2007) 311–45.

Noth, Martin. *The Deuteronomistic History*. Translated by J. Doull et al. JSOTSup 41. Sheffield: JSOT Press, 1981.

———. *Könige I (1. Könige 1-16)*. BKAT 9/1. Neukirchen-Vluyn: Neukirchener, 1968.

O'Brien, Mark A. *The Deuteronomistic History Hypothesis: A Reassessment*. Göttingen: OBO 92. Vandenhoeck & Ruprecht, 1989.

Pakkala, Juha. "Jeroboam without Bulls." *ZAW* 120 (2008) 501–25.

Peckham, Brian. *History and Prophecy: The Development of Late Judean Literary Traditions*. New York: Doubleday, 1993.

Person, Raymond F., Jr. *The Deuteronomic School: History, Social Setting, and Literature*. Studies in Biblical Literature 2. Atlanta: Society of Biblical Literature, 2002.

Provan, Iain W. *1 & 2 Kings*. UBCS. Grand Rapids: Baker, 2012.

Quell, Gottfried. *Wahre und falsche Propheten: Versuch einer Interpretation*. Beiträge zur Förderung christlicher Theologie 46. Gütersloh: Bertelsmann, 1952.

Rabinowitz, Chaim Dov. *Da'ath Sofrim (Torah, Prophets, Sacred Writings): Commentary to the Book of Malakhim*. Translated by Y. Starrett. Edited by Shalom Kaplan and N. Vogel. New York: Vagshal, 2002.

Rad, Gerhard von. "The Deuteronomic Theology of History in I and II Kings." In *The Problem of the Hexateuch and Other Essays*, 205–21. Translated by E. W. Trueman Dicken. Edinburgh: Oliver & Boyd, 1996.

———. *Old Testament Theology*. Vol. 1, *The Theology of Israel's Historical Traditions*. Translated by D. M. G. Stalker. London: SCM, 1975.

———. *Studies in Deuteronomy*. Edited by T. W. Manson et al. Translated by David Stalker. SBT 1/9. London: SCM, 1953.

Rehm, Martin. *Das erste Buch der Könige: Ein Kommentar*. Würzburg: Echter, 1979.

Reinhartz, Adele. *Why Ask My Name? Anonymity and Identity in Biblical Narrative*. New York: Oxford University Press, 1998.

Reis, Pamela Tamarkin. "Vindicating God: Another Look at 1 Kings XIII." *VT* 44 (1994) 376–86.

Rendsburg, Gary A. "Word Play in Biblical Hebrew: An Eclectic Collection." In *Puns and Pundits: Word Play in the Hebrew Bible and Ancient Near Eastern Literature*, edited by Scott B. Noegel, 137–62. Bethesda, MD: CDL, 2000.

Rice, Gene. *1 Kings: Nations under God*. International Theological Commentary. Grand Rapids: Eerdmans, 1990.

Rofé, Alexander. "Classes in the Prophetical Stories: Didactic Legenda and Parable." *SP* 26 (1974) 143–64.

———. *The Prophetical Stories*. Jerusalem: Magnes, 1988.

Bibliography

Römer, Thomas, and Albert de Pury. "Deuteronomistic Historiography (DH): History of Research and Debated Issues." In *Israel Constructs Its History: Deuteronomistic Historiography in Recent Research*, edited by Albert de Pury et al., 24–141. JSOTSup 306. Sheffield: Sheffield Academic, 2000.

———. *The So-called Deuteronomistic History: A Sociological, Historical and Literary Introduction*. London: T. & T. Clark, 2005.

Rosenberg, Joel. *King and Kin: Political Allegory in the Hebrew Bible*. ISBL. Bloomington: Indiana University Press, 1986.

Schenker, Adrian. "Jeroboam and the Division of the Kingdom in the Ancient Septuagint: LXX 3 Kingdoms 12.24 A—Z, MT 1 Kings 11–12; 14 and the Deuteronomistic History." In *Israel Constructs Its History: Deuteronomistic Historiography in Recent Research*, edited by Albert de Pury, Thomas Römer, and Jean-Daniel Macchi, 214–57. JSOTSup 306. Sheffield: Sheffield Academic, 2000.

———. "Jeroboam's Rise and Fall in the Hebrew and Greek Bible. Methodological Reflections on a Recent Article: Marvin A. Sweeney, 'A Reassessment of the Masoretic and Septuagint Versions of the Jeroboam Narratives in 1 Kings/ 3 Kingdoms 11–14,' *JSJ* 38 (2007) 165–95." *JSJ* 39 (2008) 367–73.

Schmidt, Uta. "Center or Fringe? Positioning the Wife of Jeroboam (1 Kings 14, 1–18)." In *Samuel and Kings*, edited by Athalya Brenner, 86–97. A Feminist Companion to the Bible 2/7. Sheffield: Sheffield Academic, 2000.

Seitz, Christopher R. *The Character of Christian Scripture: The Significance of a Two-Testament Bible*. Grand Rapids: Baker Academic, 2011.

———. "The Place of the Reader in Jeremiah." In *Reading the Book of Jeremiah: A Search for Coherence*, edited by Martin Kessler, 67–75. Winona Lake, IN: Eisenbrauns, 2004.

———. *Prophecy and Hermeneutics: Toward a New Introduction to the Prophets*. STI. Grand Rapids: Baker Academic, 2007.

———. *Word without End: The Old Testament as Abiding Theological Witness*. Grand Rapids: Eerdmans, 1998.

Seow, Choon-Leong. "The First and Second Books of Kings." In *New Interpreter's Bible*, edited by Leander E. Keck, 3:3–295. Nashville: Abingdon, 1999.

Sharp, Douglas R. *The Hermeneutics of Election: The Significance of The Doctrine in Barth's Church Dogmatics*. New York: University Press of America, 1990.

Simon, Uriel. "A Prophetic Sign Overcomes Those Who Would Defy It: The King of Israel, the Prophet from Bethel, and the Man of God from Judah." In *Reading Prophetic Narratives*, 130–54. Translated by Lenn J. Schramm. ISBL. Bloomington: Indiana University Press, 1997.

———. *Reading Prophetic Narratives*. Translated by Lenn J. Schramm. ISBL. Bloomington: Indiana University Press, 1997.

———. "I Kings 13: A Prophetic Sign-Denial and Persistence." *HUCA* 47 (1976) 81–117.

Sonderegger, Katherine. *That Jesus Christ Was Born a Jew: Karl Barth's "Doctrine of Israel."* University Park: Pennsylvania State University Press, 1992.

Stacey, W. D. *Prophetic Drama in the Old Testament*. London: Epworth, 1990.

Sternberg, Meir. *The Poetics of Biblical Narrative: Ideological Literature and the Drama of Reading*. ISBL. Bloomington: Indiana University Press, 1985.

Strawn, Brent A. *What Is Stronger than a Lion? Leonine Image and Metaphor in the Hebrew Bible and the Ancient Near East*. OBO 212. Göttingen: Vandenhoeck & Ruprecht, 2005.

Bibliography

Sweeney, Marvin A. "The Critique of Solomon in the Josianic Edition of the Deuteronomistic History." *JBL* 114 (1995) 607–22.

———. *I & II Kings: A Commentary*. OTL. Louisville: Westminster John Knox, 2007.

———. "A Reassessment of the Masoretic and Septuagint Versions of the Jeroboam Narratives in 1 Kings 3/ 3 Kingdoms 11–14." *JSJ* 38 (2007) 165–95.

———. "The Wilderness Traditions of the Pentateuch: A Reassessment of their Function and Intent in Relation to Exodus 32–34." *SBLSP* 28 (1989) 291–99.

Sweeney, Marvin A., and Ehud Ben Zvi. "Introduction." In *The Changing Face of Form Criticism for the Twenty-First Century*, edited by Marvin A. Sweeney and Ehud Ben Zvi, 1–12. Grand Rapids: Eerdmans, 2003.

Taylor, J. Glen. "How Can the Wrathful God of the Old Testament Be Reconciled with the Gracious Lord of the New Testament?" In *Guide for the Christian Perplexed*, edited by Thomas P. Power, 25–43. Eugene, OR: Pickwick Publications, 2012.

Thon, Johannes. "Das Grab des 'Lügenpropheten' im Dienste der Wahrheit (1 Kön 13,11–32; 2 Kön 23,15–18)." In *Die unwiderstehliche Wahrheit: Studien zur alttestamentlichen Prophetie: Festschrift für Arndt Meinhold*, edited by Rüdiger Lux und Ernst-Joachim Waschke, 467–75. Leipzig: Evangelische Verlagsanstalt, 2006.

Toews, Wesley I. *Monarchy and Religious Institution in Israel under Jeroboam I*. SBL Monograph Series 47. Atlanta: Scholars, 1993.

Tomes, Roger. "1 & 2 Kings." In *Eerdmans Commentary on the Bible*, edited by James D. G. Dunn and John W. Rogerson, 246–81. Grand Rapids: Eerdmans, 2003.

Van Leeuwen, Raymond C. "Form Criticism, Wisdom, and Psalms 111–112." In *The Changing Face of Form Criticism for the Twenty-First Century*, edited by Marvin A. Sweeney and Ehud Ben Zvi, 65–84. Grand Rapids: Eerdmans, 2003.

Van Seters, John. "The Deuteronomistic History: Can It Avoid Death by Redaction?" In *Future of the Deuteronomistic History*, edited by T. Römer, 213–22. Bibliotheca Ephemeridum theologicarum Lovaniensium 147. Louvain: Peeters, 2000.

———. "On Reading the Story of the Man of God." In *The Labour of Reading: Desire, Alienation and Biblical Interpretation*, edited by Fiona Black and Roland Boer, 225–34. Sources for Biblical and Theological Study 8. Atlanta: Society of Biblical Literature, 1999.

Van Winkle, D. W. "1 Kings XII 25—XIII 34: Jeroboam's Cultic Innovations and the Man of God from Judah." *VT* 46 (1996) 101–14.

———. "1 Kings XIII: True and False Prophecy." *VT* 29 (1989) 31–43.

Vaux, Roland de. *The Bible and the Ancient Near East*. Translated by Damian McHugh. London: Darton, Longman & Todd, 1971.

Walsh, Jerome T. "The Contexts of 1 Kings 13." *VT* 39 (1989) 355–70.

———. *Old Testament Narrative: A Guide to Interpretation*. Louisville: Westminster John Knox, 2010.

———. *Style and Structure in Biblical Hebrew Narrative*. Collegeville, MN: Liturgical, 2001.

———. *1 Kings*. Berit Olam. Collegeville, MN: Liturgical, 1996.

Way, Kenneth C. "Animals in the Prophetic World: Literary Reflections on Numbers 22 and 1 Kings 13." *JSOT* 34 (2009) 47–62.

Weippert, Helga. "'Histories' and 'History': Promise and Fulfillment in the Deuteronomic Historical Work." In *Reconsidering Israel and Judah: Recent Studies on the Deuteronomistic History*, edited by Gary N. Knoppers and J. Gordon McConville, 46–61. SBTS 8. Winona Lake, IN: Eisenbrauns, 2000.

Bibliography

Werlitz, Jürgen. "Was hat der Gottesmann aus Juda mit dem Propheten Amos zu tun? Überlegungen zu 1 Kön 13 und den Beziehungen des Textes zu Am 7, 10–17. " In *Steht nicht geschrieben? Studien zur Bibel und ihrer Wirkungsgeschichte: Festschrift für Georg Schmuttermayr*, edited by Johannes Frühwald-König et al., 109–23. Regensburg: Pustet, 2001.

Williamson, H. G. M. "The Prophet and the Plumb-Line: A Redaction-Critical Study of Amos vii." In *The Place Is Too Small for Us: The Israelite Prophets in Recent Scholarship*, edited by Robert P. Gordon, 453–77. SBTS 5. Winona Lake, IN: Eisenbrauns, 1995.

Wiseman, Donald J. *1 & 2 Kings: An Introduction and Commentary*. Tyndale Old Testament Commentaries. Downers Grove, IL: InterVarsity, 1993.

Wolff, Hans W. "Das Kerygma des deuteronomistischen Geschichtswerks." ZAW 73 (1961) 171–86.

Würthwein, Ernst. *Die Bücher der Könige, 1 Könige 1–16*. Das Alte Testament Deutsch 11/1. Göttingen: Vandenhoeck & Ruprecht, 1977.

———. "Die Erzählung vom Gottesmann aus Juda in Bethel: Zur Komposition von I Kön. 13." In *Wort und Geschichte: Festschrift für Karl Elliger zum 70. Geburtstag*, edited by Hartmut Gese and Hans Peter Rüger, 181–89. Alter Orient und Altes Testament 18. Neukirchen-Vluyn: Neukirchener, 1973.

www.ingramcontent.com/pod-product-compliance
Lightning Source LLC
Chambersburg PA
CBHW052059230426
43662CB00036B/1701